Trans

secure in my house – my sanctuary in a life that has felt in constant chaos. I break down in tears, crying for thirty years of feeling like an outsider, twenty years of knowing this to be related to my gender, ten years of exploring it, three years of transition and two years of writing about it, with all their stresses and traumas simultaneously hurtling to the fore.

For four days, everything makes me weep. At first it's painful, then cathartic, and finally just annoying – having not cried when I expected to for years, the sight of every ornament, every poster in my house sets me off, and I don't know when it'll stop. Eventually, I realise I need to get out: I visit old friends in Brighton, who indulge me as I discourse about the run-up to surgery and my feelings about it.

I return a day before admission: having to address the practicalities pulls me together, as I ensure I have everything I'll want or need during the seven-day stay. I've never been seriously ill or injured, so I've sought advice on what to take: I buy slippers and a crossword book. Once I've got everything on my list, and packed, I feel completely relaxed. I go to bed content, close my eyes, and then see a car crash outside my bedroom window. It's so vivid, it takes several moments to realise that the flaming wreckage is no more than the invention of my hyperactive subconscious, but once I do, I get a solid night's sleep – my last for some time.

Obsessed with being brave and independent, I'd travelled alone to my previous surgical appointments. This time, on advice, I've arranged for my friend Tania Glyde to take me to hospital. She arrives around midday: we eat in my favourite café and then get the Tube to Hammersmith, well before I have to report to Charing Cross hospital reception at 4 p.m. We say little, putting our arms round each other, but once I've checked in, she gives me some earplugs and a cuddly tiger ('You'll need a soft toy, trust me'). Then she goes,

1

Transgender Journey

Six weeks before sex reassignment surgery (SRS), I am obliged to stop taking my hormones. I suddenly feel very differently about my forthcoming operation. I'd previously seen transition as a marathon: surgery was like breaking the tape, but the race was won far earlier. Now I reconsider: perhaps this is more like a difficult cup final after some hard previous rounds.

It consumes my conversations as it inches closer. I am constantly asked how I feel: everyone expects a mixture of excited and nervous, and they are right. Above all, I'll be glad when it is over.

I take a little holiday in late June 2012, staying with friends in Scotland, and travel back on the first day of July. Then, for the next fortnight, my concerns over the practical, physical and psychological effects of SRS intensify by the day.

My psychotherapist, whom I've been seeing all year, tells me that I've barely touched on the surgery, so I devote my final pre-surgical appointment to it. After an hour of airing my anxieties, I feel calm and able to continue.

Five days before checking into hospital, I sign off. Returning from the Jobcentre, a man with a taste for 'she-males' (his word) follows me home, making me feel far less names have been changed to protect anonymity where necessary.

I am grateful to friends who spoke to me about past experiences, helping me shape them into the 'constructed reality' of the book, and then checked over the text to corroborate my memory: Corinne Atherton, Alice Black, Carl Boardman, Sarah Bradley, Lindsey Dryden, Tania Glyde, Jason Hall, Helen King, Jet Moon, Joe Stretch and Phil Vallon. Several people offered to read the manuscript, and some suggested changes, corrections and improvements: Christine Burns, Petra Davis, Scott Esposito, Hannah Gregory, Olivia Laing, Huw Lemmey, Alexis Lothian, Roz Kaveney and Nina Power.

I had kind words of support from plenty of people, including Jo Dawson, Dawn Foster, Lorna Scott Fox, Jean-Philippe Toussaint and Zakia Uddin, and finally Ker Wallwork, who came to me just as I began the final draft, took my hand and hauled me over the line.

Acknowledgements

This book grew out of the *Transgender Journey* series that I wrote for the *Guardian* between 2010 and 2012. The first chapter reprints my article 'Time for Sex Reassignment Surgery at Last' as it was published on the *Guardian* website on 30 August 2012, with a few minor alterations – thanks to Pamela Hutchinson for sub-editing it (and sharing my love of silent cinema), Kate Carter and Rachel Dixon for editing each piece, and Chris Borg for helping me get it commissioned. Parts of the text also appeared in articles for the *New Statesman* and *Aeon,* so thanks to Helen Lewis and Marina Benjamin for commissioning and editing those.

I must thank my agent, Jamie Coleman, for his encouragement and advice, and my editor at Verso, Leo Hollis, who constantly fought my corner and restrained my most aggressively meta-textual impulses. Thanks to all at Verso, including Sarah Shin, my publicist, Bob Bhamra for the book production, Rowan Wilson for getting it into shops, and Mark Martin and Sophie Hagen for copy-editing. I am also grateful to Joanna Walsh for her beautiful artwork, and Sheila Heti for giving up her time for the epilogue.

This also seems an appropriate time to thank my parents (or perhaps apologise to them) for their patient understanding of the difficulty and necessity of writing about them, and more generally. I should also mention that some

For Robbo (1952–2009)

First published by Verso 2015
© Juliet Jacques 2015
Epilogue © Juliet Jacques and Sheila Heti 2015

1 3 5 7 9 10 8 6 4 2

Verso
UK: 6 Meard Street, London W1F 0EG
US: 20 Jay Street, Suite 1010, Brooklyn, NY 11201
www.versobooks.com

Verso is the imprint of New Left Books

ISBN-13: 978-1-78478-164-4 (HB)
ISBN-13: 978-1-78478-417-1 (Export)
eISBN-13: 978-1-78478-166-8 (UK)
eISBN-13: 978-1-78478-165-1 (US)

British Library Cataloguing in Publication Data
A catalogue record for this book is available from the British Library

Library of Congress Cataloging-in-Publication Data
A catalog record for this book is available from the Library of Congress

Typeset in Fournier by MJ&N Gavan, Truro, Cornwall
Printed and bound by CPI Group (UK) Ltd, Croydon CR0 4YY

Trans

A Memoir

Juliet Jacques

VERSO
London • New York

telling me to surrender myself to the nurses, and I find my bed in F bay on the Marjorie Warren ward.

There are six beds, with most but not all occupants also undergoing SRS. Reassuringly, there are two people who had surgery a day before, who can hold conversations and move unaided. We chat before the nurses take my weight and blood pressure, measuring me for stockings to fight deep vein thrombosis as I'll be spending so long in bed. I order dinner and then sleep, struggling more with the sweltering temperature than anything else.

At 5:30 a.m. I'm woken for an enema: they have to thoroughly clear my bowels before the procedure. It's not pretty but I take it, shower and return to bed. At 7 a.m. the surgeon enters with two consent forms – one for the hospital, the other for me. He asks if I will allow the 'tissue removed' to be used for medical science. In the hazy half-light, I agree (to the disappointment, I imagine, of friends who've asked if they can have it). 'I'll see you soon,' the surgeon says. The anaesthetist comes soon after and asks several questions before I lie back down.

At 8:20 a.m. I'm escorted upstairs. I take the lift to the fifteenth floor in my slippers, white hospital gown and navy stockings. The chattering voices in my head silence themselves, with just the closing bars of Laurie Anderson's *O Superman* soaring through my mind, and I am ready.

Ha, ha, ha, ha, ha, ha, ha, ha, ha, ha, ha, ha, ha …

Yuri, who assists the anaesthetist, lays me on a trolley and takes my blood pressure and temperature. The anaesthetist enters, attaching a cannula to my right wrist. She asks if I have any questions. 'This'll definitely work, right?' Yes, she says, irked. 'It's just that I studied nineteenth-century medicine,' I say. 'It didn't fill me with confidence.'

'It'll be fine,' she says, raising a needle. 'You may feel a shooting sensation in your arm …'

I wake in the recovery room, dehydrated, my lips bone dry. I demand water, but it's nil by mouth until I return to the ward. I'm slow to come round, though, and they won't move me until I'm fully awake, however much I ask. After what seems an age, – I've no idea how long – they wheel my bed into the lift, and then back to F bay.

The women there are glad to see me back: I tell them that it went well, before finding a wave of 'good luck' messages on my phone. I go on Twitter to say that I'm conscious again; throughout my stay, social media keeps me sane, providing contact with friends, family and well-wishers at any time, saving dozens of energy-sapping conversations.

The nurses set up intravenous morphine, which goes towards compensating for the hated catheter bag strapped to my thigh. The machine bleeps whenever morphine is administered, which is not every time I press it, and it does bizarre things to my sleep: I close my eyes for what feels like several hours, only to find it's been five minute; but I get through the night. Dizzy and nauseous, I try not to be tetchy with the nurses, who do their best, but I struggle with the shared ward, wanting my own space and getting annoyed when they open the curtains without asking, feeling guilty about occupying myself with my headphones although everyone else is perfectly understanding.

One day after the operation, the morphine is removed. The nurses say it's to stop me getting addicted: I argue, unsuccessfully, that we can cross that bridge when we come to it. It's replaced by paracetamol and ibuprofen, which doesn't always shift a headache, and proves woefully inadequate. With vaginal packing to keep me open, I'm in severe discomfort: the lights go out at 10 p.m. and, laid flat on the hard mattress, as resting on my side impossible for the foreseeable future, I cannot sleep; the excess light, sound and heat driving me crazy.

At 3:30 a.m. I ring for the nurse. She comes, and I beg for sleeping pills, or stronger painkillers. I needed to ask earlier for pills as they have to be prescribed, and I've had my allotted pain relief, so there's nothing she can do. I ask when the packing comes out. 'Monday', she says, which I repeat in disbelief: it sounds an eternity. Then she leaves. Trying not to scream, convinced that no operation could ever be worth this level of pain and cursing myself for signing up, my outlet is Twitter. I post that this is the worst night of my life, and that I feel like I may never sleep again, and a handful of kind responses from insomniac friends and transatlantic contacts give me a little cheer.

At 6:30 a.m. I fall asleep. I wake an hour later to find nothing has changed, and it feels like this night will last forever. A nurse enters to take my blood pressure and I start crying, having promised myself I wouldn't, for the loss of independence, privacy and dignity, symbolised by the hospital staff changing me like a baby. 'You surrender those when you walk in, I'm afraid,' she says: harsh as it sounds, the reminder that these feelings are to be expected provides comfort, and night eventually rolls into day, clearly demarcated by the nurses turning on the lights, opening the curtains and offering breakfast.

The nurse specialist comes to check the wound, removing the pad over it. I look down and start hyperventilating: it's encircled by heavy bruising, the pad splattered in blood and pus. She insists I tell her what's wrong: I say it's discombobulating and looks disgusting. Worse, there's a 'phantom limb' sensation, as I think I can feel the old organ moving in the itchy cloth underwear like it used to, even though I know it's gone. Psychologically it's unbearable. This will pass, she says; there are no complications, so all will heal.

My old friend Joe Stretch is coming down from Manchester to visit. With time passing so slowly, the prospect of his company keeps me going: I text to say that as he's coming before dedicated visiting hours, he must meet me in the day room, and that as I've not slept and am in absolute agony, I won't be at my best. Even though it hurts to laugh, his reply is perfect: 'Stop moaning! It's probably just a cold!'

At 10 a.m. he arrives and I shuffle to the day room, moving like a toddler who's learned to walk by watching John Wayne films. Gently, he hugs me, and we sit. I take the sofa as I need to stretch my legs out, and talk him through everything from leaving my house to the present. I keep stopping, holding my forehead as the physical and psychological pains engulf me, but after an hour, I'm done. I pause, then ask: 'Anyway, how are things with you?'

We laugh, but I insist he tells me: other people's lives reintroduce normality, and discussing our usual subjects becomes really important. To make myself feel more human, I've put on makeup. We joke about the contrast between that and my 'sexy' catheter.

Feeling less tired and looking better than I'd expected, I change my pads and empty the catheter myself, passing time by watching Georges Méliès films and Paul Merton's programme on Buster Keaton on my laptop. Billie, who's had her operation days earlier, introduces herself. We click, sharing a love of sport, political theatre and literature; she looks at my books, and I tell her that the only one I can handle is a favourite volume of poetry, Jacques Prévert's *Paroles*. She's intrigued, and suddenly, in this rarefied environment, there's an unanticipated moment of beauty. She sits, takes my hand and reads:

To Paint the Portrait of a Bird

First paint a cage
with an open door
then paint
something pretty
something simple
something beautiful
something useful
for the bird
then place the canvas against a tree
in a garden
in a wood
or in a forest
hide behind the tree
without speaking
without moving ...

Before she even finishes this beautiful little poem we're firm friends, swiftly united in subverting our routine as much as possible. Just as the nurses are putting everyone to bed, she sneaks in and disconnects my catheter from the night bag so we can go and watch GB's Olympic football team play Brazil. The match is uncompetitive, sterile and meaningless but here, all the aspects of the BBC's football coverage that usually induce apoplexy, particularly Garth Crooks's endless banalities, are strangely soothing, and I go to bed far happier than when I rose, having requested sleeping pills well in advance.

I sleep deeply for four hours, then wake, fixated upon the question of inequality. Gradually realising that I'm in no fit state to resolve this longstanding problem, it takes time to settle back down. I take them again the following night, and something similar happens: I rise with this singular sensation of disconnect from my body. At 3:30 a.m. I go to the day room to read. Billie joins me and we watch more football together.

Soon I weep again, through tiredness and pain. I venture out into the garden for the first time. Just seeing London life – a tower block, a single car and a pedestrian – makes me realise that soon I'll be out, with the pain subsiding, and this and the fresh air makes me feel infinitely better.

That night I meet Katya, who'll be having her operation tomorrow, and I tell her that although she'll be sore, she'll be fine if she asks for sleeping pills and gets friends to sneak in food, and that the joy at resolving her gender dysphoria will make it all worthwhile, as it has for me.

As soon as I wake on Monday, I ask the nurse when the packing and the catheter will be removed. 'After breakfast,' she replies. Suddenly, I've never wanted tea, toast and cereal so much. When it comes, I eat voraciously, impatient for her to return. Eventually, she does: the removal is traumatic, taking longer than anticipated, and seeing the blood-soaked gauze makes me hyperventilate again. She calms me by saying I can shower and wash my hair, and that if I relieve myself efficiently, I'll be discharged tomorrow. Later, I manage to pee: it goes everywhere, but that'll fix itself, and the discomfort is outweighed by knowing that I'm a massive step closer to leaving. My morale is boosted further as I put on my own clothes.

I start dilating, using lubricating jelly and two five-inch dilators, one two inches wide, the other three. I have to use the smaller one for five minutes, then the larger for twenty to keep the neovagina open, three times daily for now. (In Scotland I met someone who was down to once a month, three years post-SRS.) This is very dull, and I make it tolerable by listening to music. It goes fine, so there's just one final barrier to my exit: I need to open my bowels. On Monday night, after I've ducked across the road for takeaway pizza – the first time I've left the hospital grounds – the nurse gives me laxatives, and I prepare for the most important dump of my life.

You don't need me to describe this – I couldn't top the toilet scene in *Ulysses* and even if you've not read it, you know what it's like – but later I triumphantly tell the nurses that I've done the business, and they say I can go now if I wish. I call my parents, my housemate Helen and others, deciding not to leave in a rush. This proves wise as the nurse specialist, who's not back until morning, must see me dilate. She's satisfied that I do it properly, and now the only thing keeping me is the wait for the pharmacy to send my medication. Helen comes to help me home: I'm overjoyed to see her, and we chat for an hour before my painkillers and taxi arrive.

When the car pulls up at my house I drag my suitcases inside before collapsing on to my bed, overwhelmed by the simple pleasure of seeing my own home.

Guardian, *Thursday, 30 August 2012*

2

September 2000. I opened the little purse, given to me by a friend at Collyer's, my sixth-form college in Horsham, which held my makeup. The black mascara came from Superdrug; I'd been too nervous to take it to the counter myself, so Jennie had done it for me. When the cashier told her it would look good on her, Jennie laughed and replied, 'It's for him.' Liquid foundation, on offer at Boots, which I bought after Jennie helped me realise the world wouldn't end if the shop assistant knew *I'd* wear it. Glittery eye shadow, a birthday present from Corinne, who'd sat next to me when the register was taken. She'd seen the pictures of transsexual punk singer Jayne County and Manic Street Preachers lyricist Richey Edwards – in his leopard-print blouse and eyeliner – in my ring binder and asked who they were. When I explained, she told me how she loved *Priscilla, Queen of the Desert*, the Australian movie about a transsexual woman, a transvestite and a drag queen who toured their cabaret act across the outback. After I told her that I was 'gay' and 'a crossdresser', she gave me her old tops, shoes and cosmetics.

At least I don't have to hide this from my parents any more, I thought as I stood at the mirror in my room in Oak House, one of the biggest (and cheapest) student halls in Fallowfield, the university district in south Manchester. I shaved my face for the second time that day and then rubbed on the foundation. *Would blusher be too much?* I wondered as I put more gel into my short, spiky hair. I decided to do just my eyes, and that I'd stick with my Joy Division T-shirt, denim jeans and DM boots. *What did people wear to these places anyway?*

I met Lynne and Lauren, who lived above my flat, at the bus stop. They asked the standard questions: *Which degree are you doing?* History. *Which A-levels did you do?* English Literature, History, Theatre Studies and AS-level Performing Arts. *Where did you go to school?* A comprehensive called Oakwood in a town called Horley, and then college in Horsham. *Is Horley where you're from?* I nodded. *Where is it?* Near Gatwick Airport. *I've never heard of it,* said Lynne. No one has, I replied. *What's it like?* I think it was once voted the dullest town in Surrey, I told her.

Then she asked: *Have you been to a gay club before?*

'There aren't any gay clubs near Horley,' I said. 'There's only one club, and I'd get my head kicked in if I went like this. I wanted to go to Brighton but it's a mission, and my mates weren't up for it.'

'Why not?'

'They're all straight, and they don't like the music.'

'Where did you go out?'

'Pubs and house parties, mostly. Sometimes London for a gig. I'm not big on clubbing.'

We walked into Canal Street, the heart of the Gay Village, near the red-light district. It was busy on a Tuesday night: not just younger people – most likely students – but also older men with Mancunian accents who probably resented the invasion of southerners, those who'd most likely learned about the area from the TV series *Queer as Folk*, broadcast on Channel 4 the previous winter. I'd not watched it: the trailers, all cheesy pop songs and *Titanic* references, had put me off, so I had no idea what to expect from 'the scene'.

Canal Street itself was mainly trendy bars, or chains like the Slug and Lettuce and people eating outside in the early autumn weather. Older-looking venues like Napoleon's were on side streets, with eye-catching adverts for drag queen shows, karaoke or Men Only evenings. From the outside, these looked like the traditional pubs that had been the only places to go out in Horsham: I wanted to try them out, but their old-fashioned butch/femme gay culture didn't appeal so much to the straight women I was with.

Lynne and Lauren led me on to Princess Street, past another old bar called the New Union which had cabaret at weekends, to a club called Paradise Factory.

'There are lots of women here,' I said as we queued.

'It's the only place we can dance without getting hassle,' said Lauren. 'Are you with anyone at the moment?'

'No, I'm single.'

'You might meet someone. Come on.'

Inside there were three levels with glass floors, connected by steel stairs. I found out later that it had once been the Factory Records offices, built just before the label went bust in 1992. I watched the clubbers. They didn't look like the people I'd seen on late-night TV as a teenager, in programmes and films about gay, lesbian and transsexual culture. Most of the men had shaved heads and stubble, tight tops and trousers; the women mainly had long hair and wore lip gloss and gold lamé tops. No butch dykes and no drag queens. 'Not on Tuesday,' Lynne said. 'Maybe at the weekend. Or somewhere else around here.'

I tried to dance. I didn't recognise the house tracks with their upbeat melodies and dreamy vocals. This was worlds away from the miserable 1980 bands that had attracted me to

Manchester when I was hoping to form a group. I didn't meet anyone, but nor did I leave feeling like Morrissey, standing and leaving on my own, going home and wanting to die.

———

The previous weekend, my parents had driven me from Horley, where we'd lived since I was four, with my books and CDs, bass guitar and amp, stereo and television, and T-shirts, jeans and boxer shorts all in the boot. I'd brought my makeup but left my dresses, skirts, tights and high heels in my bedroom. I wasn't sure if I'd want them: as a sixth-former, I'd only worn them to the occasional house party with Jennie's friends, or at home after everyone had gone to bed, turning out the lights whenever I heard someone get up. Otherwise I'd dressed as a boy, only occasionally letting friends put eyeliner or nail varnish on me because I couldn't be bothered with the argument with my mum that would follow. She'd kept trying to throw out the black velvet dress that Rob, one of several openly gay guys in my year, had made for me for 'Transvestite/Kinky' Day in the college's annual Rag Week for charity. I'd kept putting it back above my bed, and she'd asked me when I was going to grow out of this 'phase'.

I don't know, I'd told her, grinning. I didn't think I would.

I'd never told my parents that it had started when I was ten, but I wasn't sure if that made me a 'cross-dresser', which seemed the least loaded term, or 'transvestite' or 'transsexual'. I didn't much like any of those labels. Describing himself as a 'male lesbian', comedian Eddie Izzard had reclaimed 'transvestite' from the old stereotypes of high-powered men secretly masturbating in their wives' lingerie. In his brilliant stand-up routines about being an 'executive transvestite', he had created a memorable image of himself 'running, jumping, climbing trees, and putting on makeup when I'm up there'. But the word still felt sexual in a seedy, lonely way – the kind of thing featured on *Suburbia Uncovered* shows on late-night television. It was not a term I wanted to apply to myself.

'Transsexual' wasn't accurate either. You needed to be someone who'd been through some medical process to alter your body, right? I hadn't, and didn't plan to: *they're not like me either*, I thought. All the documentaries and articles I'd seen told the same story: someone, usually decades older than me, who'd been born male but 'always knew' they 'wanted to be a girl', keeping their feelings secret while they started a family and a career. When they finally came out, they faced a desperate struggle to stop people disowning them until their lives settled back into normality.

It wasn't that I thought they weren't sincere, but rather that I was already 'out' and convinced that marriage, children and a nine-to-five job weren't for me. I felt more inspired by Candy Darling, who'd lived as a woman and been in Andy Warhol's films, or the African American and Latina queens who'd fought the racist and homophobic police in New York's Stonewall Inn riots in 1969. Where were people like that in those stories? And what were the terms for them?

Moving to Manchester will let me work out who I really am, I'd thought.

I had requested mixed accommodation but had been put in an all-male flat when I returned my form late. I promised myself that I'd make the best of it, joining my new flatmates at the Oak House bar. *Will they be cool with me wearing makeup?* I wondered. *Be open from the start,* I decided, tentatively putting on mascara. *If you're not, it'll only be more difficult later ...*

We talked about what we were studying, where we had grown up and how well we knew Manchester. They were all on different courses. We didn't all like the same books or bands, but they shared my love of *The Simpsons* and didn't poke too much fun when they asked which football team I supported and I said, 'Norwich City'.

'Why *Norwich* when you're from Surrey?' asked Huw.

'Oh, I don't know. There wasn't a team on my doorstep, and they were alright at the time. How was I to know they'd become so shit?'

'Do you wear your eyeliner to the games?'

'Not often,' I replied, laughing. 'I only go a few times a season. I wear it to gigs occasionally.'

'I wear foundation on my nose sometimes,' said Nathan, who had a beard and lots of piercings and wore fluorescent clothes from a shop called Cyberdog. He had already come out to us as gay. Everyone else smiled and started to talk about where to go out. Nathan knew some places in the Village, offering to show me around, but the others preferred drum and bass or techno clubs – music genres that had passed me by.

That weekend, the first of the post-club parties started. There were several per week, rarely ending before 8 a.m., and I realised that getting stoned until I passed out would be the only way I'd get to sleep. On the next day, we would start smoking skunk in the early afternoon, watching funny videos – Bill Hicks, *The Day Today* or *The League of Gentlemen*, a late nineties sitcom that merged humour and horror. In the opening scene of the show, a young man, new to a small Northern town, jumps into a taxi. We see the back of the woman driving, who speaks in a deep, gruff voice: 'Are you here for work or pleasure?' She tells him about the shop 'where I get my dresses'; there is laughter on the soundtrack and in our living room. The camera focuses on a hairy foot in high heels, the man looking nervously at her large hand on the gearstick. 'I couldn't go into Dorothy Perkins once my bust started showing,' she continues, followed by a shot of thick chest hair growing through a red blouse. More guffaws. 'I've only been on the hormones eighteen months, my nipples are like bullets.'

I laughed: less than my flatmates, and later. The scene felt cruel and crude. The transsexual characters I'd seen in 1990s films like *Priscilla*, *I Shot Andy Warhol* and *Stonewall* weren't like that. Instead, they showed real people with relationships and careers, hopes and dreams, and humour about themselves. *Why was everyone laughing at this cheap stereotype?* I didn't know, but now I didn't want to tell the guys that my 'cross-dressing' went much further than a little mascara. *Perhaps*, I thought, *I might have to look elsewhere for a safe place to find out just* how *much further.*

———

Days after moving into Oak House, I got a letter from my pen-friend Sarah, a Mancunian living in Scotland who I'd met through the music pages on Channel 4's Teletext system. I'd made plenty of friends at Collyer's but none of them shared my obsession with the Factory bands; I'd been taken by Sarah's appeal for correspondents who loved Joy Division and New Order, the Durutti Column and Section 25 as much as she did. I'd long planned to study in Manchester, and thought she might be able to guide me around the city.

You'll have been in sunny Manchester for a few days now, she wrote, *and I hope you're settling in alright. In order to help you as best I can, I've compiled a little list of the city's best hangouts, bars, shops, live venues etc.* The timing was perfect. I was still trying out the student bars with their cheap drinks, and I was getting bored. *Time to explore*, I thought, heading to the bus stop.

I got the Magic Bus and headed towards Platt Fields and Moss Side. The area was notorious for its gang wars and gun crime in the 1980s and early 1990s, but, we were told, it had calmed down now. We went through Rusholme, the Asian district known as 'the curry mile' due to the sheer number of restaurants, and I felt miles away from Surrey's overwhelmingly white, middle-class suburbs. Then came the university. Freshers were loitering on the steps of the Student Union, a stone building with a flat roof and lots of pillars. Next to it were the Whitworth Park halls and art gallery, several shops and bars and the 150-year-old John Rylands Library. I liked that the Student Union was opposite the Holy Name Church, referenced in one of my favourite Smiths songs, 'Vicar in a Tutu'. Then we passed the BBC building and the Cornerhouse Cinema advertising foreign films, then the Music Box and Jilly's nightclubs. We waited for the trams to pass at the top of Oxford Road before the bus reached its destination, Piccadilly Gardens.

The city was reinventing itself after the IRA bomb of 1996 had torn it apart. The 'Gardens' were a construction site, and I saw that the centre offered the same chain stores as those in the commuter belt town centres in Surrey. I entered the ugly Arndale Centre with its orange tiles, baffled by the number of possible exits, before coming out near the Northern Quarter, which Sarah had suggested I seek out.

I entered Affleck's Palace, the five-floor 'alternative' shopping centre. There were numerous stalls selling retro shirts and studded jeans, hoodies with logos of punk bands, Mod-style suits and ties. But I was drawn to the vintage dresses, blouses and skirts. I looked through them for ones that might suit me before realising I had nowhere to wear them. If I was going to spend money on clothes, I told myself, I should replace the coat and T-shirts I'd had since I was sixteen. Wanting to leave with *something,* I got a few posters – Picasso's *Guernica,* Joy Division on a rooftop, the Smiths outside Salford Lads' Club – in the hope of brightening up the stony white walls of my room.

Pulse, the independent record shop, had been the only thing in Horley that I'd loved. There I'd met Rob and Gary, who were always recommending things I didn't know, both old and new that I liked far more than the Britpop and grunge groups popular at school. Now I'd found Oldham Street, full of similar shops. I tried Vinyl Exchange, which Sarah had said would be 'a great place to spend your student loan'. I left with the Smiths' 12" single 'Sheila Take a Bow' featuring Candy Darling on its cover, and a compilation of the Commodore 64 music that I'd heard so often in my youth, playing computer games in my room.

I saw the Night and Day Café, which Sarah called 'the best place for new bands', but was drawn to Dry 201, the bar that Factory had built just a year or two before their new offices. The bar still had its wooden floor and hanging lights, soft yellow walls and stage for DJs. There, I bought a Coke, took out my pen and paper and started writing:

Hi Sarah,
I'm in Dry 201, where our heroes drank together, ten years ago. They're auditioning for the Factory film, 24 Hour Party People. *Are you coming? You can sleep on my floor if you need somewhere to stay – as long as you don't mind my flatmates playing drum and bass until stupid o'clock in the morning, Maybe we could be Stephen and Gillian from New Order? I don't mind which of us is which …*

Three weeks later, Sarah rang the bell at Oak House. We'd never met but she was instantly familiar in her stripy yellow-and-black dress with matching tights. Even in her heels, she was several inches below my 5'8", but I envied the defiant way she walked around the city, not giving a fuck about the looks people shot at her. *I wish I'd been that sure of myself when I was sixteen,* I thought as we hugged.

'You went with the New Order T-shirt then?' said Sarah in a soft Mancunian accent, laughing.

'I've hardly got anything else,' I said. 'I *hate* clothes shopping.'

'You're just going to the wrong places. When I move back we'll go out together.'

'You're moving down?'

'Yeah, with my friend Dave. You'll like him, he's into the same music as us.'

'Great!' I said. 'We can hang out, my flatmates are good guys but they're doing my head in. The noise and the smell … you'd think there was a fucking war on.'

'Can't wait,' she replied as we got a bus to the venue – a pub on Princess Street called Joshua Brooks.

'What parts do you reckon we'll get?' I asked Sarah.

'One of the wreckheads at the Haçienda, probably,' she replied.

A man beckoned me over.

'Where are you from?' he asked.

'Surrey.'

'Sorry, your accent won't be right.'

There was no point arguing. I went back to the bar, trying not to look too despondent.

'How did you get on?' I asked Sarah.

'I got a second audition! How about you?'

'They didn't want me. Too southern.'

'Oh, honey, I'm sorry,' said Sarah. 'Let's go to Dry Bar, I'll buy you a Coke.'

I smiled, and we walked up to the Northern Quarter.

'The towns where I grew up had no identity at all,' I said as we walked up Oldham Street. 'People here seem much more proud of their past.'

'There's a few City heroes up there,' Sarah replied, pointing at a building with six panels on the side, three men in sky blue shirts and another three in red.

'Bell, Lee and Summerbee?' I said, referring to Manchester City's trio of 1960s stars.

'Yeah. Legends.'

'Next to Best, Law and Charlton,' I continued.

'Scum,' she said. I laughed, looking at the pavement. There were slabs celebrating the 'Madchester' groups – James, the Inspiral Carpets, the Happy Mondays, 808 State and others who played at Factory's Haçienda nightclub during the ecstasy-fuelled Summers of Love in 1988 and 1989.

'That's the Walk of Fame,' said Sarah. 'None of the bands we like, you'll notice.'

'Joy Division were too miserable, New Order were too erratic, the Fall were too weird and the Smiths were too poncey. This lot were happy and laddish, which is how Manchester wants to be seen, right?'

She laughed. 'What shall we do tonight? Canal Street?'

'Not really. I went with the Gay and Lesbian Society in the first week and had nothing to say to anyone. Nathan took me to Cruz 101. I did my eyes and nails, and this guy sat next to me and started stroking my hand. When I told him that I wasn't interested, he yelled "What the fuck are you doing here then?" and stormed off.'

'Jeez,' said Sarah. 'Let's go to one of the indie clubs. They're not great but we might like some of it.'

We went to Fifth Avenue instead. Wandering back to the bus stop afterwards, we laughed about how the DJ had played the first Stone Roses album on repeat while lads in Adidas shirts shouted the choruses. Pointlessly, I hid my nails in my pockets, worried that blokes leaving the pubs would hassle me, forgetting that I'd made up my eyes again.

We sat, happily, at the bus stop. A man who I'd seen at a trashy bar called Mutz Nutz where I'd been with the guys in the flat next door came over.

'Hi,' I said, nervously.

'You okay?'

'Fine, thanks,' I told him – Surrey speak for *Please leave me alone*.

He kissed me on the lips.

'I knew he was gay because he wears makeup,' he said to Sarah.

'Doesn't mean he wants you to kiss him though, does it?'

'He doesn't mind,' the man continued, grabbing me again.

There was no one else around. I pushed him away.

He stared at me for a moment. As he reached for my wrist, a bus turned up. Sarah and I rushed on, making sure we were near some people at the back, wondering how keen they'd be to defend a girly-looking student from the advances of a gay man. Luckily, they weren't tested: he didn't follow us. I stared out of the window, trembling. Sarah took my hand.

'I'm sorry.'

'It wasn't your fault,' I told her. 'I'm done with the scene, that's it.'

'Oh, love. I bet you never got this in Horley.'

'I never dared go out like this in Horley. A few of my mates in Horsham wore makeup around town and got beaten up.'

'We'll find some good places for you,' she said. 'I promise.'

I kept holding her hand, thinking about how I missed my old friends. I wondered if the ones who'd moved to Brighton – particularly Steve, who'd been in a punk band with me that we'd tried and failed to launch during my teens – were having an easier time. *I should have joined them rather than coming here*, I thought. Here, I knew nobody, and, it seemed, nothing. But at least Sarah and I had got on well 'in real life', and together, I felt sure we'd find a group of people just as good.

———

I took the tram to Dave and Sarah's flat in Prestwich. Dave had said he had 'an exciting project' for me but wouldn't give any further information. I'd only met him twice since Sarah had moved in and become his girlfriend, but I'd already noticed that he liked to generate some mystery around himself. After finishing his degree in popular music at Bretton Hall in Wakefield, he was playing guitar in a group called Five Years Later. The band had a singer but I wondered if they wanted me to play bass. In my head I had a brilliant band already: a fusion of post-punk, drum and bass and militant Marxism called Zinoviev Letter. Admittedly it hadn't become a reality – no doubt because I spent so much time smoking skunk. It was nonetheless the only band in Manchester that I was prepared to pursue and Sarah had promised to join once I arranged some practices.

Wearing a black suit and tie, his hair dyed the same shade, Dave opened the door.

'Nice eyeliner,' he said. 'Very Richey.'

'Thanks,' I replied.

He led me upstairs and showed me a folder of laminated papers labelled 'Valentine Records', and packed with logos, flyers for club nights, album covers, balance sheets and graphs. 'After My Bloody Valentine, right?'

Dave smiled: by getting the reference to his favourite band, I'd passed the first test. 'Way better than recreating Factory, right?' he said. 'You in?'

'Sure,' I said. 'What would you want me to do?'

'DJ at our nights, help us promote them, listen to new bands and tell us if they're any good. Generally be awesome.'

'I can do that. Well, maybe not the awesome bit.'

'Oh, stop trying to be self-deprecating and roll us a spliff,' said Dave, laughing. Then we spent the rest of the evening celebrating the creation of the main committee.

Our first club night was planned for the UMIST (University of Manchester Institute of Science and Technology) union, at the start of my second academic year. Back in Manchester after a summer in Horley and wanting an outfit that would feel worthy of such an event, I went shopping. The vintage clothes in Affleck's Palace were out of my price range. So were the simple, elegant frocks at La Femme in Withington, where I was now living, with eight people who'd lived next door at Oak House, after deciding that staying with the drum and bass crowd would mean failing my degree.

I tried the charity shops. Ignoring the woman at the counter who told me that 'the men's clothes are over there', I found a beige button-up blouse with a subtle floral motif. I silently handed it to the assistant, gave her the money for it and left. Back home, I tried it on with some brown women's jeans, size fourteen, that fit better than any men's trousers I'd ever owned and that I'd bought from Oxfam Super Savings on Oldham Street. Then I packed a bag with records and CDs and hopped on the bus, doing my makeup while I rode.

Since starting at sixth form, I'd had my hair spiky, holding it up with gloopy gel that smeared down my forehead when it rained. My mum didn't like it but as she wouldn't let me have my hair long, this had been our compromise. Now, 250 miles from home, I let it grow to my neck, with a fringe at the front. This had happened by accident: I simply hated going to the barber's. I'd gone to meet Dave, Sarah and a couple of new Five Years Later members in a Northern Quarter pub, taking another Mancunian soaking. 'It looks much better like that,' Dave told me, and Sarah and the others agreed. Realising that I could no longer be bothered to spike it every day, I let it go, and it soon felt like it better suited me.

I could dress how I liked at our club nights, I thought. I trusted Dave and Sarah to make sure I was safe, partly because they both wore as much eyeliner as me. I got through my first DJ set without fuss: the small crowd made no comment on what I wore, surprising me by dancing enthusiastically to the Smiths and the Fall. *Which is how it should be,* I thought as I went home, sleeping in my makeup as I couldn't bear to take it off.

I wanted something subtler for our monthly DJ slot at Zumbar on Oxford Road. The owner wanted us to play 'quiet' records and I wanted to dress in soft fabrics and colours to match the sounds. I went into Cancer Research in Withington, near La Femme. The old lady on the counter was the only person there, watching as I instinctively went to the books. Then she eyed me with suspicion as I passed the men's section to the dresses and blouses. Listening to music on my Discman to drown out my self-consciousness, I hurriedly rooted through the racks until I found a crushed velvet top, purple, with short sleeves and a round neck. *Don't try it on*, I thought to myself. *Just give it to Sarah if it doesn't fit.*

I took it to the counter, trying to act casual.

'Is that for *you?*' she asked.

'No,' I replied. 'It's for my girlfriend.'

'I should hope so too,' she concluded, hiding it in a bag.

I handed her £2.50 and left. *She didn't believe the lie that she made you tell her*, I thought. *Go back and tell her not to treat customers like that.* But then I thought about how I'd have to explain the issue to some branch manager, who might be even more hostile – surely it'd be easier to go elsewhere for clothes. I trudged back to my bedroom, hid the top in a drawer and took out a little bag of marijuana.

That week, I'd spoken to a friend about how doing dope was making my bad moods worse. This time, though, I hoped that it would *stop* me thinking about how lonely I was. I'd never felt comfortable talking to my housemates about my gender – once, while we were all smoking in my room, one of them had looked at my pictures of Audrey Hepburn in *Breakfast at Tiffany's* and Lena Olin in *The Unbearable Lightness of Being* and said: 'For a gay guy, you've got a lot of women on your walls.'

'It's camp,' I'd replied, before another had said, 'But they're *all* women!' Too tired to explain that I wanted to look like them, not sleep with them, I'd shrugged. Now, I put my copy of 'Sheila Take a Bow' on my lap, rolling the tobacco, paper and dope over Candy Darling's sad, beautiful face before lighting up.

That night, my housemates had gone to Robinski's in Fallowfield – another place where you paid £4 and then every drink was 50p. By now I'd stopped going with them, feeling that I'd lost touch with my 'feminine side' by playing up my interest in football and putting a hold on my cross-dressing to fit in with the guys around me. I decided to explore it through the movies and bought a coffee-table book to familiarise myself with Marilyn Monroe, Mae West and other 'gay icons'. However, I soon became more interested in world cinema, spending hours in the Cornerhouse or at home giving myself a crash course in European film. Nobody from my house or my degree ever joined me, so yet again I was alone with a video. I'd seen, and liked, several films by gay German filmmaker Rainer Werner Fassbinder, whose films were bleak, pessimistic and furious. I'd been particularly impressed with *The Marriage of Maria Braun* (1978), in which the symbol of West Germany's post-war 'economic miracle' – Herbert Zimmermann's radio commentary on the country's unexpected World Cup Final win in 1954 – played caustically as Braun died in an explosion. Fassbinder's next work, *In a Year of Thirteen Moons* (1978), about a transsexual woman, was apparently his most personal film – and one of his greatest.

The film followed Elvira (formerly known as Erwin), who went to Casablanca for sex reassignment surgery after the man she loved, Anton, said 'I'd love you if you were a woman.' Yet he still rejected Elvira, as did everyone she ever cared for. The film starts with the words 'He says he's a woman.' Elvira is beaten by strangers and dumped by a male partner who tells her, 'You have no soul, you're nothing but an object – someone ought to squash you to death!' I felt nauseous during a scene in which she returns to the butcher's shop where she once worked, talking hysterically with a friend about her surgery, the implication being that what was done to her body was mutilation, rather than consensual or desirable. Elvira's loneliness and humiliation become ever more unbearable as she is disowned by her family, her friends and Anton, until her grimly inevitable suicide. I didn't know much about the 'sex change' process, but I knew it went through some sort of clinic, and that they'd never let anyone do it on such a whim. Yet *In a Year of Thirteen Moons* still terrified me. Was cross-gender living really that harsh? Were transsexual lives as disposable as the film seemed to suggest? Or was Fassbinder's worldview just relentlessly bleak?

———

At least I felt safe with the Valentine Records crowd. We were soon putting on nights all over Manchester, giving me an excuse to blow my student loans on records and clothes, as well as films to play as backdrops to performances or to watch with Dave and Sarah after meetings.

Sarah would be back in Scotland for our biggest night of the year, at Font near Piccadilly Gardens, but she helped Dave and me to plan it. She suggested we show one of my favourite films while the bands were on, a silent from Weimar Germany starring Louise Brooks called *Pandora's Box* (1928). I was hunting at Affleck's Palace for an outfit that Brooks might have worn when I got a text from Dave, telling me the bar was in a rough bit of town and that 'it might be best if you don't dress up'.

'I'll be alright, won't I?' I replied.

'Sarah's away and I'm going to be busy so I think it's better not. Really sorry x'

I went home and tried to sleep – yet another afternoon nap that failed to compensate for my worsening insomnia. Then I faced the sad task of deciding what to wear. Grudgingly, I settled on black trousers, a blue T-shirt and suit jacket with my DM boots. I added a little makeup, if only to tell myself that one day, things might not be like this.

I got to Font and had a drink with Dave and John from Doublejo(H)ngrey, an electronic band featured on our recent compilation CD. One of John's bandmates, Graeme, walked in. He had a clip in his hair, pink eye shadow and shiny lip gloss, and wore a lilac dress with matching tights and high heels. *I didn't know he did that*, I thought, as Dave and John put down their drinks and stared at him.

'I heard they told you not to dress up,' said Graeme. 'I thought that was really fascist, so I did this to support you.'

'Err, yeah, thanks,' I said, trying not to look at Dave and John, who left to set up for the bands. I decided to escape the tension too, going to the record decks as I was DJ-ing first. I put on *Pandora's Box* and gazed at Brooks on the screen. I wished I had her black bob and blazing brown eyes, and that I could express myself as freely as she did, ignoring the glares of the lecherous men as she danced happily with another woman. *Hell, I wish I could express myself as freely as Graeme*, I thought. The film reached its conclusion – with Brooks's character's death – and my heart sank, another brutal end coming to someone too honest about themselves.

Nobody gave Graeme any trouble, though, and at the end of the night I thanked him. For all the awkwardness, he had given me a little courage. *Perhaps I'll stick up for myself more*, I thought. The next time I saw Dave, he apologised: it hadn't been right for him to make that request, and it wouldn't happen again. I accepted his apology, and it never did.

———

I still wasn't sleeping. The questions I asked myself grew harsher with each passing hour, and every joint. *Why don't you have any friends? Why doesn't anyone* love *you? Why don't you enjoy the gay clubs? You're not really 'gay', are you? Why aren't you getting out of this cross-dressing 'phase'? What happens when your parents find out? Why are you so depressed again? Wasn't getting out of Horley supposed to fix this?*

I need help, I concluded. *Perhaps there's a university thera- pist. No – that's for Americans with more money than sense. I'll speak to someone I know. But* who?

I decided to talk to my personal tutor. The last time I'd spoken to a teacher about this was at school at the age of fourteen, when I'd told a couple of them that I felt life was pointless. They were mostly sympathetic but unsure of how to help, but one had asked me, 'Why carry on if you feel like that?' Even then I'd thought: *That's not what you say to a depressed teenager, is it?*

It was impossible to talk about this – another feeling that I'd bottled up when my parents insisted I'd not tried hard enough to get on with my classmates. I'd alienated my few friends at Oakwood by talking endlessly about how miserable I was, so I worried about telling people in Manchester, especially as Dave was suggesting that I wasn't trying hard enough to get on with my housemates. Nearing the end of the year, I'd realised that they just weren't the right people for me. But who were?

I stood outside the door, staring at the nameplate: DR S. H. RIGBY. It seemed so official: he was an affable man, with pictures of the Chemical Brothers (who he'd taught) and Manchester City teams on his walls. I was taking his class, a people's history of medieval Britain, and so I saw him every week, but I was still very nervous about bringing this up. I took a deep breath and finally knocked. He invited me to come in and I sat, hunched, my elbows on my knees, tense.

'Is everything okay?'

'I'm really depressed,' I told him. 'I'm thinking of leaving.'

'I'm sorry to hear that,' he said. 'Is it the course or the students?'

'The course is alright – I'm enjoying the Intellectual History bit. But I miss my mates from college. They're all in Brighton and I want to finish there. I don't get on with my housemates and I haven't made any friends on the degree.'

'Look,' he said. 'Most students are very bourgeois, wherever you go. They're not interested in art or ideas – they just want to get drunk. It gets better in the third year – you'll meet more people with the same interests. My advice would be to go away for the summer, see your old friends, come back refreshed and finish here. I know it's a bit early, but are you thinking about a Masters?'

'Yes,' I told him. 'I want to do Literature and Visual Culture at Sussex.'

'Great, I'll write you a reference. But concentrate on here – you'll enjoy your final year.'

'Okay, thanks,' I mumbled as I left, not completely reassured but feeling that he had probably spoken wisely. In any case, I couldn't move away from myself. For now, I thought, I should start revising for my exams.

Home Movies

I hadn't known about it at the time, but in 1988, when I was seven, Margaret Thatcher's Conservative government passed Section 28, which banned the 'promotion' of homosexuality in schools. This law virtually silenced any positive discussion of sexuality or gender in British classrooms, and meant we only had one hour on sexual diversity at Oakwood, delivered in Religious Education, weeks before our final exams.

Our teacher announced that we were going to watch a video. 'It's about two boys who ... well, I think it's just a phase, but ... well ... they're ... umm ... they're *homosexual*.' He rushed the crucial word under his breath.

Bill, who'd been made to sit at the front, raised his hand.

'Sir ...'

'Yes?'

'What's a homosexual?'

The teacher went red. 'Watch the film,' he told us, hoping to avoid any follow-up questions.

In the film, two young male students quiver through a lesson in which they are told that 'one in ten people is homosexual.' Another pupil stands and shouts, 'That means there's two in here! Is it you?' He points at the two young men. I rolled my eyes as Richard did the same in our classroom, and laughed wearily as the two boys in the video, probably filmed in the early 1970s, ran away to go camping together.

I'd never dared talk to *anyone* about my gender identity, or my sexuality. At school, I got told that I sat 'like a queer' just for crossing my legs, so I felt that being open about who I was would end badly. There was nothing to help me in Horley Library either, so everything I learned about the subjects came from films and TV programmes – the ones I'd chosen to see by myself.

Ace Ventura: Pet Detective (1994) wasn't something I'd wanted to watch. The main reason I'd rented it from my local video shop was because the boys in my Year 10 History class endlessly quoted it, and I wanted to be able to laugh with them. Mostly, I didn't care for it: the film's brand of gross-out humour wasn't my thing. The comedic climax hit me hard, but not, I suspected, for the same reason as it did everyone else I knew.

Unravelling the mystery at the core of the plot, Ace Ventura (played by Jim Carrey) realises that Lois Einhorn, the Miami Police lieutenant whom he has kissed, is transsexual. She was once known as Ray Finkle, a former American football player whose disappearance has formed part of Ventura's investigation. 'That's it!' he yells. 'Einhorn is a *man!*' His face fills with disgust. 'Oh my *God!* Einhorn is a *man!*' He races to the toilet and is sick. Then he squeezes a whole tube of toothpaste and a plunger into his mouth, before burning his clothes and jumping into the shower, crying, 'No! No!' Then he leaps into his car and drives off to seek revenge. Finding Einhorn in a room full of people, Ventura points and screams: 'She is *not* Lois Einhorn! She's a *man!*' When Einhorn says he's lying, he yanks at her hair, hoping to pull off a wig. No luck: it's real. He rips open her blouse, saying, 'Would a real woman be missing these?' She has breasts, so Ventura turns, laughing, and shouts, 'That kind of surgery can be done over the weekend!' Nobody stops him: Ventura strips off her trousers and then looks astonished. Where is 'big old Mr Kanesh'? Dan Marino, the Miami Dolphins' star quarterback, tips him off. Ventura turns Einhorn around, showing the crowd that the deceptive Einhorn has tucked her male genitalia between her legs, and screams: 'That's why Roger Podacter [whom Einhorn has supposedly killed] is dead! He found Captain Winky!'

Every man pukes in unison: clearly, I was meant to puke with them, or at least laugh. I couldn't, but I still felt sick.

———

Ace Ventura's cruelty had come as a shock. In response, I looked for films that might be more sympathetic. I tried *The Crying Game* (1992), directed by Neil Jordan. I already had some idea of its famous 'twist' from *The Simpsons*, when Mayor Quimby told a crowd of voters: 'The chick in *The Crying Game* is really a man!' When they booed, he back-tracked: 'I mean, *man* that was a good movie!' So I watched as IRA member Fergus fell in love with Dil (Jaye Davidson), the girlfriend of a hostage held by Fergus's group and then accidentally killed. Their relationship was handled with admirable sensitivity, the romance growing as Fergus pro-tects her from hostile men in the nightclub where she sings, until he gets her to the bedroom: she drops her knickers, 'revealing' her male genitalia.

'I thought you knew …' says Dil, as Fergus rushes off to throw up. Apparently, he didn't, and the idea was that Dil 'passed' so well as a woman that viewers didn't either. I was seeing that the 'surprise' was a convention – or cliché. I didn't realise for years that Fergus soon apologised and carried on dating Dil – seeing her draw that kind of response from him had made me turn off the TV, and look elsewhere for people who I thought might be like me.

Soon, I discovered that transsexual people should not 'deceive' anyone about who they were, but shouldn't be open about it either. I watched a short documentary on Channel 4 called *Murder and the Feather Boa* (1996) about the killing of La Vanessa, who organised the first gay rights march in Chapias State, Mexico, and then of twenty-nine other trans-vestites and transsexual women, many of them sex workers.

I saw that for many people around the world, expressing themselves as they wished meant risking death. For once, I felt grateful to have grown up in the suburbs of southeast England – my anxieties paled next to the challenges faced by these women in Latin America, not least at the hands of the police. I also had a far easier life than Brandon Teena, a trans man killed in Humboldt, Nebraska, in 1993, played by Hilary Swank in *Boys Don't Cry* (1999). Brandon's struggles to fit in with the guys in a small American town while keeping his gender secret ended with him being raped – for which he was blamed – and then murdered. I only saw the film after I came out as transsexual, but I could well remember the fear that came with those youthful conversations about what I enjoyed doing or who I fancied, as I sat terrified that giving the wrong answer would lead to bullying, exclusion and violence.

But the tragedies were collective as well as individual. In secret I watched documentaries about drag queens, transvestites and transsexual people who'd survived the HIV/AIDS epidemic of the 1980s talking about how it had changed queer subculture forever. In one documentary a character sat in a London cab with tears in her eyes as she spoke about her friends 'dropping like flies' and how she missed the 'family' she'd fought so hard to find. I liked the sound of the community she described, feeling sad that I'd never know such comradeship, but I also felt relieved, as I struggled to comprehend the scale of the crisis, that the worst of it was over, at least in the West.

A world had changed, perhaps been lost – something I started to understand as I watched *Stonewall* (1995), directed by Nigel Finch. The film opened with someone putting on lipstick, and then a tracking shot along a bar where there had been a fight. It cut to archival footage of Richard Nixon and various moments in the 1960s civil rights movements; the people interviewed recalled that 'every other group had made their point' and that it had been time for the 'faggots' to make theirs. But the heroes weren't the ultra-cautious, white 'homosexual rights' activists who insisted that men wear suits and women wear dresses to their peaceful protests, but the African American 'drag queens' of colour who sang and danced in New York's dimly lit Stonewall Inn.

Stonewall didn't feature Sylvia Rivera or Marsha P. Johnson, who were at the riots and then set up the Street Transvestite Action Revolutionaries to advocate for homeless queens and queer youths; it was only years later that I found out how central they had been to the struggle of July 1969. This story belonged to Miranda, originally from Puerto Rico. She was at the bar, explaining to Matty Dean, a young gay man who had just arrived from the southern states, that he had to keep his identity secret. 'We're all Smiths in this place,' the queens told him – just before the police broke in and demanded 'ID', targeting anyone not 'wearing at least three items of clothing appropriate to their gender as ascribed by nature'. The police were smug, arrogant and cruel. During the first raid, a cop walked up to Miranda, sarcastically saying, 'So classy and dainty *it* is' before taking off her glasses and ordering her to the washroom. They dunked her face in dirty water to ruin her makeup, laughed at her and called her a 'sissy'; when she put her lipstick back on and Matty Dean stood up for her, they were both arrested, along with the other queens.

I loved how Miranda revelled in a position between male and female – she preferred to be called 'she' and went to the army headquarters in women's clothes after being ordered to enlist for the Vietnam War. The recruiting sergeant called her 'lady' at first, and she replied: 'I ain't no lady, that's why I walk the middle of the room.' They asked if she was 'some kind of invert' and stamped 'sexual deviant' on her application, excusing her from service. I felt so inspired by Miranda and the queens who joined arms with her outside the Inn: they refused to keep quiet and blend in, knowing that they could only bring about change by standing up for themselves, together, and fighting discrimination with radical action.

I became fascinated with New York's queer underground of the late sixties, and watched *I Shot Andy Warhol* (1996): the story of how *SCUM (Society for Cutting Up Men) Manifesto* author Valerie Solanas attacked the famous pop artist. I was starting to learn from the music of the Smiths about Warhol's Factory and the creative people who found a home there. The boys at Oakwood didn't share my obsession with the Smiths, and several hated them. 'They're really miserable, and all their songs sound the same,' said the Nirvana fans who sat around me. I disagreed: I loved Johnny Marr's jangly guitars, sometimes slow and sad, often upbeat or even funky, but it was Morrissey who drew me in. He seemed so proud to be an outsider, and so *funny* with it, making me feel so much better about not liking the same bands or films as my peers, not to mention the amount of time I spent alone.

The first Smiths song I heard was 'What Difference Does It Make'. Morrissey opened by saying that all men have secrets, and that he was going to offer his. Immediately, I was hooked: he was giving me a *language*. I found solace in 'This Charming Man', hinting at some sexual awakening with another man, and 'Handsome Devil', which was more up front about queer secrecy and desire. That made me laugh, as did 'Vicar in a Tutu' with its simple message: 'He's not strange / He just wants to live his life this way.' It made me feel that my cross-dressing was something that *just* needed to be accepted. Then I heard 'Sheila Take a Bow', in which Morrissey turned 'You're a girl and I'm a boy' into 'I'm a girl and you're a boy' with delicious ease, the gender play being all the better for its lightness. If you weren't on his wavelength, you might have missed it.

I read all I could about the band, including the people Morrissey put on their record covers, like Factory actors Joe Dallesandro and Candy Darling. Darling was one of the main characters in *I Shot Andy Warhol,* played by Stephen Dorff. I was sure I was meant to marvel at how Dorff/Darling became ever more beautiful, with scenes of her putting on Revlon eye shadow and the Factory men saying things like 'She gets realer and realer.' But what captured me was the growing tension between Candy and 'butch dyke' Valerie (Lili Tayor), who aimed to overthrow the government and eliminate the money system.

At first, they seem to get on: Valerie tells Candy, 'I thought you were a lesbian' and Candy replies, 'Thanks, a lot of people say that.' Then Candy explains that she's a 'drag queen', and the Factory is the only safe place for her. Valerie – a young hustler whose lesbian experiences and feminist politics attracted the unwanted attention of psychiatrists – thinks Candy might help her get to Warhol, hoping the Factory will produce her screenplay, *Up Your Ass.* But Warhol doesn't like her script and eventually loses it; then he angers Valerie further by telling her, 'You ought to get [Candy] to do your makeup.' Valerie comes to hate both Warhol (who she thinks has stolen her script) and Candy. In one scene, she talks about how much she loathes men, and wants to eradicate them. Getting a 'sex change' isn't a solution, she argues: 'Look at Candy Darling. He is the perfect victim of male oppression.' I didn't understand: to me, it looked like Candy was being herself in defiance of expectations about how men should behave. Candy simply says, 'Piffle.' The scene closes.

So I didn't get any sense that this conflict represented anything more than Valerie's personal grudge, and by the end of the film, it looked as though she acted purely out of rage. A disastrous TV chat show appearance ends in a fight after the homophobic host makes fun of Valerie for looking 'mannish'. I was on her side there – it seemed as appalling for him to humiliate her for her self-presentation as it did for the New York Police Department to attack and arrest Miranda and friends for theirs. But I couldn't really sympathise when Valerie furiously breaks into Candy's room, telling her that 'Andy likes you because he hates women and you're a fucking freak', calling her 'Jimmy' and hitting her, just before her unsuccessful attempt to kill Warhol.

In the coda, I learned that Candy had planned to undergo gender reassignment and began taking hormones, but died of cancer in 1974 at the age of twenty-nine. Her attempt to move away from calling herself a 'drag queen' – a term tradition-ally belonging to gay male subculture – to self-identifying as a transgender woman was cut short.

I kept watching anything that might help me to under-stand how sexuality and gender identity were separate issues, even if they had often been associated with each other and explored within the same spaces. My favourite of these films was *The Adventures of Priscilla, Queen of the Desert* (1994). It came out at the same time as *Ace Ventura*, but could not have been more different. Here, Terence Stamp, Hugo Weaving and Guy Pearce play, respectively, a transsexual woman, a transvestite and a drag queen, who travel across the outback from Sydney to resurrect their cabaret act on the other side of Australia. There are plenty of scenes with the three of them on stage, or in front of strangers when their bus breaks down, but in a way they are always performing, trying to work out when to be bold about who they are and when to keep their genders secret. On one occasion they return to their bus after a night out to find 'AIDS Fuckers Go Home' daubed across it.

I liked *Priscilla* best when transsexual woman Bernadette (Stamp), cross-dresser Tick/Mitzi (Weaving) and drag queen Adam/Felicia (Pearce) were in 'everyday' places. In a scene at a hotel bar, when Mitzi and Felicia are in colourful wigs and dresses, the owner tells them, 'We've got nothing here for people like you.' Bernadette replies, 'Why don't you just light your tampon and blow your box apart, because it's the only bang you're ever going to get, sweetheart!' Everyone laughs *with* the transsexual woman, and they all get drunk together. Towards the end, Bernadette and Mitzi are trying to keep a low profile in a small, rural town, when Felicia, bored, dresses in her most outrageous clothes and starts flirting with the toughest men around. They 'read' Felicia and corner her, calling her a 'fucking freak' and threatening to 'split his legs'. Bernadette and her lover Bob save Felicia before telling her how stupid she's been: they understand that however important it is to express oneself sincerely, they live in a world where it isn't always possible, and that often, their safety has to be put first.

One of the cool girls in my Year 11 Maths class asked if anyone had seen *Priscilla*, saying she loved it. Not wanting the questions that might follow if I praised it, I just smiled, but felt better just for hearing that someone else had seen the film and been inspired rather than disgusted by it. *If only everyone could watch it*, I thought.

Then, Dana International of Israel won the Eurovision Song Contest in May 1998, a few weeks before we were due to take our final exams and leave the school. Openly transsexual, her grace and beauty amazed the boys and girls in my Maths class: 'I thought they were just blokes who wore dresses!'

She may not have spoken to me as much as Morrissey, let alone Candy Darling or the queens at Stonewall, but at least she started a positive discussion about trans people, even if it was only because the guys thought she was hot. Back in the days of Section 28, that was probably the best I could have hoped for.

3

'I never thought I'd be so glad to come home,' I told my father as he drove into Horley, past the Chequers Hotel and the little row of shops to the house where I'd grown up.

I'd planned to withdraw and recover over the summer, securing a job at a duty-free shop at Gatwick Airport and piling up films to watch and books to read. I didn't know where to find dope in Horley, and I didn't want to look for it. Smoking only occasionally with friends from Horsham, free of the marijuana-induced haze, I started to write. I'd tried plays and scripts at Oakwood – a drama about a shell-shocked soldier written after a school trip to the First World War battlefields, a sitcom about a struggling football team inspired by Norwich's ongoing ineptitude. But back then, I hadn't been open with anyone about my gender, unprepared to go further than writing 'My name is Juliet' on my schoolbooks before crossing it out, or entering 'Juliet' on the high score tables of my Commodore 64 games.

If I can't be myself in my life, perhaps I can in my writing, I thought. *But how?* 'Transvestite' or 'transsexual' authors only seemed to write memoirs, usually when they were much older than I was, so I had no role models. I started to conceive a narrative about someone who decides to become a work of art by copying the style of Alla Nazimova in her opulent silent film version of Oscar Wilde's *Salomé*. Even at the time it was made *Salomé* was known as a 'queer' movie, and it fascinated me: it was rumoured that the entire cast had been gay or lesbian, with several of King Herod's courtiers played by men in drag. The costumes had cost $350,000, a huge sum in 1922. But I had no idea where my central character might *go* as Nazimova, and little experience of walking around in even the most subtle women's clothes, let alone her eye-catching pearl headdresses and necklaces, and dealing with the inevitable attention this would attract.

That summer I came across another reference to Wilde's play in Pedro Almodóvar's film *All about My Mother* (1999). In many ways the film was as tragic and melodramatic as *In a Year of Thirteen Moons,* but I felt totally different at the end, as uplifted as Fassbinder had left me depressed. The composition of Almodóvar's shots struck me – vivid red where Fassbinder had used dull brown – and the plot was more intricate, opening with Manuela's visit to see *A Streetcar Named Desire* on her son Esteban's eighteenth birthday, only to see Esteban run over and killed in his attempt to get an autograph from the star actress, Huma.

There were so many complex relationships in the film, and I loved watching them unfold. I identified with Manuela because, like my mother, she was a nurse. Esteban's death prompts Manuela to go in search of his father: she never told Esteban about him, and never told him that he had a son. First, she goes to a red-light district, where she saves transsexual sex worker Agrado, an old friend, from being attacked by a client. Agrado tells Manuela 'all I have that's real are my feelings' after years of beatings, frustrated that the validity of her womanhood is constantly up for debate – then she tries to pre-empt all the people working in the theatre (where she is deputising for heroin addict Nina, playing Stella in *Streetcar*) 'asking about my cock'.

In my favourite scene, after Nina and Huma hospitalise each other in a fight, Agrado takes the stage, recounting her life story rather than cancel that evening's performance. A few members of the audience leave, but Agrado holds most of them rapt with a mixture of honesty and humour. 'Look at this body, all made to measure,' she says, detailing the operations she's had on her tits, jaw and nose, only for the latter to be broken in an assault. 'It gives me character,' she says, smiling, 'but if I'd known, I would have saved my money.' Laughing with the crowd, I loved her parting message: 'The more you resemble what you've dreamed of being, the more authentic you are.'

Lola, Esteban's transvestite father, finally appears at the funeral of Manuela's friend Rosa before dying of an AIDS-related disease (having passed the virus on to Rosa). The survival of Lola and Rosa's HIV-positive child gives the film an optimistic conclusion, and I liked that Almodóvar let Agrado flourish where Fassbinder's Elvira had been obliterated.

I didn't know what I dreamed of being, but *All about My Mother* made me feel more confident about exploring it, and Agrado made me want to share experiences with other people. During the summer between school and sixth form, when I'd been thinking about how to come out, I'd spent hours online, using slow and expensive dial-up Internet, finding people, some nearby, who seemed confident in their male-to-female identities, comfortable about sharing them with strangers, if not their loved ones. Their websites featured photos of them in dresses, heels and makeup for nights with friends at house parties or bars, or in everyday clothes to show how they felt most authentic.

I'd preferred the short biographies to the pictures. The stories followed similar patterns, opening with the realisation that they wanted to be girls or liked wearing women's clothes, before discussing how they came out to family, friends and colleagues. Some had been disowned by their parents, dumped by their lovers or divorced by their wives. Others kept their relationships, maybe compromising on when or where they cross-dressed. Some had children who never wanted to see their fathers again; others had frank discussions with their sons and daughters, becoming stronger for it. Some spent time with like-minded people at 'friendly' bars and clubs; a few felt no desire to be part of any 'community'. Some were forced out of work after declaring they were transsexual; others switched jobs when they changed gender presentation. A few convinced their coworkers that they'd still be able to do their jobs competently and stayed, joking about how they could still join in with office 'banter', read maps or operate heavy machinery.

I'd also found the Sussex Transgendered Page. I'd never seen that word 'transgender' before: it just seemed like a way to cover the fact that the site was run by a 'transvestite' and a 'transsexual' woman. The site featured their life stories, an FAQ page about their identities and advice on coming out, buying clothes and presenting as female in public. Back in my first year at sixth-form college, I'd emailed Claire, the transsexual woman, and introduced myself. I told her that she'd made me feel less lonely, and asked if we could meet. She refused as I was under eighteen, but she gave me her phone number.

'You don't sound very camp,' she'd said when I called her. 'Why do you call yourself a drag queen?'

'I'm gay and I wear women's clothes,' I'd replied. 'I thought that made me a drag queen.'

'A drag queen is someone who performs on a stage,' said Claire. 'Do you?'

'No.'

'Would you like to?'

'Not really.'

'Then you're not a drag queen,' said Claire.

'Whatever,' I'd said, laughing. 'I'm worried about my parents finding out, though.'

'Look,' she told me. 'The way I see it, if you have children, then you need to be ready for anything they do. If you're not, then you shouldn't have had them. You'll find a way.'

I'd thanked her, and said goodbye. We never formally met – by the time I turned eighteen, I'd felt more comfortable talking to my college friends. Some time later, though, I recognised Claire when she came into WHSmith in the County Mall shopping centre in Crawley, where I worked on Thursday evenings. I could not find the nerve to tell her that I was that fumbling student who'd called her, and thought that perhaps she wouldn't want to discuss her gender while trying to buy a newspaper.

Now, back in Horley for the summer, I returned to her website, but rather than contact her again, I went to the Venues page. Then I called my old Collyer's classmate, Corinne and asked if she'd like to go to a club in Brighton called the Harlequin.

'Maybe – what's it like?'

'Apparently it's "Brighton's only transvestite bar." They've got drag queens and a disco at weekends. It should be fun.'

'Let's do it!' said Corinne. 'We can go shopping together, get ready at mine and then I'll drive us down.'

We met at the County Mall in Crawley.

'Have you still got that dress you bought for Rag Week?' asked Corinne.

'I kept it in a box and loads of the sequins came off. I thought it'd be nice to buy something new, anyway. I've got some tights, my wig and these heels I found in that charity shop in Horsham,' I said, showing her my shiny black shoes.

'Wow! What size are they?'

'Seven and a half. Honestly, you should've seen the looks on the little old ladies' faces when I got them.' Corinne laughed. 'To be fair, people aren't much better in Manchester,' I said, telling her about my experience in Withington.

'I'll bet. We'll try New Look first, they'll have something. And if anyone gives you hassle, I'll tell them where to shove it.'

Corinne paused, looking at a shaven-headed man coming out of Burton's and walking towards us.

'Who's that?' I asked.

'It's my fucking horrible ex-boyfriend. What was I *thinking*?'

'Hi,' he said to Corinne.

'Hi,' she replied. 'What are you up to?'

'I'm buying a suit for a wedding.'

'Whose wedding?'

'Mine.'

'Okay. Hope it goes well,' she told him as I stood silently, awkwardly. Then he walked off.

'You alright?' I asked Corinne.

'I'll be fine,' she said. 'Let's try the charity shops. Who's he bloody marrying, anyway?'

We laughed as we went to Cancer Research. I was so comfortable with Corinne that I forgot about what the sales assistant might think, rifling through the women's section, showing her things in my size.

'Too mumsy,' she said at a floral frock. A soft pink blouse was 'too girly'. A blue top was 'too low cut'. Then I found a short black dress, Lycra, with an electric blue flower on the chest. 'That's nice! Try it on.'

'I'll ask. Do you mind coming with me?'

The assistant said 'Sure.' I entered the cubicle, taking off my jeans. I'd worn my tights underneath, and tried them with the dress. I liked how it clung to my contours, without making my hips look too narrow or my shoulders too broad. After putting on the heels and looking in the mirror, I stepped out.

'That's *great!*' said Corinne. 'You've got lovely legs. You *cow!*'

'Ha! That's good enough for me,' I replied. I changed back into my T-shirt and jeans, gave three pounds to the assistant and we left.

Corinne drove us to Horsham, taking me to her room. 'I painted it myself,' she said as I looked at the walls, two of which were lime green, the other two hot pink. She had a fluffy bedspread with a cowskin print, a full-length mirror in one corner and another over the mantelpiece. I put my makeup there, next to hers.

We changed into our outfits – Corinne went for a pencil skirt and low-cut top, all in black, modelling it for my approval. Then we sat by the mirror.

'I never do makeup with someone like this,' she said.

'Me neither,' I responded as we applied mascara.

'You're holding it like a pen,' she told me, laughing. 'Hold it at the end. And do it slower, you'll get more volume.'

I followed her advice, elongating each eyelash. Then we went downstairs to find Corinne's mother watching television in the lounge.

'Mum, have you met Juliet?'

I grinned at Corinne. This was the first time I'd been introduced to anyone as Juliet, and I loved how casual, how *natural* she made it seem.

'I don't think so,' she said. 'I like the name. How did you choose it?'

'It just came to me when I was ten, and I still like it. I'd love to say it was Shakespeare but let's face it, it was probably a trailer for *Juliet Bravo* or something.' Corinne's mother laughed. 'I didn't know anyone called Juliet,' I continued, 'so I felt like it was mine.'

'It suits you,' she replied. 'Is this the first time you've been out like this?'

'Apart from Rag Week at college. Everyone kept telling me that I'd taken the dressing-up *far* too seriously,' I said, stroking my wig. 'Most of the guys just threw on a dress and smeared lippy across their faces. No point in doing something if you don't do it properly, right?'

She smiled. 'Quite! Lovely to meet you, Juliet. You girls have a good time.'

'We will,' said Corinne, as we stepped into her car, an old white Metro.

The Harlequin was behind Woolworths on London Road in Brighton. Corinne pulled into the car park at the top of the street. It was dank and dark, and reeked of piss. I tottered in my heels getting out of the car, having hardly worn them outside. I'd learned how to walk in them from a scene in *The Simpsons*, when Bart tries on Lisa's shoes: 'Heel, toe, heel, toe!' I found my balance, putting my hand on Corinne's shoulder as we approached the stairs on to Providence Place. There were three teenaged lads drinking lager, looking at us. One gave us a half-smile as we passed, and the others seemed unbothered, but I sped up anyway.

'Are you okay?' asked Corinne.

'I'm getting used to people staring at me,' I replied.

'Evening, ladies,' said the doorman, ushering us in. There was a jukebox by the stairs with a notebook for requests for the DJ, and a handful of people at the bar, which had several lights and mirrors around it. Nobody looked at us, and I immediately felt relaxed, in a way that I never had in Manchester.

'I'll get you a drink,' I told Corinne. A man with a shaved head and piercings, wearing a red shirt and tartan kilt with hairy legs, glanced at me. We went to the mezzanine floor so we could see the stage, dance floor and bar. Before long, he followed us there and came to our table.

'Do you mind if I say hello?'

'Not at all,' said Corinne.

'What's your name, darling?' he asked me.

'Juliet.'

'Is this your first time here, Juliet?'

'It's her first time anywhere, really,' Corinne told him.

'May I ask you a personal question?'

'Alright,' I said.

'Do you like men or women?'

'Men, I think.'

'How about you?' he asked Corinne.

'How about me *what*?'

'Which way do you swing?'

She paused, laughing. 'Nobody's ever asked me that before. Heterosexual, I suppose?'

'You'll get asked anything here. Don't worry, it's always friendly. I'll let you finish your drinks,' he said, going back to the bar.

'Are you into him?' asked Corinne.

'Not really – why?'

'He totally fancied you!'

'He *what*?'

'Didn't you see?'

'No, I never pick up on these things.'

'How did you miss *that*? His eyes were all over you!'

'Haha, get in!' I said, grinning.

'He didn't fancy *me*,' she said, pouting. I raised my eyebrows and smiled. As she started laughing, I got up.

'I'm just going to the toilet.'

'Which one?'

'Oh, I hadn't thought of that … I'll decide when I get there, I guess?'

I saw two doors: 'GENTS' on the left, and 'LADIES/TV/TS' on the right. *They've really made an effort*, I thought, going right. As I entered, a woman doing her makeup smiled at me, saying, 'Like the dress!' as I came out of the cubicle. I thanked her and returned to Corinne.

The lights dimmed, the music stopped and a voice-over asked us 'ladies and gentlemen' to put our hands together. To huge applause, one of Brighton's drag queens – I forget who now, perhaps Lola Lasagne, Maisie Trollette or Dave Lynn – walked into the spotlight and started lip-synching to 'I Will Survive'.

We went near the stage, looking at the lamé curtains and lights, laughing as the queen wandered around the room, picking out the most ostentatious people and poking fun at what they wore. There were a few other 'TV' or 'TS' people, all (I guessed) twenty years older than me, blending into the crowd. After a few more songs – familiar from *Priscilla* and nostalgic radio programmes in my parents' car – the show ended and we sat, watching the dance floor slowly fill to Steps, S Club 7, and Abba. I sipped my drink as an irresistible beat kicked in: 'Dud, dud, dud, dud, dud, dud, dudududududududuh …'

' "Blue Monday!" ' I shouted. 'I *love* this!' I grabbed Corinne's hand and we went to dance. As New Order faded into Donna Summer's 'I Feel Love', a man lifted the front of my wig.

'Damn!' he said. 'I wish you weren't a geezer!'

I smiled, taking this as a compliment, and he left me alone.

We danced until closing time and then wandered back to the empty car park, arm in arm to stop each other falling. I took off my wig to reveal my hair, flat and sweaty, and wiped off my lipstick before getting into the car, taking off my dress and bra, putting on my T-shirt, jeans and trainers before Corinne drove me back to Horley.

'That was amazing,' she told me. 'Thanks so much for inviting me!'

'Thanks for taking me! Now let's just hope my parents aren't up.'

'I thought they knew?'

'I tried to tell them at college, but they wrote it off as a phase. I don't think they'd be cool with it. But Mum gave me some nail varnish that she got with a magazine once, so I don't know. I'm not sure how to tell them. Now probably isn't the time.'

'Do you want me to take your stuff back, and you can pick it up later?' said Corinne.

'Yeah, that's really kind, thanks.'

She drove on to our street.

'Slow down,' I said, looking up at my parents' bedroom. 'I just want to check the light's out.' I kissed her goodbye before sneaking up to the house, cursing the proximity light for announcing my presence, hoping the dogs wouldn't bark. I opened and closed the front door and tiptoed to the bathroom, washing off as much of my mascara and eyeliner as I could before falling asleep, euphoric in the sense that a whole new world had opened up in front of me.

———

My old flatmate Matt and I walked back from a bar, having caught up on our return to Manchester for our final year at university. Sometimes helping at Valentine nights, Matt had become one of my closest friends. I'd not been sure about him when we'd first met at Oak House, when he said he'd been put in a flat full of girls and worried that people might think he was a 'mincer'. I'd felt jealous, already sick of the mess and the noise where I lived. Soon after he'd moved into the flat next door, however, I'd told him I was 'gay', and he'd been fine.

We'd bonded over our love of lower league football and music. He had introduced me to trip-hop, and I had played him post-punk. We both loathed the *Daily Mail* – my parents' newspaper, which had depressed me as a teenager with its endless stories about transsexual women demanding expensive surgery on the NHS, usually accompanied by a picture of a burly person in a floral dress with stubbly legs. When Matt said he came from Redhill, where I'd been born, just north of Horley, we realised that we felt the same alienation from our staunchly Conservative home towns.

On the corner of Princess Street was Manhattan's, with its decorative silhouette of the New York skyline and the Twin Towers, destroyed the previous September. I'd wanted to go there since the first year, when some American students had told me it had cabaret at weekends, with 'guys in drag' behind the bar, but every time I'd walked past, it was shut.

I stopped, finally seeing it open. 'One more drink?'

'What is it?' asked Matt.

'It's a drag bar. I've heard it's great.'

'It's not really my thing.'

'Go on, I'll buy you a pint.'

'Fucking hell, you must *really* want to go,' said Matt. 'Alright.'

It was smaller than the Harlequin, with a few tables, a small stage in the corner, a glitter ball and disco lights over the dance floor, quiet on a weeknight. I went to the bar. Someone in a black wig, pink top, short skirt and tights served me: I just smiled and said thanks, wondering if we might have struck up a conversation if I'd come as Juliet, before Matt and I sat down.

'I watched this documentary about a transsexual woman once,' he said. 'She had to go through this clinic to get her surgery. The doctors were total cunts, telling her if she didn't do everything they said then they'd stop her doing it. Did you see it?'

My mind fell back to the summer of 1996. I'd ventured out of my room, taking a break from computer games to watch football with my parents. They'd been slumped on the sofa, Mum's arm around Dad, our dog Jake across their laps. My brother was next to them, and our other dog, Daisy, had claimed her place on the armchair. I stood for a moment before a voice from the screen grabbed my attention:

'In 1979, George became Julia ...'

A male face cut to a female one, the caption saying 'A CHANGE OF SEX'. Then there had been a shot of a woman, middle-aged, with a permed haircut that I recognised from TV programmes about early 1980s music, football or politics. She'd had a breast job and was being lectured by a stern-sounding man, who told her, 'You're overstepping the mark and I don't like it one bit.' Apparently she'd needed his permission. 'Fifteen years since the landmark documentary, we catch up with Julia Grant ...' *I need to see this*, I'd thought.

'I hope neither of you ever have a sex change,' said Mum.

'Why not?' I asked.

'It's just not *normal*, is it?'

I'd sighed, not knowing what to say as my dad laughed and my brother stared blankly at the television. I'd been wearing

Mum's clothes in secret for several years, wondering how I'd managed not to get found out yet. I'd never told anyone that maybe I *would* rather be a girl. *Perhaps she knew and this was her way of telling me to stop?* Did *I* want a 'change of sex'? I had no idea, and I felt ill. I trudged back upstairs, listening to Joy Division rather than watching the match. I hadn't dared watch the programme – *what if I got caught?*

I brought my mind back to Manhattan's.

'I remember it being on but I missed it,' I said.

'Shame, I think you'd have found it interesting.'

I watched a couple of people – as at the Harlequin, they were in their forties, I guessed, either 'TV' or 'TS', wearing wigs, lipstick and heels with their dresses. I wanted to say hello, but in my second-hand T-shirt and jeans, with no makeup, I didn't know how to introduce myself. 'I'm a cross-dresser too!' didn't seem right, so I talked to Matt about how he thought Fulham would do in the Premier League, and if Norwich might finally return to the top division that season. Then I went home.

Years later, I found out that Julia Grant had opened Manhattan's. That night in September 2002, I would never have imagined then that she and I had been so close, let alone that our lives would take such similar paths.

———

I had decided that, for my final year, I would return to student halls, moving to Whitworth Park near the university. I got put in a flat with seven science students who already knew each other. On our first evening, they invited me to Horny, the Student Union disco. I declined – I was going to catch up with Dave and Sarah – and when they drunkenly wolf-whistled at some passing women, jeering when the women asked to be left alone, I knew I'd made the right choice. They got home at 4 a.m. after a fight, and later that week, I moved out, finding a room in a six-bedroom house in Withington. Donna, who was studying Fashion, had moved in after the intended tenants pulled out, on the condition that she find five other flatmates. I liked the house and told her I wanted to move in.

'One thing,' I said. 'I'm a cross-dresser. I don't do it at home much, but sometimes.'

'Fine with me,' she replied.

I started buying more dresses and skirts, women's jeans and T-shirts, wearing them around the house. The last person to move in, Sergi, was a waiter, originally from Catalonia, who did coke with his boss and kept a picture of General Franco in his wallet because he thought it was funny. 'If anyone in Lleida ever catches you with that, you're dead!' said my other Spanish housemate María José, before warning him that the strong cigarettes that he smoked, Ducados, might not be great for his health, or ours. He waved the packet in our faces, yelling 'For men! MEN!' and laughed. So I wondered how he might respond to my evolving style.

I soon found out. Sergi came home and saw me in a long black skirt and tights with my purple top, watching Almodóvar's *Law of Desire* with María. He smiled, went to the window and lit another Ducado, and we never needed to speak about it.

'My friend is doing a drag act at the Hollywood Showbar,' Donna said one day. 'Come?' Thinking that I might finally meet someone like me who was my age, I instantly said yes. I put on my makeup with a black and pink blouse, jeans and loafers, and got the bus. Donna's friends Kevin and Celeste joined us: like Lynne and Lauren, they had plenty of questions.

'Do you do this a lot?'

'Mainly when I'm out, but whenever I feel like it.'

'To the gay clubs?'

'No, I don't usually go to them. Just to gigs, pubs – wherever.'

'Do you have a girl's name?'

I hesitated – *did I want to tell them?*

'Not yet. I'm still deciding. It has to be right.'

'Do you want to go all the way?'

'What do you mean?'

'Would you like to be a woman?'

'I don't think so. I'm alright like this.'

We got to the venue, which, like Manhattan's, had been opened by Julia Grant. It resembled a Working Men's Club: wooden tables and chairs, purple walls and old carpets, with a piano bar upstairs and a black stage with lights around it. I watched, sipping a Coke, as Donna's friend, wearing a white dress and blonde wig, lip-synched through some pop song. A man tapped me on the shoulder.

'You should be up there!'

Donna and I laughed.

'I'm not a drag queen,' I told him.

'What are you then?'

'I've no idea!'

'Whatever, you should try it. You'd be great!'

Momentarily, I considered it. Perhaps I could call myself Morrissette and do Smiths covers, wearing NHS glasses and hearing aids like Morrissey on *Top of the Pops*. Certainly I'd have fun with 'Sheila Take a Bow'. Maybe somebody *could* do something a bit more interesting with drag? *But not me, not now*, I thought.

'Honestly, I'm alright,' I replied.

'Shame,' he said as Donna's friend stepped down. Donna suggested we drink elsewhere, and I didn't argue. Drag wasn't my thing, this wasn't my scene, and I never saw her friend again.

———

January 2003. I'd returned to Manchester for my final semester, having spent the Christmas break setting up my new life in Brighton. I'd applied for my Masters and agreed to live with my old friend Phil from Horsham; I'd caught up with Steve and formed another group with him, Corporate Marketing Ploy. He played drums, his friend Dan played guitar, I was on bass and Phil sang (or screamed) – we practised and gigged when Phil and I visited during the holidays. This was a side project to Steve and Dan's main band, Cat on Form, a hardcore punk act whom Factory Records founder Tony Wilson had been trying to sign to his new label. I'd contained my jealousy during a recording studio party on New Year's Eve, when Steve and Dan explained that they weren't going to sign with Wilson anyway.

I'd stepped back from Valentine, DJ-ing only at the monthly nights and engrossing myself in my dissertation (a wildly ambitious study of arts and politics in interwar Germany and Russia). It saddened me, though, that I was so concerned with the future and had written off the 'now'. *It wasn't meant to be like this,* I thought, standing on the Manchester University Union steps in my long overcoat. *Let's go home.*

'Hey!' came a voice as I walked towards the bus stop. A man approached me, his short brown hair somehow both scruffy and immaculate, wearing a black shirt and a pinstripe jacket with white beads over the pocket. Recognising him from our French revolutionary philosophy seminars, and a show with a couple of American bands before Christmas, I said hello.

'I like your coat,' he said.

'Thanks, I've had it for years.'

I couldn't remember any guys I knew saying they liked my male clothes, although Dave and John often said nice things about my makeup.

'You were at that Faint gig at the Roadhouse, weren't you?' he asked.

'Yeah, I'd gone to see Radio 4,' I replied.

'I thought they were boring,' he told me.

'I liked "Dance to the Underground". Otherwise they just sounded like Gang of Four, but not as good.'

'Did you like the Faint?' he asked.

'I found them a bit shallow.'

'Really? I thought they were *cool*,' he said. 'All those dark synths and drum loops.'

'Schneider TM were better. Like Kraftwerk, but funnier.' I replied.

'Yeah, they were great. I'm Joe, by the way.'

'Nice to meet you,' I said. 'Fancy a coffee?'

We went to Big Hands, a nearby café and venue, looking at the adverts for local gigs and clubs. We talked about what we did: I wrote short stories, I said, and after apologetically explaining that 'Corporate Marketing Ploy' had stuck because we thought it was funny, told him that I co-wrote lyrics with Phil – about America's response to 9/11, the fact that Section 28 had still not been repealed despite the efforts of Blair's government, and whatever else made us angry.

'Do you know Valentine Records?' asked Joe.

'I helped set it up!'

'My band recorded a demo, I wondered if they'd like to hear it.'

'I'd love to.'

'You'll hate it,' he told me. 'Far too pop.'

'What does it sound like?' I asked.

'Depeche Mode, Soft Cell, the Human League.'

'I *love* all that! Bring it tomorrow and I'll check it out.'

The next day, Joe gave me a C90 cassette with 'Performance' scrawled across the label, five song titles on its front. From the opening synth whirrs on 'Female Gaze', I was hooked. Jagged guitar riffs slashed across the digital rhythms and a cool Northern woman's voice sang of 'lashes draped in sin' before Joe's vocals kicked in: 'Blackened eyes and brittle lashes thickly smudged with subtle dashes ...'

The band were creating a world miles from anyone else in Manchester, anyone else in *Britain*. The songs were about the emptiness of partying, the dark side of sexuality, the insincerity of youth culture, with male and female vocals bouncing off each other, synths and guitars winding in and out of each other. It had that wit and wisdom, euphoria and melancholy that made the Smiths, New Order and the Fall so wonderful. I felt sure that they would represent Manchester's new sound just as the renovated Piccadilly Gardens, with its ordered greenery and obelisks, symbolised its new image. I played the tape a dozen times and then texted Joe: 'Meet me at the Cornerhouse tomorrow. Bring the demo.'

Valentine had a roster of groups that straddled electro-pop and post-punk, and I was convinced that I had found the band to take us to the next level, maybe even to the heart of Manchester's music scene. At the café, I wrote a note for Dave: 'This is the best new band I've ever heard. We've *got* to put out an EP.' We spent an hour trying to buy a Jiffy bag to take the tape to Dave's new flat, sharing the thrill of anticipation as we dropped it into his letterbox.

We went back to the university market. As I rooted through the books, Joe bought a couple of crop tops – a bold move for anyone, let alone a six-footer who always looked so effortlessly stylish in jackets and jeans. *How does he do it so calmly?* I wondered, thinking back to that charity shop in Withington. I got a pink T-shirt with an image from Russ Meyer's *Faster, Pussycat! Kill! Kill!* I'd found the film dull, but thought it would make me look cool. The suspicious look that Joe gave me when I showed it to him didn't quite make me reconsider.

I stuck with my brown Oxfam shirt and women's jeans the next time I saw him. He lived with Joe Cross, Performance's songwriter, near Oak House. We'd been in the same halls – he'd used the time I'd spent getting stoned to protest against the tuition fees introduced by Blair, and I wished I'd known him then. By now, we'd talked plenty of Marx and Foucault, Bush and Blair, Brecht and Camus, and I'd told him how I never went anywhere without my copy of *Alcools* by Guillaume Apollinaire, the arch-modernist whose poems were mysterious and surreal, beautiful and bleak. Joe handed me a volume titled *Twentieth-Century French Poetry*, saying only, 'Read this.'

I cast my eye over 'Breakfast' by Jacques Prévert, a simple scene of a communication breakdown between two people – both men, I imagined. I was transfixed from beginning to end:

> He put his raincoat on
> Because it was raining
> And he left
> In the rain
> Without talking to me
> Without looking at me
> And I
> I put my head in my hand
> And I cried.

'That's *incredible*,' I said.

'Isn't it? Says so much with so little.'

In return for the demo tape, I'd given Joe my short story, 'Nazimova'. I asked if he'd read it.

'I loved it!' he said. 'It's funny, smart and full of life. That club you wrote about – is it real?'

'It's the Harlequin in Brighton.'

'It sounds wonderful. Did you go as Nazimova?'

'Haha! Not quite, but I did dress up.'

There was silence. I wondered if Joe was contemplating the fact that I'd just come out to him. Perhaps he was considering what I'd come out *as*, given that I'd said 'I'm gay' to him early on. I braced myself for the usual barrage of questions. Then he asked:

'Are you coming to the anti-war march in London?'

'I can't afford it.'

'There's a free bus,' he told me.

'I've got loads of work,' I said, not wanting to tell him that I couldn't face the massive crowds and lines of police.

'Okay. You'll come to our gig at Big Hands though, right?'

'Of course!'

I went to the venue alone, pushing to the front as Performance came on. The two Joes wore suits, Cross on keyboard, Stretch behind the microphone in eyeliner, reciting poetry and drenching himself with water between songs. There were two women, sisters: brown-haired Billie on keyboard and bleached-blonde Laura on guitar and vocals, dressed in knowingly New Romantic–style blouses and necklaces. *No band would dare shamble on in sports gear with acoustic guitars after this*, I thought as they raced into 'Dotted Line', a high-octane cocktail of bleeps, beats and subtle melodies, the deliberately vacuous lyrics turning straight love songs into something ridiculous. The room seemed too small for them, Laura and Joe bursting from the stage, this electricity building between the band and the crowd. The set closed with Laura hammering her guitar, Joe hurling himself at the walls and everyone clapping and whistling.

I texted Dave: 'Did you listen to *Performance* yet?'

He hadn't. By the time he did, all of Manchester was talking about them. *City Life*, the local answer to *Time Out*, put them on the cover; American labels were calling them, and they were no longer an underground band but the leading lights of a scene laughably dubbed 'Manctronica', crowds of people in vintage clothes with their hair bleached or dyed black queuing around the block to see them. Electro-pop was coming back in: acts from America and Germany were breaking through, and I desperately wanted Performance to spearhead a similar movement here – with Valentine. But we had no money to put out an EP – I certainly couldn't provide it – so we had to be content with a single track on a compilation and a few headline slots at our club night at the Retro Bar.

One of these came on my final night in Manchester. That week, Valentine had been profiled in *City Life*. Dave, Sarah, John and I met their reporter at Retro Bar, suspicious as he didn't have a Dictaphone or even a notepad, annoyed that nearly every question was about Performance. *Are you responsible for their rise?* Sarcastically, I'd said: 'Yes, we're like Malcolm McLaren, only more self-indulgent.' This had reached print as 'We want to claim full responsibility for Performance's rise to fame,' taken without irony by one of the bands we'd released, who expressed their irritation on our website's forum. I made a mental note to be more cautious if I ever became involved with journalists again.

The issue had a feature on Manchester's greatest ever front men, with Ian Curtis as 'poet', Liam Gallagher as 'fighter' and Morrissey as 'ponce'. They rated up-and-coming singers on various criteria, giving Joe 76 per cent for 'androgyny' and four out of five for 'clothes', but just two for 'manifesto', making me feel they'd not seen the (dis)content beneath the style. With the hype around the band and the label, the night sold out, young men and women who looked like they wanted to be in Performance queuing around the block as I opened the DJ sets.

The floor was empty, so I played a recording of Vorticist artist/writer Wyndham Lewis reading his poem 'End of Enemy Interlude'. Aggressively sexist, Lewis would have hated having his work aired by me in my chocolate blouse, long skirt and black velvet jacket that Dave, Sarah and the others at Valentine had bought me as a leaving present. Joe liked it, though, striding across the room with a huge smile.

'I love this,' he told me. 'Great beat.'

I laughed. After a few more tracks, I closed with 'Once in a Lifetime' by Talking Heads.

'Oh, I love this!' said Joe. 'It's perfect pop music!'

I agreed: I remembered how blown away I'd been when I first saw the video on MTV at age thirteen. It starts with David Byrne in a bow tie, suit and glasses lunging into the frame, puffing his cheeks, water flowing behind him, four bass notes rising and falling beneath a shimmering synth line. He constantly stops, exhausted, dipping in and out of view. He starts shouting, pointing at a screen behind him: 'And you may find yourself living in a shotgun shack! And you may find yourself on the other side of the world!' By the chorus – 'Letting the days go by … Into the blue again, after the money's gone' – I was transfixed. It closed with the singer repeating, 'Same as it ever was'. Apparently life-changing experiences, Byrne suggested, often don't alter your humdrum life much at all.

I stepped down. Performance delivered another blistering set. Joe and I stood together after they left the stage, watching people dance.

'You're doing the right thing, leaving Manchester,' said Joe.

'I hope so,' I replied. 'I'm going to miss you, though.'

'We'll keep in touch. You'll come to London for Performance gigs, right?'

'Definitely!'

The end of the night came, and I got a taxi home. The next day, my father arrived to move me between Manchester and Horley for the last time. *Just a few months back in the suburbs and then I can really start living*, I thought, certain that I'd get funding to support my further studies into Literature and Film, music and gender.

A History of the Sex Change

One evening in early 2002, I was flicking through the stations on my portable TV. Channel 4 had a documentary entitled *A History of the Sex Change*. For all I'd seen about 'transsexuals' in the media, I'd never seen this kind of historical context given before, and I was intrigued. The documentary took me back to 1920s Germany, which I'd studied in A-level History and become obsessed with while in Manchester, fascinated by its modern art, Expressionist plays and films. But for all that, I knew nothing of interwar Berlin's role in 'the sex change' (as it was always called in the press); I'd never thought about how the process was developed, or where words such as 'transvestite' or 'transsexual' came from, so I kept watching.

Before the First World War, German sexologist Magnus Hirschfeld popularised the first specific term for gender-variant people: 'transvestite'. He had already founded the world's first homosexual rights group, the Scientific Humanitarian Committee, in 1897, before publishing *The Transvestites: The Erotic Drive to Cross-Dress* in 1910. Challenging assumptions that cross-dressing was intrinsically linked to homosexuality, he interviewed hundreds of 'transvestites', male-to-female and female-to-male, finding them split roughly evenly between heterosexual, homosexual and bisexual people; he also distinguished cross-dressing from narcissism, masochism and fetishism. Hirschfeld divided 'sexual intermediaries' into four categories: 'hermaphrodites in a [narrow] sense' who 'give enough cause to be mistakenly identified regarding their sex at birth'; people with unusual 'physical characteristics' such as 'men with womanly mammary tissue ... and women without [it]'; men who were sexually 'passive' and women who were 'aggressive'; and 'men who more or less dress themselves as women or live totally as such' or 'women of manly character [or] who more or less lead the life of a man'.

Nearly a hundred years later, I questioned Hirschfeld's ideas about the way 'feminine emotions and feelings are reflected in ... manner of love, direction of taste, gestures and manners', and thought he should not have associated 'passive' with 'female' and 'aggressive' with 'male'. But his work had contributed so much to the self-realisation of transvestites and transsexual people throughout the twentieth century, and now it was helping with mine.

Gender variance had a far longer history than Hirschfeld's 'transvestites', appearing in Greek mythology concerning Dionysus, the androgynous god of wine, ritual madness and ecstasy. The designation of clothing as male or female and the practice of cross-dressing (and by implication, the classification of behaviour as masculine or feminine), were ancient enough for Deuteronomy 22:5 to declare that 'a man's item shall not be on a woman, and a man shall not wear a women's garment: for all that do so are an abomination unto the Lord'.

In Western Europe, Christianity did not permit large 'third gender' communities like those in Eastern and Southern Asia. In India, the *hijra* were eunuchs who adopted 'feminine' gender roles and dress – in the past and present, they have been on the margins of society, but allowed to perform religious ceremonies at births and weddings. In Samoa, the *fa'afafine* – people who were born male but who adopt both traditionally masculine and feminine traits – are more integrated into the country's social life; not all parents try to stop boys from behaving in this manner. Thailand's third gender community, the *kathoey*, are perhaps best known in Britain: people who often identify as 'gay' but display varying levels of femininity, from wearing women's clothes to having 'feminising' surgeries.

The Old Testament also outlawed homosexuality, and Protestant Britain introduced the first law against 'buggery' in 1553. There were no rules against cross-dressing, but men who wore 'female attire' were believed to be sodomites, and it was commonly thought that people who presented as feminine must be attracted to men. As London and other industrial cities grew, offering new levels of anonymity, people began to cross-dress in semi-public or public spaces. In the eighteenth century, men dressed as women had sex in 'molly houses', entrenching the perceived link between cross-dressing and sodomy: parish constables raided Mother Clap's molly house in Holborn in 1726 and arrested forty men. Three were hanged.

During the Victorian period, male-to-female cross-dressers on London's streets were arrested by the new Metropolitan Police, usually for soliciting or public order offences. After the farcical arrest, trial and acquittal in 1871 of Ernest 'Stella' Boulton and Frederick 'Fanny' Park, who argued that their appearances *en femme* in notorious London nightspots were extensions of their theatrical 'drag' personas, sexologists took greater interest in cross-dressing. Motivated by their opposition to British and German laws that outlawed homosexuality, late-nineteenth-century writers such as Edward Carpenter and Havelock Ellis theorised about 'inverts': people who were physically male but spiritually female, or vice versa. But it was not until Hirschfeld and others explored the possibility of sex reassignment that his separation of gender variance and sexual diversity became more widely accepted.

In 1919, Hirschfeld established the Institute of Sexual Science in Berlin, meeting many people who wanted to change their bodies. Having coined the word 'transsexualis-mus' in 1923, he supervised the first reassignment operations, including a mastectomy on a transsexual man in 1926 and a penectomy and vaginoplasty on Dora Richter in 1931. Most notable were those surgeries performed on Danish painter Lili Elbe, who moved from Copenhagen to Paris with her partner, artist Gerda Wegener, in 1912. Gerda's work often featured a short-haired, brown-eyed woman, who, it shocked Parisian art circles to learn, was her husband. In 1930, having spent time during the previous decade living as a woman, Lili went to Germany to have her testicles removed. She had four more surgeries: the second to remove her penis and attempt to transplant ovaries from a twenty-six-year-old woman; the third and fourth to remove these, due to biological rejection. This caused a sensation in Denmark: the king invalidated Lili's marriage to Gerda in October 1930, but allowed her to have her sex and name legally altered. The fifth operation, to 'create a natural outlet from the womb' and transplant a uterus, led to her death from heart failure on 13 September 1931, just after she accepted a proposal from a man who promised to help her become a mother.

Before coming to power, Hitler called Hirschfeld 'the most dangerous man in Germany'. The Gestapo visited his Institute as soon as the Nazis took power, most interested in finding correspondence he had conducted with Party members. Hirschfeld was abroad on 6 May 1933 when he heard that most of the Institute's papers had been removed, along with 20,000 books and 5,000 images. Four days later, these materials were burned at Berlin's Opera Square along with works by Jewish authors, pacifists and Communists, and the bronze of Hirschfeld's head made for his sixtieth birthday. Around the fire, students chanted, 'Against decadence and moral decay! For discipline and decency in the family and state!' Joseph Goebbels arrived to address the crowd – over 40,000 people – hoping that nobody would remember that he had studied literature with Jewish professors and praised the writers whose works were in flames. Hirschfeld – Jewish and socialist as well as homosexual – never returned to Germany and died two years later in France. But long after the collapse of the 'thousand year Reich', his work continued in America and Britain and throughout the world to give people words, identities and possibilities.

4

A letter dropped into our family home, informing me that the Arts and Humanities Research Board would not pay the tuition fees for my Masters or provide a living allowance. I'd made plans to become an academic, but that prospect was now looking bleak. Phil – one of my closest friends from childhood who was going to do a Masters in International Relations – had found us a flat near the seafront. But moving in that September, I soon realised I'd have to study part-time and find a job – quickly. Leaving full-time education meant adult responsibilities: for my twenty-second birthday I got £20 from my grandmother and a £1,000 council tax bill.

Declared a city for the new millennium, Brighton and Hove wasn't that big. But unlike Manchester, where a straight line had led from the centre past the university to the student district, its layout always confused me. It was a lovely place to get lost, however: I enjoyed exploring the Lanes, narrow streets of antique and jewellery shops, and the North Laine, a trendy grid with cafés, vintage clothes, book and record stores. It took me some time to understand how they connected to London Road – further attempts to visit the Harlequin always ended with my giving up and finding a 'straight' pub, although perhaps I'd have tried harder if I'd come as Juliet. Gradually, I worked out how to find the Free Butt, the pub and gig venue where Steve was a sound engineer, and which of the Seven Dials led where. I often stopped to gaze at the terraced houses that sprawled across the hills, wondering who lived in them and what their lives were like.

Little interested me in Hove, and most of the places I wanted to go to in Brighton fell between Preston Park, where the Pride party was held every August, St James's Street, which led into the Kemp Town gay district, and City Books, the independent shop on the Brighton–Hove border – all of which were within half an hour's walk from our flat, at most. Gradually, I identified my favourite places: Wax Factor for second-hand vinyl, and Borderline or Edgeworld for new music; the Great Eastern for a cosy, quiet drink or the King and Queen to watch Cup finals with a big crowd; the Duke of York's, opened in 1911, for art house and independent movies, and the Cinematheque, an amateur-run club screening anything from Marx Brothers comedies to avant-garde shorts by the London Film-Makers' Co-operative, which I thought was the best thing in town.

Every Thursday, the *Brighton & Hove Argus* billboard near our flat promised: 1000S OF JOBS – INSIDE! Every Thursday, I opened the paper and thought: *These all look fucking shit*. There were graduate training schemes in banks or the police, and if I'd known as an eighteen-year-old that I'd be expected to put my studies into the service of those bastards, I might not have bothered. Then I realised my prospects and ambitions weren't shaped by university but school. I remembered the Kudos software I'd used at Oakwood, which asked 'yes or no' questions about what type of work I'd enjoy in order to find my ideal job. After a sequence of questions, the computer concluded:

THERE ARE NO SUITABLE JOBS FOR YOU.

The Argus kept proving Kudos right until I saw an advert for charity work, reasonably paid at £7 per hour. I showed up at the office only to realise that this meant standing on Brighton's streets, badgering consumers into regular donations. I left, deciding to hand my CV into shops. The Co-operative Department Store – the most antiquated building on London Road – gave me an interview.

'You're over-qualified,' said the branch manager. 'You'll leave.'

'It'll take two years to do my Masters,' I replied. 'You'll have me for that.'

He grudgingly hired me, with Mondays off for my Psychoanalysis, Literature and Film seminars. So I began to sell televisions and toasters, radios and refrigerators for £5.09 per hour, with £1 commission for every item over £100 sold. My income secured, I went to the Co-operative Bank for a Career Development Loan.

'What's your Masters in?' asked the clerk.

'Literature and Visual Culture.'

'Sounds interesting,' she said. 'There are a lot of people doing useless degrees like History.'

'My degree was in History.'

'I'm sorry …'

'No, it probably is useless, you're right,' I said. I laughed to break the tension so that I wouldn't start weeping, feeling all that optimism I'd felt six months earlier vanish. I told myself that at least I could afford to stay in Brighton and *do* my degree, which I would enjoy for its own sake. Just as well, because if History was bunk, what good was Literature?

———

Unlike Manchester, the University of Sussex had a film library and Queer Studies centre. I went to my first seminars in a pink shirt and makeup, replacing my overcoat with a brown fake-fur-lined women's jacket from Oxfam. My new course mates were the people I'd hoped to meet as an undergraduate: Jimmy liked Werner Herzog movies as much as I did, and was usually up for a trip to the Duke of York's or the Cinematheque. Max, a Tottenham fan, would come with me to watch football matches in pubs. Jennie introduced me to avant-garde writers such as the early-twentieth-century feminist and futurist poet Mina Loy. Alice, who wrote papers on arty French erotic films and who always looked great in her neon-pink coat and her beaded polka-dot tops, said she liked to go to what we called 'gay clubs' around Brighton, but which were being rebranded as lesbian, gay, bisexual and transgender (LGBT) venues.

The inclusion of the 'transgender' made me feel I could go to these places as Juliet. Phil didn't care what I wore, laughing just about how I'd spend my money on dresses when my men's clothes were falling apart. I became relaxed at home – I knew I could wear what I liked without feeling judged – and soon I became confident in going out.

I was far more comfortable shopping in Brighton: the city prided itself on its 'alternative' culture, with punks, goths and electro-pop fans blending in as much as the LGBT clubs stood out. Some places fell over themselves to show how accepting they were: I grew fond of a nameless shop on Trafalgar Street, whose owner responded to my request to try on a cocktail dress with stories about her 'drag queen' friends, asking about my size and style before throwing whatever she could find at me.

I would get ready in our bathroom, shaving my face and chest, arms and legs, and then get the lift from our floor to the street, hoping nobody saw me. As I couldn't afford a bus, it was a long walk to the Harlequin, or Kemp Town for 'T-friendly' places such as the Queen's Arms, Charles Street or R-Bar, and I worried that people would ridicule me, threaten me, or worse. I preferred the walks in winter. Light and heat made me feel exposed, my makeup running as both fabrics and fear made me sweat. In the dark and cold, nobody looked at me much. Sometimes, crowds at the nearby church would stare as I approached. Worried about my voice, I'd mouth, 'Excuse me' and walk faster, trying to ignore their obvious disapproval.

In general, groups of young men would be more openly hostile. Often I'd get to Seven Dials, hesitating when I saw people over the road by the cash point. Sometimes, they'd yell 'I'm a lady!' at me – a catchphrase from the sketch show *Little Britain*, uttered by 'rubbish transvestite' Emily Howard. I'd rush off, hoping they'd be satisfied with just laughing at me. I knew that standing up for myself would result in a kicking.

It was safer to stick to quiet back streets. One night, avoiding busy North Street, I looked down an alley. Thinking it was clear, I carried on. Three men sat at the other end, drinking. One sized up my legs, licking his lips. Another wolf-whistled. I knew what that meant: *I've read you and I'm calling you out.* Terrified and humiliated, I dropped my head, but the verbal attacks just got worse. Over time, I realised that however vulnerable I felt, the only way to stop them was to hold myself up and try to look fearless. And after the difficulties of getting to my destination, meeting my friends always made these hazardous journeys worthwhile. I'd feel liberated, particularly in the newer venues with their largely female crowds. The men in older joints such as the Queen's Arms tended to ask intrusive questions about what was in my bra. I preferred to sit in the corner and chat.

Alice and I soon became close, finding plenty of common ground in our musical and aesthetic tastes. She preferred tops and skirts on casual nights out to appear not to have tried too hard, and soon I ditched my dresses for similar outfits, including some that she gave me. I'd tease her because her friends in bands were so style-conscious; *mine*, on the other hand, were in guitar acts and wore jeans and plain T-shirts. They declared that 'fashion is fascism' and decried keyboard-led groups like Miss Pain with their 1960s clothes and songs that included diary extracts. My friends claimed that *their* lyrics were seriously political, unlike this confessional froth, and I agreed.

'Where do *you* fit into that?' asked Alice. Perhaps she sensed that my friends' criticisms made me uncomfortable after yet another declaration of Performance's brilliance. I'd been convinced that they were going to be huge by their high-octane Islington Academy show with Pink Grease in December 2003, which ended with Joe yelling from the rafters over a wall of digital noise. I hadn't stopped talking about it since.

'I'm not sure,' I replied, laughing. Corporate Marketing Ploy had fizzled out, and Cat on Form's original drummer Eva – one of the few women on that scene – had left. The atmosphere at Free Butt gigs felt even more macho, and I had started spending less time there and more at LGBT venues, where I thought I could safely be myself.

Beneath my anxieties about where I went and what I wore, and how I was perceived and treated as a result, was a growing discomfort with my body. Often, my choice of clothing was an attempt to make this visible. I felt no happier with the labels of 'transvestite' or 'transsexual' than I had during my teens, and I'd never seen this sensation of discomfort expressed other than in phrases such as 'trapped in the wrong body', which had never quite spoken to me. I didn't like my facial hair, flat chest or genitalia, but I'd long known that I could change them. The more I read about Hirschfeld's patients, or transsexual women such as April Ashley whose marriage had been declared void when her husband wanted to divorce her in 1970, a precedent which still stood, the more I felt trapped not by my body but a society that didn't want me to modify it.

One evening, I came home from a bar to find Dan and Jamie from Cat on Form talking to Phil. My arrival initiated a discussion about how I didn't like the clubs.

'I hate the music, and they're usually pretty empty …'

'Do you have to go there?' said Jamie.

'I don't *have* to … I'd feel too nervous anywhere else, though.'

'Do you want to go all the way?' asked Dan.

'Change my body? I don't know,' I said. 'It looks so difficult.'

'I think it's one of the most damaging things you can do,' said Phil.

'Why?' asked Jamie.

'Besides what you do to your body, you've got to deal with how everyone reacts.' Phil gestured at me. 'I mean, look at how much shit you get just walking to a bar.'

I sighed and nodded, and we changed the subject. I hardly ever wore dresses or makeup at home, no longer feeling the need. In public, I was playing with my style, telling friends that the notion of 'male' and 'female' clothes was absurd. I didn't challenge anyone who called me 'madam', just smiling if they apologised. At work, though, I had to be unambiguous, inauthentic in polo shirts and trousers, trying as hard as I could to convince people that they really *needed* that television.

One afternoon, a familiar face walked in: Martin Nichols, my form tutor at Collyer's. I'd always liked him – when he'd asked what we wanted to *do* and I'd said 'writer', he'd been one of the few who hadn't told me to 'get a proper job'. Instead he replied, 'Being a writer is fine, as long as you don't mind being poor.' Back then I'd thought: *I'm poor now – how bad can it be?*

I was finding out, trying to balance my job, studies and social life with writing a play called *A Rational Death*, based on the story of an Arkansas man diagnosed as schizophrenic on death row who could not be executed until he had completed a course of forced medication. It wasn't going well: Joe hated the first draft, and while the second was better, the gulf between my ambition and my experience seemed unbridgeable. This was especially clear in the flat, stilted scenes between the alienated central character and his psychiatrist.

Perhaps Mr Nichols can help, I thought.

'Are you still involved with the New Venture?' I asked, thinking back to our A-level Theatre Studies trips to see plays that he'd put on there.

'Yes, I'm directing *Antony and Cleopatra*. I need a young man to play Eros. Fancy it?'

'Sure.'

I sold Martin a cooker and met him for rehearsal a few days later. There, I met Carl, who was playing several minor roles. I liked him immediately. Fifteen years older than me, thin with short black hair, a little taller than me, he seemed far more genuine than any man I'd met on the 'scene'. He didn't fit the butch or camp stereotypes, being gentle and soft-spoken without any affectations, and he shared my love of minimalist composers, particularly Steve Reich, and European film. We made a date to see Almodóvar's *Bad Education* at the Duke of York's.

After putting on my favourite blouse (the beige one I'd bought in Manchester), I made up my eyes and painted my nails, wondering how Carl would react. *Best to be open*, I thought. But when I showed up to meet him, after all my agonising, he just kissed me and we entered the cinema. The film was about a filmmaker, Enrique, and an actor called Ignacio, trying to deal with the sexual abuse they experienced at a Catholic boys' school in 1970s Spain by writing and directing a movie about it. I admired Almodóvar's fearlessness in tackling such a 'taboo', and found Gael García Bernal irresistibly beautiful as 'drag queen' Zahara in a green dress and brown wig, shot with great love. But *All about My Mother* had shown damaged people finding ways to *live*; *Bad Education* showed Ignacio trying to blackmail the priest into paying for sex reassignment surgery before becoming addicted to heroin and being murdered. Here was yet another film in which a transgender character was systematically destroyed. Seeing Ignacio shoot up and die, I was filled with self-loathing. The idea that *any* man, yet alone one so smart and sweet, might love me just made me want to run away.

Nonetheless, I kept going to Carl's Kemp Town flat after that first date. He'd cook, and I'd bring videos. Often these were collections of short films made before the First World War. 'What do you like about these?' asked Carl as we watched Georges Méliès' sumptuously hand-coloured *Voyage beyond the Possible*, a science-fiction fantasy with primitive sets and special effects.

'You can see they're working out a language,' I replied. 'When to use close-ups or long shots, when to cut and how often, when to use colour, everything.'

'Your nail varnish is chipped,' said Carl, smiling. I shrugged. 'Shall I fix it?'

Carl took a box from a cupboard. 'This is from the theatre.' I gave him my hand and he redid my nails, hot pink.

'What else have you got?'

'I don't know if I've got anything that'll suit you ...'

'Don't worry,' I replied. 'It'll be fun.'

He found a black dress, red bangles, false eyelashes and a blonde wig. I put them all on.

'This is weird,' he said as he finished my makeup. I smiled at him.

'Are you going to stop then?' He laughed. I posed for a few photos, and then we kissed. For a moment, I forgot every street heckle and intrusive question, every newspaper cartoon and TV comedy sketch, and relaxed, letting him love me, letting him fuck me.

I wore more makeup the next time I saw him, straightening my hair for the first time. We'd been seeing each other for two months. I suspected that he wanted a more serious relationship than I did, and the time had come to discuss it.

'The cross-dressing was fun once,' he said, 'but it doesn't turn me on.'

'But it's who I am. I don't think I can be with anyone who feels like that.'

'Be with anyone?' he asked. 'What *are* we doing, anyway?'

'I don't know. Maybe we should stop.' I watched his face drop, feeling awful, wondering if there was any way things could be different.

'I know people always say this, but it's not you, it's me. I need to figure all this out.' Silence. 'I hope we can still be friends.'

'I knew this was coming,' said Carl, 'because you were late. You're never late.'

'I was doing my makeup.'

'I was wondering who else to invite for dinner.'

'I'm sorry,' I replied. 'I hope you find the right person.'

'I think I'll always love you,' he told me.

I hugged him until he was ready to let go. I took the stairs to the street and walked home, trying not to look back, wanting to cry, not knowing what was stopping me.

———

A family friend ran an antique book magazine, and I'd asked her about work. She'd commissioned me to review a biography of Sir Winston Churchill. She liked my piece, and in spring 2004 I was offered a contract. I quit the Co-op and supplemented my writing income with part-time work in a shop called Avatar Jewels in the Lanes. A colleague there set me up with Marino, a former priest from Bari, who (I thought) looked like Michel Foucault with his shaved head and glasses. We got on, talking about Blair and Berlusconi, and after dinner, we went to bed together. He wanted to suck me off. I hated it, not wanting him to *see* my penis, let alone touch it. 'It's soft!' he said, angrily, and we went back to kissing.

The next time I saw him, I put on foundation, mascara and lipstick – and replaced my boxer shorts with briefs from the women's section of Marks & Spencer. We ate and went to my room. We kissed, then he undid my belt and pulled down my jeans. 'I'm sorry,' he said, seeing my underwear, 'but I don't like your lipstick. It's not attractive.'

'You didn't mind earlier, but you hate it *now*?'

'Maybe it's because it's taboo' – *he actually said taboo*, I thought – 'but I can't do this.'

He put on his jeans and left. I cried, and never saw him again.

———

A card arrived from Dave and Sarah, postmarked Manchester.

We're doing the last Valentine night at Retro Bar in July. See you there! PS Don't forget the 'dress code'.

I packed some CDs, as well as a 1920s-style black dress, fake pearl necklace, headscarf and a tube of deep red lipstick. I met Joe at Piccadilly Gardens: we agreed that not getting any Performance EPs out on Valentine had meant that both parties lost momentum. So far they'd released just one single, on Guilty Feet, created especially for them by local journalists; Joe played me their next one, 'Love Life', due out soon, saying that although he wasn't satisfied with it, they were in negotiations about signing for a major label.

'Sign for an independent,' I insisted. 'You'll get more freedom.' But Joe said the band were adamant that a big company with more resources would better suit them. I met Dave, Sarah and the rest of Performance at Retro Bar, changing into my dress and doing my makeup in the disabled toilet. Andy, the gay guy who ran the place, to whom I'd never found a word to say, gave me a smile.

'Love the dress!' said Sarah. 'Can I take a photo?'

'Sure,' I said. 'With me, Joe and Joe.'

'You look amazing!' Sarah said as her camera clicked.

'Thanks!' I replied. 'A guy in Brighton said I looked like Marlene Dietrich.'

'He must have been drunk!' yelled Andy. 'Or fucking *blind*!'

I pouted as Dave and Sarah laughed, wishing that I had quick answers to this sort of banter. It just wasn't how I spoke to my friends.

'How's the writing going?' asked Joe.

'I'm redrafting *A Rational Death*, but I've got this idea for some short stories about transgender people ...'

'Transgender?'

'Cross-dressers, transvestites, transsexual people, whatever.'

'Do that, it'll be great,' said Joe. 'It's a commercial project.'

'Maybe,' I replied. 'I've got my dissertation and journalism for now.' We went downstairs, where Performance played another exhilarating show. Then we talked, briefly recapturing that excitement we'd felt about the future just before we graduated. Now we had to make so many decisions about where we worked, what we worked on, who we even *were*. Neither of us had ever imagined how complicated these decisions would be, and even though spring 2003 was only fifteen months past, the optimism of that time already felt like a lifetime ago.

———

Back in Brighton, I needed a job again. I'd lost the freelance contract in a wave of cuts and couldn't find any journalistic work besides writing for *Filmwaves*, a quarterly magazine devoted to independent film and artists' video, with only nominal payment. Alice worked at Legal & General, Brighton and Hove's main student employer alongside American Express and Lloyds TSB. She said it wasn't terrible – her colleagues were friendly, the office was relaxed, and she thought I wouldn't have to deal directly with the public. One afternoon, having stayed out all night, she'd asked if I could lend her some clothes for work. Her boss complimented her on my knee-length floral print skirt and told her that 'only you could stay out all night and then turn up late having borrowed a skirt off a bloke'; this made me think the place sounded alright, but my main reason for wanting the job was because it was over the road from our flat.

So I went to the agency and got a temporary post, working 4 to 9 p.m. five days a week, checking tax figures on people's insurance policies because the company's expensive new system didn't do it properly. There, I recognised Alexis Lothian, having met her on campus, and we started talking. I said I was writing about *Berg* by Ann Quin, a brilliantly dense and dark 1960s novel about a man who'd come to Brighton to kill his father, a dismal end-of-the-pier entertainer long before the 'Pink Pound' had gentrified the city. I described a scene where Berg tried to disguise himself as his father's lover, and Alexis said it sounded fascinating – she was taking the Queer Studies MA and 'reading a lot of transgender theory'.

'Really? I'm transgender.'

'How do you mean?'

'I'm still working *that* out,' I replied. 'But I'm somewhere between male and female.'

'Have you read *Gender Outlaw* by Kate Bornstein?'

'No! But it already sounds great …'

Excited, I found it in the university library. '*Gender Outlaw* [1994]', read the back cover, 'is an account of Bornstein's transformation from heterosexual male to lesbian woman, from a one-time IBM salesperson to a playwright and performance artist.' *Great!*

Bornstein wrote about how she'd never seen anything in Western culture encouraging her to discuss her gender: 'Those who came out were either studied under a microscope, ridiculed in the tabloids, or made exotic in porn books, so it paid to hide.' In therapy as an adult, she was told to invent the girlhood that she'd never been allowed, rather than be honest about her past. Her ambition was to find a transgender writing style that would help outsiders to relate to our experiences. This would make it harder for the 'gender defenders' – those invested in conventional ideas of 'male' and 'female', or how people with 'male' or 'female' bodies should behave – to speak for us, or over us.

I expected conservative newspapers like the *Daily Mail* or anti-political correctness columnists such as Richard Littlejohn to be 'gender defenders'. I was stunned to find that certain feminists hated people like me just as much, if not more, than those on the right. If I bought a paper, ignoring Phil's disdain for the mainstream press, I'd get the *Guardian*, and I spent most of my time on Legal & General's website reading the news and football. I often disagreed with it, but I expected a liberal-left broadsheet to display a basic level of respect for minorities. If *they* didn't, who else would?

Alexis mentioned an article from earlier in 2004 titled 'Gender Benders, Beware', by feminist journalist Julie Bindel. I found it in the *Guardian* archive: it had been published at the same time as the activist group Press for Change had managed to pass the Gender Recognition Act, overturning the April Ashley verdict by allowing transsexual and transgender people to change their birth certificates and other documents without undergoing sex reassignment surgery. However, this law was not Bindel's concern. She began with a critique of the Human Rights Act, which had confirmed the fears of many feminists about 'fancy lawyers defending all sorts of scum'. Then she celebrated the British Columbia Supreme Court's decision in Vancouver to bar transsexual Kimberley Nixon from training as a rape counsellor: 'For now ... the law says that to suffer discrimination as a woman you have to be, er, a woman.' She launched a more general attack, accusing all transgender people of conforming to stereotypes: 'fuck-me shoes and birds'-nest hair for the boys; beards, muscles and tattoos for the girls. Think about a world inhabited just by transsexuals. It would look like the set of *Grease*.'

I'd never seen *Grease* and had no idea what anyone in it looked like, and it seemed to me that it wasn't transgender people doing the stereotyping. Bindel's tone annoyed me throughout, reminding me of Germaine Greer's petty attack on journalist Suzanne Moore's 'hair ... bird-nested all over the place, fuck-me shoes and three fat inches of cleavage' back in 1995. The most important issue was buried within a similar string of invectives: 'We're comfortable in our own skin, let's be women but subvert what that means.' I *wasn't* comfortable in my own skin or in the expectations that came with it. I slapped my palm against my forehead: *how could you raise such a crucial point and* still *completely miss it?*

Everything I knew about cross-gender living suggested that being open meant potentially exposing oneself to verbal or physical attack. I understood why Nadia, the winner of that year's *Big Brother* on Channel 4, told the public but not her housemates about her transition. Along with Jackie McAuliffe, the transsexual sex worker from the BBC's *Paddington Green* documentary series, Nadia and Bornstein made me feel that the stereotypes upon which Bindel's position relied could be broken down. However, Julie Burchill's 'Gender bending' piece from 2001, which read like Bindel's after several cans on Stella, was a reminder that the *Guardian*'s editorial position was as hostile as the *Daily Mail*'s.

Now I had a better understanding of 'transgender' as a term that opened space between male and female. I told Alice about Carl and Marino, and how the widening gap between my body and mind had ended both relationships.

'I think I'm transgender first and gay second,' I told her.

'I thought it was the other way round,' she replied. I didn't know how to make it any clearer to her or to myself that my gender identity was a more pressing issue than my sexuality. .Did I need to read more, write more, or live more?

I went to see *Transamerica*, presented as a landmark in transgender cinema at the Duke of York's. In the film, Bree (Felicity Huffman) is due for sex reassignment surgery when Toby, the seventeen-year-old son she never knew she had, calls from New York asking for 'Stanley' (her 'old' name) to bail him. Fearing Toby's response if he finds out who she is, Bree pretends to be a Christian missionary and takes Toby on a road trip. Toby ultimately realises that she is transsexual and accuses her of lying, forcing her to admit to being his father.

Exploring what was possible within the mainstream, *Transamerica* seemed an exercise in compromise. I was glad that the first person on screen is a trans woman, Andrea James, teaching Bree how to feminise her voice, and that Bree attends a party full of trans women, played by trans women, discussing their lives and loves. I'd never seen this on screen, but it only partially compensated for Huffman, famous from TV's *Desperate Housewives*, becoming yet another outsider to play a leading transgender role, whose gender identity is established through predictable clichés – putting inserts in her bra, wearing pink while putting on makeup, seeing a psychiatrist who tells her, 'You look very authentic.'

But *Transamerica*, and Bree, didn't *feel* 'authentic', even though I knew that plenty of her experiences were typical, particularly her anxiety about being 'read'. I didn't trust the way she considered surgery the start of her 'new life'. Wouldn't coming out as transsexual have caused far bigger changes? Did the film *need* that scene where Toby sees Bree standing to piss, outdoors? What would have been different if a trans woman had played Bree – or written her dialogue?

I persuaded Lindsey, who'd been in my English Literature classes at Collyer's, to watch *Wild Side* with me, also at the

Duke of York's. We'd been close for years, calling each other when we lived in separate towns around Horsham, and emailing when we were studying in separate cities, talking plenty of how I wanted to write and she to make documentaries. Now she worked for a TV company in Brighton, and we often watched films together, or discussed art and literature, feminism and body image over coffee.

The French film, named after Lou Reed's *Walk on the Wild Side* and directed by Sébastien Lifshitz, was about a ménage à trois between Russian army deserter Mikhail, Algerian rent boy Djamel, and transsexual sex worker Stéphanie. It opens with Antony Hegarty, from Antony and the Johnsons, singing in a Parisian café. The audience were all trans women, listening to Hegarty's 'I Fell in Love with a Dead Boy', its chorus repeating: 'Are you a boy or a girl?' I was so familiar with this question – from music, such as David Bowie's 'Rebel Rebel' or Jayne County's cover of 'Are You a Boy or a Girl' by the Barbarians, and from my life. Usually, violence lurked behind the enquiry: when I got asked it, in makeup by day or dresses by night, I tried not to reply, unsure if there were any answers that wouldn't get me beaten up.

I recalled a school trip, at thirteen, when a girl in trousers, well built, explained our destination and asked if anyone had any questions. Barry, from the football team, asked: 'Are you a boy or a girl?' Nearly everyone on the bus laughed. She trudged back to her seat, trying not to cry, and I'd felt awful for her.

Deeply poetic, *Wild Side* avoided the clichés of so many transgender films. Stéphanie's history was quickly established by a phone call asking for 'Pierre'. Lifshitz had cast transsexual actor Stéphanie Michelini as the main character: her performance was subtle and tender, her character wearing black rather than pink, not *needing* to do anything to prove her gender identity to the audience. The revelation that her mother is ill leads her from Paris to her home village, where she tries to make peace with her past, with flashbacks to being bullied at school, or playing with her sister.

I could relate to Stéphanie's sadness when her mother greets her as 'my little boy', calling her 'Pierre', and telling her that her father would have hated her transition. 'Maybe he would have just wanted me to be happy,' says Stéphanie, and her mother is sensitive enough to ask if these questions are hurting her feelings. Stéphanie's relationship with her father, like so much in *Wild Side*, is left unresolved; the film ends with her mother's death and the trio catching a train to Paris, quietly in love.

'That was beautiful,' said Lindsey. I felt ambivalent, uneasy at the occasional voyeurism, especially in a scene where a man pays to watch Stéphanie having sex. Was I meant to identify with him? The camera, switching between his viewpoint and his face, suggested I was. There had been a few shots of her genitalia already, which I'd thought unnecessary, but still I felt sympathy with Stéphanie, who had probably been excluded from most other work. I went home happy to have seen Michelini allowed to lead with such dignity and grace. Perhaps the way to the 'authenticity' that Bree and Agrado craved was to let transgender people speak for themselves, rather than assuming that audiences would not accept this, just as Stéphanie's mother had assumed that her father would not accept her.

———

I finished my MA in September 2005, with no idea of what to do next. One afternoon at work, I sat with Matt, a Sussex postgraduate in Social and Political Theory, and Zach, studying for his MSc in Astrophysics. Zach asked Matt why he was still at Legal & General when he had a Masters. Matt went around the room, pointing out that he and I, as well as Neil and Paul, had a Masters, 'and Manisha and Abhisek have got two.' I sighed, returning to yet another *Guardian* story about car bomb deaths in Baghdad.

I applied for numerous administrative jobs at the University of Sussex, hoping they might pay the tuition fees for a PhD as the Arts and Humanities Board had declined to fund my proposal on British surrealist writing. There were always dozens of applicants, and I was terrible at interviews, never able to pretend that I wanted these jobs for any reason other than to pay my bills. When I got an interview for a position I thought I might like – writing e-learning courses run by a company called Epic – I froze:

INTERVIEWER: This job is about telling stories. What's your Masters dissertation about?

ME: An English author called Rayner Heppenstall.

INTERVIEWER: Tell me about him.

ME: He was born in Huddersfield in 1911 and became one of the most interesting writers of his time, but nobody really reads him now. He's best known for his first novel, from 1939. It's called *The Blaze of Noon*, told by a blind masseur. Because the central character can't see, there are lots of beautiful descriptions of how objects feel, including the people he has sex with, and the narrator's not reliable so you have to work out what's happened and what's just in his imagination …

INTERVIEWER: I'm bored already.

ME: He published eight novels, a really interesting range of styles. I really love *The Connecting Door*, from the early sixties, where he takes all these ideas from modern French literature and makes something new, where there are three main characters and it turns out they're all the same person at different points in time ... [*Interviewer looks blank.*] He's most famous for having a fight with George Orwell when they lived together ...

INTERVIEWER: That's brilliant! Why didn't you start with that?

ME: I don't know.

I didn't get the job, and returned to the office, deflated. I'd sent *A Rational Death* to various London companies: none of them wanted to produce it, but the Soho Theatre liked it enough to invite me on to their Young Writers' Programme. I went every Wednesday for ten weeks, doing work experience at artists' video organisation Lux, which involved watching some fascinating films but didn't lead to further work.

I couldn't even pass an interview for my own job. Our new manager, Ray, announced himself by emailing our entire team to accuse us of not doing enough work, which we responded to with unanimous contempt. He decided to turn the temporary posts into permanent positions. My answer to 'Why do you want this job?' was to say that a proper contract would provide sick and holiday pay; later, he said this was why he'd not offered one. Our mutual hatred effectively got me fired, but then everyone who'd been there longer than me left, and Ray grudgingly extended my contract. He introduced several new recruits, hoping I'd show them the ropes before he sacked me again.

'This is Clare,' said Ray, introducing a young-looking woman in black trousers and red hoodie. At his request, I showed her around, then bought her coffee. Like me, she was part-time, so I asked what else she did.

'I'm studying Digital Music at Brighton University,' she said.

I smiled. I'd barely discovered any new music since leaving Manchester, disillusioned by those on the scene who only talked to people they thought might offer them something, and by Joe's experiences with Polydor, who had ordered Performance to decide 'if they were a pop band or an indie band' and told Joe to dumb down his lyrics for daytime radio.

'I'm getting into electronica,' I said. 'Recommend anything?'

Before long, we were swapping cases of CDs. I gave her experimental films downloaded from file-sharing networks and websites like Ubuweb, and she gave me brutal, glitchy artists such as Venetian Snares, 'intelligent dance music' by Autechre, µ-Ziq and Ulrich Schnauss, taking me to the experimental Wrong Music nights at the Volks. I most liked Chicks on Speed, though: female artists making electronic dance music and often covering post-punk bands. Their vocals were cool and detached, exuberant and defiant, drawing me in with their declarations that 'my body is a weapon' and that glamour could be powerful rather than passive. I watched their videos on YouTube – their emphasis on style felt as radical as any of the sloganeering I'd heard on the punk scene, and I loved their brand of feminism – funny, fashionable and fierce.

'I *hate* feminism,' Clare told me as I explained what I'd enjoyed about the band.

'I think it's really important,' I said, 'but I'm excluded from it.'

By now, we'd become close. Clare was questioning her sexuality, feeling more drawn to women but worried about what her parents would think. I'd kept my gender issues quiet, only occasionally turning up with nail varnish on, but I'd immediately felt comfortable with Clare. I'd been encouraged by her fierce insistence that 'You *are* a writer' when I complained that nobody was interested in my journalism, even though Dalkey Archive Press had agreed to publish my work on Heppenstall. I soon told her I was 'gay', but often visited bars like the Harlequin as Juliet. I asked her not to tell anyone, and if she'd like to join me. Unlike me, she felt no need to endure their terrible playlists, but she'd often notice my shaved arms, remarking, 'You've been out,' and smiling to assure me that my secret was safe.

'There's this line of feminism that hates transgender people,' I said. Clare looked puzzled. 'It's a long story but basically, they argue that by transitioning, we uphold traditional gender roles.'

'*What?*' she said, laughing. 'That's *ridiculous!*'

'Well … yeah,' I replied, realising that I'd never discussed this with anyone who wasn't taking a Gender Studies course.

The radical feminist perspective didn't come up in the office again, but hostility towards transgender people did. I'd asked Alice if I should be 'out' at work, and she'd told me that there was a transsexual woman, Fay, on her team: 'the things that get said … they're not kind.' I'd decided not to ask what those were, but as Fay made occasional trips to our department, I found out. I'd hear sniggers across the room as she walked in, with a couple of boys telling me how ridiculous they thought she looked in her skirts and heels, and inviting me to laugh with them.

I kept my head down, but my pretence of working did not convince anyone given how much time I spent on the Internet, in the canteen or in the courtyard, even though I didn't smoke. I thought back to my final weeks at Oakwood. I used to walk home with a boy called Chris who had a brutal sense of humour, impersonating people with cutting precision. He didn't always try to be so sharp: once he just pointed at a passing car and yelled, 'Look at that tranny!' I'd shrugged, pleased with myself for not joining in, but now I hated myself for the same response. *I know how that feels,* I thought. *I can see the cruelty. Why don't I tell people to leave her alone? Why can't I tell them how difficult this is?*

———

I spent another evening at the Harlequin. We'd already sat, bored, through yet another lip-synching drag queen, and I was telling Sam and Jen – PhD students at Sussex – where I'd found my black-and-white top when I saw someone I knew.

'I've met that guy,' said Sam. 'He had the biggest gay porn collection I've ever seen.'

'That's Ed, I work with him,' I replied. 'He sits with a couple of women, bitching about everyone.'

I decided not to avoid him. I thought that, as a gay man, Ed would understand why I wasn't out at work, and if he came here, then surely he'd be sensitive.

'Oh my *God*!' he yelled, pointing me out to his boyfriend.

'Hi,' I said, wearily.

'Are you a tranny, then?' asked Ed's partner.

'I'm transgender.'

'Have you had a sex change?'

'No,' I replied.

'But I thought "transgender" meant people who … you know … cut off their bits.'

For fuck's sake, I thought. 'Transgender' had given me space within the Harlequin's tired old 'TV/TS', but seemed to confuse outsiders as much as it had helped me.

'Don't worry,' I said, going back to my friends. I knew that my secret would be all around the office before I even started my Monday shift, and walking past Ed and our colleagues, I heard the same giggles that often greeted Fay. *This is like being back at school,* I thought, catching him whisper 'tranny' as I went to the canteen.

I tried to let Ed know how annoying I found this without losing my temper, but it didn't make him stop. While my co-workers and I were discussing what we'd wanted to do for work – rather than what Matt called 'the work the computer finds too boring' – I said that when I was young, I'd dreamed of being an astronaut.

'You could be the first tranny in space!' shouted Ed. 'Look at me! I'm flying a space shuttle in my high heels!'

Everyone laughed.

'Can you stop it?' I said, snarling.

'Oooh,' went Ed. 'The tranny's—'

'I mean it! I'm sick of everything I say being met with this bullshit! Fucking stop it! Prick!'

I shook my head and stormed back to my desk. *Was this my life?* We'd just moved to a new office, a mile from my flat, which I'd dubbed Surveillance Park, with rows of desks to leave workers exposed, and meeting rooms with glass façades. The head of security had explained that the Union office would be 'frosted' so nobody could see who was in there, glaring at me when I said it was in the middle of an open-plan office so everyone would know who'd gone in. He boasted that the complex had 158 CCTV cameras – 'fifty-four in this building alone'. 'Don't pick your nose,' he said, 'they'll see you.'

'That's not funny,' I'd muttered as people laughed.

Then, inevitably, he concluded with: 'If you've got nothing to hide …'

On the bus to the old office, I'd told Clare that I found the new place depressing.

'You could find *anything* depressing,' said a colleague. *They were right,* I thought, staring at another circular on Microsoft Outlook. I emailed Clare.

Everyone knows. They're all laughing at me. I can't take
much more of this.

So I was 'out' in nearly every walk of my life. It felt *awful*,
and just made me more worried about what my parents would
think if I told them. I didn't want to say I was 'transgender',
though – it would raise more questions than it answered.
I couldn't help thinking that they'd write it off as another
'phase', and I had enough on my plate as it was.

Soon, I realised that bumping into colleagues in supposed
'safe spaces' was the least of my worries. Alice joined me at
Charles Street with her boyfriend Russell, who worked for
a mental health trust and played bass in an indie-pop band
called the Sussex Heights Roving Artists' Group, or Shrag
for short, who were starting to gig around Brighton. As they
went to the bar, a man came over to me.

'I've been watching you all night.'

'Right,' I said.

'It's alright – I know what you are.'

I sat, stunned. *What kind of chat-up line is that? Am I supposed to be flattered that you've 'read' me and not run off to be
sick?* Before I'd had a chance to ask why he'd spoken to me
like that, he'd started kissing me. I shoved him away.

'I just want to talk to you. I know what you are,' he
repeated, almost crying. I explained what was happening to
Russell, who told him to leave me alone.

'Are you alright?' asked Alice.

'Occupational hazard, isn't it?' I said, remembering her
remark that every man should go to a gay club to see how
it felt to be hit on. She nodded, hugged me and called a taxi.

I'll still be welcome at the Harlequin, I thought, weeks later.
I had my usual anxious walk, but nobody hassled me. I texted
my friend to let her know I'd arrived. A man walked over.

'Can I buy you a drink?'

'Okay, sure.'

He bought me a vodka and Coke.

'I used to live in Thailand,' he said.

'What were you doing there?'

'Just working. The girls there ...' He sidled closer. 'Honestly, you'd never know.' He raised his eyebrows. I didn't return his gaze. He rammed his hand up my skirt, grabbing my genitals. 'You like that, don't you?'

I yanked his hand away. He tried to put it back. I shoved him, hard.

'Come on, darling. Don't be upset.'

'Leave me alone,' I replied. He didn't move. 'I mean it – fuck off.'

He looked at me to suggest I was mad, and left.

Another transgender woman – in her forties, I guessed – asked if I was okay. I explained. The casual air of resignation in her reply cut me to the quick: 'He did that to me, too.'

We hugged, and soon my friend arrived. I decided not to tell her – I worried she'd blame herself – but I did tell the story later to Elizabeth and Tatiana, friends from my course.

'If someone buys you a drink, that means they want something,' said Elizabeth.

'No one ever taught me that.'

'No one ever gets taught that,' replied Tatiana. 'Are you going to report it?'

'First I'd have to go to the police and say, "I went out dressed as a woman ..." All I know is that he wore a black shirt, has a beard and lives in Sussex. Even if they bothered to find him, I'd have to go to court, relive it and explain why I was dressed like that. Then it'd be my word against his, and no jury is going to favour me over some respectable businessman, are they?'

Tatiana sighed, and I tried not to think about how that man might have treated the women he found in Thailand. Weeks after, the Harlequin closed. It briefly reopened as a club called hQ, its flyers covered with images of gay skinheads in leather, but Brighton already had the Bulldog for that. Soon it disappeared for good, and I didn't know where else to go.

———

'Are you going to Pride?' asked Clare across the desk. 'This year's theme is *Carry On*.'

'I write about British experimental film. I'm fucking *ashamed* of *Carry On*.'

'Oh, come on!'

'Maybe there's something better on later,' I said, scanning the websites of several venues. 'The Alternative Pride Party looks great – Performance are supporting Chicks on Speed. We should go to that!'

'I'm in London in the evening,' she replied, 'but let's hang out during the afternoon.'

I decided to do both – which meant spending a whole day as Juliet for the first time. Excited, I did some shopping. On eBay, I bought inserts for a bra that a friend had given me – no way was I going to spend so much time with itchy cotton wool pressed to my chest. I got a Kohl pencil, lip liner, lipstick and a pocket mirror from Boots, wearing them with a red polka-dot top from Rokit, a black skirt from a London Road charity shop, fishnet tights and flat shoes. I headed to the unisex salon on Western Road, trying to ignore the stares.

'Your hair's thinning at the front,' said Lucy, showing me where it was receding.

'Is that because I keep straightening it?'

'No, it's just your hairline moving back.'

Fuck, I thought. I knew that oestrogen would stop male pattern baldness from worsening, but wouldn't repair what I'd lost. I was worried. *If I transition, will I have to wear a wig? Will I look less 'authentic'?* Then I caught myself: this was the first time I'd thought about my body in terms of reassignment, rather than just thinking of ways to make it easier to 'pass'. Stunned, I was silent as Lucy cut my hair into a bob, with a fringe. I paid £30, stepped outside into the searing heat and sweated as I walked to the Old Steine, immediately making my hair curl.

I couldn't find Clare, so I went alone to the parade. I soon got bored with the floats – they all seemed the same to me, and I didn't care that Barbara Windsor was waving. I paid more attention to who was marching, spotting the NHS and Mind Out, the LGBT mental health service, alongside the police and representatives from the Labour Party.

After half an hour, I wandered up to Preston Park. I was overwhelmed by the crowds and the noise, so many sights and sounds clashing with each other. There were rides – chair-a-planes and a merry-go-round – and tents recreating Brighton's gay clubs from Revenge to Dynamite Boogaloo. Drag queens, familiar from the Harlequin, were doing cabaret, and there were stalls advertising sexual health services and places to shop, as well as inviting people to sign up for trade unions or the military. Remembering the *Onion*'s spoof headline mocking the 'fight for the right to love men, kill men', I went to find Alice.

We sat in the shade, talking. Here, for once, I could be Juliet and be left alone, and my main concern was getting Norwich's result at Leeds, as I couldn't get phone reception with one hundred thousand people in the park. I walked back to London Road, seeing that we'd lost 1–0. *Performance must be here by now,* I thought, looking up angrily as someone in a passing car yelled 'faggot' at me. *This is my day, you shit-stack,* I thought, but I said nothing. I called Joe and met him on St James's Street, where most of the evening's parties would be held. It was already heaving, all pumping house music and whistles, so I joined the band for dinner.

'Nobody at Polydor understands us,' said Joe. He made nothing of how I was dressed, nor did anyone else in the bar, and for the evening, I almost forgot that I'd ever been made to feel that it was an issue. Recently, I'd become less convinced that Performance would make it. Like the *Observer,* who'd earmarked them in December 2004 as one of five bands to watch, I'd thought that 2005 would be their year. But, despite its explosive synths and surging chorus, their only single, 'Surrender', had failed to chart, and the label weren't backing them. 'They've done nothing to promote the new EP.'

Joe Cross, Laura and Billie nodded sadly. I was amazed: the title track, 'Short Sharp Shock', was just as arresting as 'Surrender', and I'd become obsessed with the second song, 'I Want Out', an anthem for the generation that I saw trapped in pointless, soulless work.

'How's the writing?' asked Joe, after telling me that the novel he'd written, *Friction,* was with an agent and about to go to publishers.

'The Soho Theatre turned down the play I wrote for the course, I can't make *A Rational Death* work, I can't make the short stories work, I can't get an article commissioned and the office is driving me mad,' I said. 'I'm thinking about psychotherapy.'

'It might be an idea. You should be able to cope with being in your mid-twenties and not liking your job.'

'You're right. But I'll worry about it on Monday.'

Alice and Phil joined me at Concorde 2 for the gig. It was half empty, missing the intimacy that had made

Performance's early gigs so special, but I loved the new songs, and felt excited about their album even if Polydor still hadn't approved it. Phil and I argued about Chicks on Speed all the way home: he thought them shallow, insubstantial, but I loved their colourful stage show as much as their records, and I'd danced the night away. Then I got home, undressed, looked sadly at my body and struggled to sleep in the stifling heat.

———

I reached the station on time, though I didn't know where I was going. I got on a train. As it pulled out of Brighton, I fell asleep. Later, an announcement woke me. *This train is leaving Paignton.* Why am I in Paignton? I wondered, thinking back to childhood holidays there. I jumped off and ran to the other platform. I've missed work, I thought. They'll fucking fire me. As it departed, I remembered: My books! My films! My clothes!

I saw the guard – a stern-looking woman. 'My suitcase is on that train!' I yelled, pointing. 'Can I call anyone?' She looked away.

'No.'

'Please?' I started crying.

'Shouldn't have left it there, should you?'

I tried to argue.

'Can I see your ticket please?' I found my wallet and showed her.

'That's not valid. You'll have to pay a fine.'

'On top of the fare home?' Fuck ...

I woke: just a dream. At least I hadn't spent another night back at school, wondering why I had to re-do my GCSEs, or watching an aeroplane fall and explode. *It wasn't meant to be like this,* I thought as the letter arrived from the Arts and

Humanities Research Board, informing me that they would not pay my tuition fees for my PhD, nor provide a living allowance. Clearly, I was stuck at Legal & General, who had finally given me a permanent contract, and I somehow found the energy to throw on a shirt and trousers and trudge to Surveillance Park.

You're never going to get out of here, I thought, staring at another spreadsheet. *All that study was a waste of time, nobody cares about your pointless articles about the London Film-Makers' Co-op, nobody's going to read your book, everyone's laughing about you being a 'tranny', and why do you keep wasting your money on dresses when your work clothes are falling apart and you can't even be bothered to shave, you utter failure?*

Oh FUCK OFF, I told myself. Bypassing Ray, I asked the senior manager for a chat. We went to a meeting room. Nervously, I wondered who was looking in, and what they'd think we were discussing. Then, finally, I found some courage.

'I'm really depressed,' I said. 'My mum thought I might get a therapist through work.'

'Yes, you can get five free sessions through the Employee Support Programme.' He found a phone number, and I called it.

'What are the issues?' asked the receptionist.

'Mostly work,' I replied. 'I feel isolated and bored, I hate the job, and I hardly get on with anyone. Time's slipping away and I'm getting nowhere with the things I want to do.'

'How long have you felt like this?'

'Forever, really. It was worse at school but it's never gone away.'

'It sounds like your job is bringing a lot of underlying things into focus. I'll recommend you for counselling. Come to the Wilbury Clinic on Friday at 5 p.m.'

I checked a map. The clinic was on Wilbury Road, five minutes from our flat, fifteen from the office. I got there in good time, 4.50 p.m., ready to sit in the waiting room. I walked up to where I thought it was. I saw nothing: just a house like all the others. *Where is it?* I asked a passer-by if he knew where it was. *No.* I walked up the street. *Where IS it?* I ran into an estate agents and asked them.

Sorry, we don't know where that is, they said. I panicked, racing down the street, swearing, cursing, furious at myself, *you know you've got no sense of direction, now you're going to miss it,* hyperventilating, *it's there you stupid cunt, right at the top of the street, knock and try to calm down* … A friendly looking woman with silver hair and rosy cheeks, middle-aged, opened the door. 'I'm here for my appointment,' I said, gasping. She showed me into the living room, where two chairs faced each other, gesturing at me to sit down. Then she sat opposite, smiling, waiting for me to speak.

Gender Outlaws: The Birth of Transgender Theory

It wasn't just in the cinema that trans people became more visible during the 1990s. Unknown to me as a teenager, there was an explosion of theory in North America during the decade, as authors explored their identities through a mixture of autobiographical, historical and feminist writing.

This was a movement that had been a long time coming. In the decade after the Second World War, a handful of transsexual people, including Roberta Cowell and Michael Dillon in Britain and Christine Jorgensen in the United States, attracted mainstream media attention purely *because* of their transitions. During the 1960s, it became clear that trans people were moving from being seen as isolated individuals to members of identifiable categories, if not a group. Harry Benjamin – an associate of Magnus Hirschfeld who had fled first to New York and then San Francisco after the closure of the Institute for Sexual Science – became the leading US specialist on medical treatment for gender variance, understanding that not everyone he saw wanted physical interventions on their bodies, but handling hundreds who did. He classified different types in *The Transsexual Phenomenon* (1966) by how likely they were to want a 'conversion operation', and this book became the standard reference as gender identity clinics began to manage reassignment, demanding that people meet the requirements of psychiatrists for living in their desired gender before they received hormones and surgery.

At the same time, there were splits in the second-wave feminist movement along lines of gender and sexuality. Betty Friedan, author of *The Feminine Mystique* (1963), aired anxiety that lesbian participation in feminism would impede its progress due to the homophobia that would be aimed at the movement. Lesbians who had seen post-war feminism as too heterosexual and establishment-oriented focused on linking straight and lesbian women around shared oppression, with male-defined gender roles seen as an instrument of power. They rejected the 'butch' and 'femme' models within lesbian erotic culture as mimicry of heterosexual relationships, and posited an androgynous, gender-neutral style in an effort to break the expectation that female bodies, 'feminine' behaviour and sexual orientation towards men should be linked. They set up women-only organisations, and soon the eligibility of trans people to enter those spaces was hotly contested.

Not everyone argued for their exclusion. In the controversy over transsexual singer and activist Beth Elliott being expelled from the lesbian group Daughters of Bilitis after a vote on her presence went 35–28 against, with another vote at the West Coast Lesbian Feminist Conference in 1973 similarly split, *Lesbian Tide* newspaper publisher Jeanne Córdova defended Elliott. Córdova called Elliott 'a feminist and a sister' and expressed her frustration at the movement for devoting so much energy to the tiny numbers of trans people within its orbit.

Eventually, the loudest and most hostile voices came to dominate. The most virulent anti-trans text was *The Transsexual Empire: The Making of the Modern She-Male*, published in 1979 by Janice Raymond, a former nun who had become an academic. Three years earlier, women-only Olivia Records had appointed transsexual woman Sandy Stone as a recording engineer. When this became public knowledge, Olivia were asked to remove her. Olivia supported Stone, stating, 'For many women, evolving a consciousness of class and sex oppression involves uncertainty, anger and the turmoil which accompanies any major life process. For transsexuals, who are simultaneously evolving through confronting their true sexual identity, these processes are doubly difficult.' Despite this, Stone soon left voluntarily to minimise damage to Olivia's business.

Describing the importance of Raymond's book as 'a sourcebook for anti-transgender opinion and a goad for transgender theorising', historian Susan Stryker quoted Raymond's explicit identification of reassignment with rape: 'All transsexuals rape women's bodies by reducing the real female form to an artifact, appropriating this body for themselves. It is significant that in the case of the transsexually constructed lesbian–feminist, often he is able to gain entrance and a dominant position in women's spaces because the women involved do not know he is a transsexual and he does not happen to mention it.' Raymond claimed that Stone did so by working at Olivia without announcing her gender history, ignoring the fact that Stone most likely knew that if she had, she would have taken plenty of abuse and Olivia would not have been able to utilise her skills at all.

Raymond wrote that 'The Transsexual Empire' was ultimately a medical empire based on a patriarchal medical model that in turn provided a 'sacred canopy' of legitimations for transsexual treatment and surgery. Raymond only spoke to a handful of service users – thirteen at most – and failed to engage with the structural conditions they were forced to navigate, or acknowledge the antagonism that often characterised the relationship between the clinics and transsexual people. Using male pronouns for trans women throughout, Raymond concluded that 'the problem of transsexualism would be best served by morally mandating it out of existence', advocating 'consciousness-raising therapy' as an alternative to the existing system.

Carol Riddell's 'critical review' *Divided Sisterhood*, published a year after *The Transsexual Empire*, argued that it was Raymond who was making an issue of trans people's inclusion, writing that 'in the British women's movement, there seem to be two transsexuals' and maybe a dozen in the United States. Riddell also wrote that the clinics 'were not regarded with favour by most of the medical patriarchy', with the 'gender-amendment training' arising from the fact that 'like all marginal institutions, they strove to justify themselves by their conformity', hence the often oppositional relationship with their patients.

A crucial intervention came at the end of the 1980s when Sandy Stone, by now a computer expert and artist, circulated her essay 'The Empire Strikes Back: A Post-Transsexual Manifesto' on early digital networks, before its first print publication in Routledge's anthology *Body Guards: The Cultural Politics of Gender Ambiguity* in 1991. This was Stone's response to Raymond, but unlike Riddell and some of the others who had replied to *The Transsexual Empire* at the time, she did not argue on Raymond's terms but attempted to change them, aiming to work around both the medical and feminist discourses on transsexual people, and break the silence they imposed.

Stone wrote about how, before coming out, many transsexual people seek relevant literature: autobiographies but more importantly medical texts, notably *The Transsexual Phenomenon*. It took GIC researchers years to establish that the reason why so many people fitted their 'transsexual' profile was because they had read Benjamin's work and knew what to tell their psychiatrists – primarily that they realised at a very young age that they were born in the 'wrong body' and that this impulse had never dissipated.

Stone suggested that ' "wrong body" has come, virtually

by default, to *define* the syndrome' as managed by the GICs, and called for a 'deeper analytical language for transsexual theory' in which authors explored the territory between male and female and were more honest about their personal histories. This was difficult, however, if it remained easiest for transsexual people to accept a contract with the GICs in which they were programmed to disappear, and so couldn't challenge writers such as Janice Raymond who claimed that they were too irrational or irresponsible to express themselves sincerely. Answering Raymond's accusation that transsexual women reinforced gender stereotypes by conforming to antiquated models of femininity, Stone called for them to go beyond 'passing' in their acquired gender (thus erasing their histories), at least in their writing or creative work, and enter the theoretical discourse around transsexuality. Otherwise, 'radical' feminist calls to prevent people from medically real-ising their identities would remain unopposed: Stone knew open discussion of specifically transsexual experiences would make their attacks untenable, and help gender-variant people to become more politically organised.

Kate Bornstein was one of many writers to answer Stone's call. She wrote in 1994 about how the only things that trans people could get published were 'the romantic stuff which set in stone our image as long-suffering, not the challeng-ing stuff'. Then she gave a long list of people, many of whom were her contemporaries, whose stories resonated with hers. These narratives included those of photographer Loren Cameron, who took portraits of lesbian and trans people; essayist Jamison Green, who wrote about transsex-ual men and visibility in a culture where far more attention was given to trans women; *Transsexual Menace* activist Riki Ann Wilchins, who talked about the need for trans people to reclaim the terms created for us by the medical establishment and come up with our own ways of framing our experiences.

In *Gender Outlaw*, Bornstein was open about her past, revealing her 'old' name and pictures of herself before her transition, discussing what had happened to her body in considerable detail – her reaction against 'a world that tells people like me … to not reveal that I'm transsexual, to not reveal my truth'. In particular, I liked her insistence that 'everyone has to work at being a man or a woman', implying that *everybody* had a gender identity to manage, but that 'transgender people are probably more aware of doing the work'. Bornstein identified neither as male nor female and talked about how culture *created* gender, and gender roles. 'No one had ever hinted at that, and so, standing outside a "natural" gender, I thought I was some monster, and that it was all my fault.'

It wasn't surprising that she had failed to see this conditioning for so long, she said, given that most cultures assign a sex to babies at birth depending on whether or not they have a penis. The enforcement of masculine or feminine behaviour followed almost immediately from the words 'It's a boy' or 'It's a girl', despite the fact that people rarely talked about what 'male' or 'female' really were. If they did, the expectations that came with physical bodies could be shown to be absurd.

Bornstein quoted Suzanne J. Kessler and Wendy McKenna, two psychologists who had explored the processes by which people assign genders to others, based on (often unacknowledged) rules. For example, anyone who displays any 'male' characteristics is usually assumed to be male until proven otherwise. 'Consider a list of items that differentiate females from males,' wrote Kessler and McKenna in *Gender: An Ethnomethodological Approach* in 1978. 'There are none that always and without exception are true of only one gender.' Seeing how much space this opened between traditional ideas of the sexes, Bornstein played with this idea, even setting games for the reader:

Exercise: Make a list of all the genders you observe in a week.

Exercise: Make a list of all the genders you've been in a week.

Exercise: Make a list of all the genders you can imagine in a week.

Bornstein further allowed me to see that comedy shows and films – such as *Ace Ventura* – were able to laugh at transgender people, and to portray us as sex objects or psychotic murderers, because the community was so disparate. We were forced to develop our views in solitude. We had no cultural norms to work with or react against, and no shared history.

This was something Leslie Feinberg addressed in *Transgender Warriors: Making History from Joan of Arc to Dennis Rodman* (1996). The book interwove Feinberg's personal journey with a survey of gender variance from ancient Greece and Rome to the present. This intriguing story included the Two-Spirit people of Native America who did work and wore clothing associated with both men and women, as well as Boulton and Park and other cross-dressers in Victorian London, the Stonewall rioters and many more.

Language was an important issue for Feinberg, who wrote that 'there are no pronouns in the English language as complex as I am,' preferring to be addressed as *ze* and *hir* (as in 'ze is here' and 'this belongs to hir'). Feinberg acknowledged that the words used in *Transgender Warriors* might soon become outmoded as the terminology evolved, but the important thing was to construct a past that accounted for positions beyond male and female. Historians must not be allowed to casually dismiss cross-dressing or other gender-variant behaviour; thus a present might be created in which people's right to control their bodies and to determine their identities was respected. This was a matter of personal safety above all: 'When I say I am a gender outlaw in modern society, it's not rhetoric. I have been dragged out of bars by police who claimed I broke the law when I dressed myself that evening. I've heard the rap of a cop's club on the stall door when I've used a public women's toilet ... I shouldn't have to prove my sex to any police officer who has stopped me ... and my body should not be the focus of investigation.'

In addition, Feinberg criticised the attempts of Janice Raymond and others to 'define "woman" as a fixed entity', noting, 'No matter what definition is used, many women who should be inside will be excluded.' Hir definition of 'transgender' was broad, aiming to unite groups of people that had historically been disparate, even antagonistic. 'I asked many self-identified transgender activists ... who they believed were included under the umbrella term. Those polled named: transsexuals, transvestites, transgenderists, bigenders, drag queens, drag kings, cross-dressers, masculine women, feminine men, intersexuals, androgynes, cross-genders, shape-shifters, passing women, passing men' and plenty more.

The term 'transgender' *did* assume a narrower definition, though; as somebody living some or all of the time 'in the gender opposite to their anatomy', I liked Feinberg's inclusiveness. 'Transsexual' and 'transvestite' still didn't feel right for me: 'transgender' offered me space to explore myself, as well as a way of understanding the oppressions shared by anyone who transgressed gender norms.

In response to this first wave of radical critique, Viviane K.

Namaste published *Invisible Lives: The Erasure of Transsexual and Transgendered People* in 2000. A transsexual activist based in Montreal, Namaste worried that 'transgender' failed to recognise differences among gender-variant people, acknowledging that the existing language did not deal well with positions between or beyond 'male' and 'female'. Across the world, the failure of language to illuminate the complexities of gender had disastrous consequences: for example, trans women put in male prisons, or HIV/AIDS services placing trans people into binary categories according to their anatomy, which might clash with the way they saw themselves, and how they actually lived.

Another problem, which Namaste addressed in a chapter entitled 'Genderbashing', was that, during the form of violence known as 'gay-bashing', people were attacked not because of their sexualities – which weren't visible – but because their presentation was deemed threatening to male and heterosexual domination of public space. Although very little research had been conducted on trans victims of violence, she quoted a 1992 study that found that 52 per cent of trans women and 43 per cent of trans men in London had been physically assaulted, in comparison to the data gathered by a 1989 American telephone poll that found that 7 per cent of lesbians and gay men had been attacked that year.

Namaste noted that people were beaten up more in gay and trans spaces, especially if they were black, usually for being effeminate, and that cross-gender living was most dangerous for sex workers and poorer people living in densely populated, high-rise housing with lifts where they could not be protected, more conspicuous on public transport and under the stark lights of subways.

Importantly, Namaste pointed out that 'passing' male-to-female people became subject to the same violence as other women, but that their upbringing meant they did not learn strategies to deal with it during their adolescence, compounding the problem of gender clinics not teaching them how to look after themselves. More than anyone else, Namaste gave me an indication of what transgender *living* would entail, and how I might manage the challenges that I had already experienced, and some of the others that might follow.

5

I took a deep breath.

'Ever since school, I've felt that life is pointless,' I said. 'It may be depression, I can't tell any more. I'm always bored, tired, unable to enjoy anything. Nothing ever fixes that. I don't fit in anywhere, especially work, and it'd be better if I left, but I can't afford to. I'm never satisfied with anything I do and always feel I have to justify myself.'

'To other people?'

'And to myself. I feel so isolated, so rootless.'

'Slow down,' she said. 'We need to *find* those roots. Where did you grow up?'

'Horley. There wasn't much there – a little library and a few shops, a couple of youth clubs.'

'When you were very young, did you make friends there?'

'Yes, but they kept moving away.'

'So how did you spend your time?'

'Reading, or playing computer games. I was mostly alone at school.' I paused. 'When I was seven, this kid called Terry from the year above invited me to play this game where you had to get across the playground without running into anyone. I said no as I didn't want to get hurt, and he said: "We've got to make you more masculine." I told him I was fine and he ran off.'

'That's a strange thing for an eight-year-old to tell you,' she said. 'How did you feel?'

'Lonely,' I replied. 'Who did he mean by "we", I thought, and why did it matter?'

'*Did* it matter? To you, I mean?'

'Not then. It became more important when I was ten.' I drank some water. 'I was watching *The Chart Show* on TV. Erasure were number one, doing this cover of "Take a Chance on Me". The video cut between two guys singing and two people in leggings, sequins and feather boas. Then I saw the singers were dressed as the women from Abba. They looked like they were having fun, so I copied them.'

'What did you do?'

'I went into the spare room, where my mum kept her dresses. I never saw her wear them, but she had them for special occasions. I checked to make sure everyone was out, then tried on this blue dress with a pleated skirt, over some tights ...'

'How did that feel?'

'I've never quite been able to express it,' I replied. 'There was this huge rush of energy ...'

'Was it sexual?'

'Isn't everything when you're ten?' She smiled. 'Maybe it was, partly, but I already knew it meant far more than that. It just felt *natural*. Calmer. More comfortable. Then I heard my parents' car pull up the drive. I got changed, trying to make everything look like I'd never touched it. After that, whenever they went out, I'd ask how long they'd be so I could plan to do it again. I just felt confused – I didn't know what it made me, or what would happen if anyone found out. I just knew that I wasn't supposed to do it, but that I felt happiest when I did.'

'What was stopping you?'

'Fear of getting caught. I didn't tell anyone for six years, I spent that whole time thinking about killing myself. I still can't be myself around my family, I'm always holding back.'

'Have you told them anything?'

'When I was eighteen, I got a phone call from Chris, my friend from school. I'd tried to cut everyone off when I went to college, but we were still in touch. He said, "I've heard this horrible rumour that the girl across the road saw you in your room, wearing a dress."'

'What did you do?'

'I screamed, "That's bollocks!" and hung up. I thought my parents would hear from someone, so I told my mum I was gay. I didn't think she knew much about identity politics so I hoped that would cover anything.'

'How did she react?'

'She was angry at first,' I said, 'but after a few days we talked, and she realised I'd still be the same person. I don't know if she told my dad, but nothing really changed. I've never spoken to my brother about it.'

'You're not gay,' she said.

'I'm attracted to men.'

'Maybe. But I know lots of gay men and you're not like them.'

'I consider myself transgender,' I replied.

'What do you mean?'

'I have a male and female side … I don't know how they relate.'

'You're not depressed, but you have some intense conflicts to resolve. Do you paint, or draw?'

'I loved to as a kid, but I don't any more.'

'Why did you stop?'

'We had to choose our GCSE subjects and everyone I wanted to avoid did Art because they thought it'd be a laugh.

And people kept telling me to pick things that'd help me get a "proper job". Look where that fucking got me.'

'Have you considered kickboxing as an outlet for your anger?'

'No,' I replied, laughing. 'I write.'

'Good. You should address these issues creatively. Plenty of authors and artists felt the way you do.' I thought of writers I loved, from Russian revolutionary poet and playwright Vladimir Mayakovsky to English novelist and filmmaker B. S. Johnson, who hated their governments, their contemporaries and often themselves, and how I'd drawn comfort from them.

My fifty-minute session ended and I left, feeling so much lighter than when I arrived. That night, having aired my long-standing anxieties about achieving nothing as time passed, I woke at 3 a.m., obsessed with what I'd do on New Year's Eve, even though it was two months away.

I returned to the counsellor a week later. The night before, I'd gone to London to see Performance, frustrated at how hard I found it to concentrate on their set, voices in my head clamouring about money, work, health, fitness, diet, family. Joe said *Friction* had been accepted for publication. I felt pleased for him, but reproached myself: *Why hadn't I written a novel?*

'What can be done about these feelings?' asked the counsellor. I closed up.

'The female expresses your loving side, that your family never let you show,' she said.

'*Nobody* let me!' I replied. 'I had to spend years at school pretending to be male. I bought T-shirts with "No Fear" on them, baggy jeans, record bags, trying to be like the boys. No one was fooled, especially not me. But if I didn't do it, I thought I'd get beaten up.'

'This is where your anxiety comes from,' she told me, handing me some leaflets on relaxation techniques. *Self-help bullshit*, I thought. But once I'd gone home, I decided to read them, trying the breathing exercises designed to shift my focus from mind to body. I lay on my back, taking in air and holding my breath, trying to slow myself down. I didn't think it was working: it felt like the anxiety was too deeply ingrained. It filled my brain and colonised my body, in particular my arms, making my fingers shake whenever I held out my hands. I reported back at my third session.

'You don't respect your body. You don't love it.'

'I want to escape it. I wish I could just be a spirit.'

'You have a split personality,' she insisted. I looked at her, resentful of such pathologising language. 'You need to integrate these sides with each other, and with your body. List all the ways you neglect it, and work on them.'

I left. For a beautiful moment, the internal chattering stopped: for once, my mind felt clear. I decided not to put my MP3 player on, noticing the trees without their leaves. The noises of pedestrians and traffic stopped feeling like a dull background buzz and became sharper, stronger signs of life. I focused on the minutiae of existence, rather than my big ambitions, understanding that achieving the latter wouldn't be possible without taking care of the former. I made a point of cleaning my teeth twice a day, and playing football with friends.

Continuing to address the anxiety cycle that put writing so far above self-care, I finished my five sessions. I wanted to continue, but couldn't afford my counsellor's rate. I called the Rock Clinic in Kemp Town, which offered hour-long sessions at £10.

'I suffer from depression and anxiety,' I told the receptionist. 'I also have gender dysphoria.'

'What's that?'

'It means there's a gap between my mind and body. I'm transgender.'

'Sorry, but that's too much for our counsellors, I'm afraid.'

I phoned Joe.

'That does sound like a lot,' he said. 'I think it's worth paying whatever it takes to stay where you are.'

Taking his advice, I persuaded my counsellor to accept £30 per session. Gradually, my anxiety subsided, at least at times. I started going to house parties as Juliet, wearing the kind of tops and skirts that Alice had suggested a few years earlier. For the most part, it wasn't a big deal – my friends just talked to me the same way as ever, and I preferred being with them in private to clubs – but every now and again, someone would ask if I wanted to 'go all the way' or 'have a sex change'.

'Maybe in a few years,' I would reply. I gave my counsellor the same answer when she asked how I felt about myself.

'I consider myself male in body but female in spirit,' I told her. 'I'm happy with that.'

'Then I think we're finished.'

'Thanks for all you've done for me.'

'Thank yourself,' she told me. I stepped outside, ending nine months of therapy, and made a point of listening to the birds singing on my short walk home.

———

I went back to one of my favourite computer games – *Alter Ego*, a text-based life simulator by clinical psychologist Peter J. Favaro. To create the game Favaro had interviewed hundreds of men and women about their most memorable experiences; he highlighted those that 'many people shared', along with others he devised himself. There were male and female versions; I'd only been able to find the male version, perhaps because the audience on its release in 1986 had been mostly male.

The play began with twenty-six True/False questions. My answers set opening personality scores in twelve fields: Familial, Intellectual, Physical, Social, Vocational, Calmness, Confidence, Expressiveness, Gentleness, Happiness, Thoughtfulness and Trustworthiness. It had seven Life Stages, from Birth, Childhood and Adolescence to Adulthood and Old Age. During those, I could make choices in given scenarios, which would change my Personality scores.

I became addicted: the Narrator was funny, friendly and smart, and I loved seeing how the decisions I made in my youth affected my adult life. But I'd known in my teens that the path it offered – marriage, children and a career – wasn't for me, and that not everything that shaped my existence was a choice.

Now that the game had been put online, I could try the female version. This stopped me from idealising the girlhood I never had. After my first period, the Narrator told me: 'Getting used to all of the changes in your body makes this time of life difficult. It's like walking into a house that you've known for years and finding all of the comfortable furniture has been replaced by new pieces.' But still, the moments of warmth between parents and daughter – simple things like buying my first bra with my mother – made me cry. I was starting to see how my childhood had been lost to gender dysphoria: I had never been *myself* at school, feeling like I'd grown up in black and white, and now I had to work out how to live in colour.

Trying to find other people in that grey area, I downloaded films from sites such as Ubuweb and peer-to-peer networks like eMule. I began with *Flaming Creatures*, made by Jack

Smith in 1963 and swiftly banned across the United States, with police seizing the print used at its premiere at the Bleecker Street Cinema in New York. As Susan Sontag put it, 'there are no ideas, no symbols, no commentary on or critique of anything ... [It] is strictly a treat for the senses.' After opening with a prolonged, harrowing rape scene, the film gives way to an unscripted, dreamlike orgy with drag queens, poets, vampires and mermaids dancing and screwing. It suggested that although life on the margins of sex and gender could be traumatic, it could also be beautiful, offering so much pleasure as well as pain. I thought back to how *Stonewall* and *I Shot Andy Warhol* had touched on this subculture when I was still at school: ten years later, I finally had access to the films that were made within it, and I carried on exploring.

Paul Morrissey's *Women in Revolt* (1971) featured Warhol's three transgender 'superstars' but no transgender characters. Made in the Factory, it spoofed the radical feminist movement three years after Valerie Solanas had shot Warhol. Candy Darling, Jackie Curtis and Holly Woodlawn improvised most of their dialogue as members of Politically Involved Girls (P.I.G.), a militant group destroyed by infighting, self-interest and a lack of coherent goals. As well as enjoying the send-up of the nastiest extremes of radical feminism, I loved seeing Darling and company playing non-transgender people. It opened up possibilities beyond even *Wild Side*'s bold employment of Michelini as its lead.

Then I watched Jennie Livingston's documentary *Paris Is Burning* (1990) about African American and Latino people of various gender identities who competed in glamorous 'voguing' balls in New York during the 1980s. Contestants would walk down a runway and be judged on their dancing skills, as well as the 'realness' of their clothes in categories ranging from Schoolboy/Schoolgirl to Executive – aiming to 'look as much as possible like [our] straight counterparts'. The film showed the communities that had formed by contestants who could finally celebrate their difference. The cast spoke candidly about facing racism, homophobia, transphobia, poverty and the AIDS crisis, being thrown out of their homes, shoplifting or doing sex work as they struggled to survive in 'a rich, white world'. Their stories were often sad; Venus Xtravaganza, who spoke about how she wanted to be a spoiled, rich, white girl, and how a man had touched her 'down there' and then 'flipped out' and threatened to kill her, was murdered during filming, and several others died young. But the film remained exciting and inspiring, and full of defiance.

———

I looked online for a different queer scene. I joined a mailing list for Queeruption, an annual festival featuring performance art, games and workshops. Things had changed since my time in Manchester: now, the city had an event called Get Bent, with a mission statement declaring it 'a safe space for all genders and sexualities to engage with and foster the possibility of creating queer-positive spaces'. It showed short films about 'trans youth', hosted talks on mental health activism and queer theory, and presented stand-up comedy, cabaret and underground bands. I'd missed Get Bent and something called the Transfabulous Festival of International Transgender Arts in London, but an email invited me to join Queer Mutiny Brighton in the Pride parade, protesting against the army and police having stalls at the event and the Labour government's reluctance to accept LGBT asylum seekers.

I put on a black dress, tights, a wig and makeup. I worried: *Did I look too 'femme'?* As I got to the Old Steine, several men in a passing car shook me out of my introspection.

'Bender!' they yelled.

There are thousands *of us,* I thought. *This is the one day you're not going to beat us.*

'Hi, I'm Jo,' said a woman, several inches shorter than me with short black hair, a dress with stripy stockings and a placard that said 'Cunts Not Cops'.

'I'm Juliet.'

Jo smiled. She was about to do a Masters in Cultural History in Manchester, and I asked what she would be studying.

'Radical feminism and trans people,' she said as we stepped into the parade with our banners and flags, surprised that no one even seemed to notice, let alone try to stop us.

'Is that still going on?' I said, nervously.

'In some places, yeah. Don't worry, this is a safe space. It's mostly in the *Guardian* now – Julie Bindel's just written another article saying trans people shouldn't be allowed surgery.'

I'd seen the piece. Published earlier that week and entitled 'My Trans Mission', it opened with two sentences saying that 'good liberals' should fight discrimination against 'transsexual people' before 'However …' Bindel apologised for the tone of her 2004 piece, as the 'sarcasm I used … was misplaced and insensitive', but then proceeded to observe that 'any criticism of transsexuality seems to be deemed unacceptable outside of homophobic, rightwing circles'. But this didn't ring true: it seemed to me that she was setting the terms of debate, arguing that 'sex change surgery is unnecessary mutilation' and 'modern-day aversion therapy treatment for homosexuals'.

Bindel continued: 'My concerns about the increasing acceptance of "transsexuality" as a diagnosis are based upon my feminist belief that it arises from the strong stereotyping of girls and boys into strict gender roles.'

Her argument had barely changed since 2004, but my self-understanding had. I'd never felt I fitted into traditional ideas of 'masculine' or 'feminine', but increasingly, when I told people I was 'transgender', they asked about my body – not whether I liked dresses or dolls as a child. Jo did neither, aware that I didn't *want* to be bombarded with questions about it, and we talked about Manchester instead.

As we approached Preston Park, I felt it was someone else's turn to hold the 'No Pride in the Army' sign. As I handed it over, several policeman charged towards us, wrestling away our flags and banners, hauling us off the route. They didn't arrest anyone, but after a debrief in which we tried to convince ourselves that we'd made our point – we had marched most of the way, after all – I went home, exhausted.

In the evening, I went to a Queer Mutiny party at the Cowley Club on London Road. The venue was the home of Brighton's radical counterculture, serving cheap drinks and vegan food, hosting anarchist meetings and punk gigs. I met Alice outside and buzzed for entry. We didn't know anyone, and felt awkward at the looks we got – perhaps I *was* too 'femme' for this scene, however inclusive it claimed to be. Nobody had seemed particularly interested in talking to me, but soon Alice told me that someone had asked her to 'Pull your skirt down, please.'

'Who did that?' I asked, angrily.

'The woman on the door,' she replied. 'I don't want to stay.'

'Me neither,' I said, and we went to a house party. If this scene wasn't going to welcome my friends, could it ever feel like home?

———

My book on Heppenstall came out in September 2007 – the beginning and end of my academic career. That month, my parents used some money from selling my grandmother's house to get me on to a short National Council for the Training of Journalists Diploma course. Having left Legal & General, I felt freer, more open to new experiences. I went to Lacies, a shop in Hove for transgender women. It sold clothes, underwear, makeup, wigs and inserts for bras, and books and magazines that covered 'the community'.

'Are you coming to Miss Transgender?' asked the shop-keeper, handing me a flyer. Lacies had organised the pageant to raise money for the Clare Project, a drop-in centre in Kemp Town that provided information and counselling, and for the Gender Trust, which helped people transitioning at work. It was at the Old Ship Hotel, with three categories: Miss Transgender, Mr Transgender and Miss Mature.

'Are you going to enter?' asked my friend Susanna.

'I'm not sure,' I replied. 'I don't like the idea of a pageant, but I might watch. It could be good to write about.'

'Come on!' she said. 'You can't spend your whole life sitting on the sidelines. Write about it if you want – it's obviously important to you – but get involved.'

I considered it. 'Yeah, it'll be a laugh. Why not?'

I applied for the competition., I registered as Juliet Jacques, using my grandmother's maiden name, and made up some vital statistics. The contest had a James Bond theme, and I thought I knew the conventions: dark lipstick, long black gloves and 'exotic' accents for the women, short hair and sharp suits for the men. I'd never seen a Bond film (and still haven't), so I arbitrarily picked *From Russia with Love,* and then went online to find a 'favourite *EastEnders* character', assuming that most of the people in the show when my mum used to watch it would have left. Then I looked for clothes that I thought would suit. I bought some elbow gloves and dark lipstick, and then found a boutique having a closing-down sale.

The shopkeeper welcomed me with a smile. I returned it and told him I was looking for a dress for a beauty pageant. Unfazed, he picked out a few things he thought 'might suit'. I settled on a black dress with a silk skirt and a bodice covered in gold and silver glitter, marked down from £250 to £100.

'I *love* this,' I said, modelling it in the empty shop. 'But it's a bit out of my range.'

'Have it for £50,' he replied, and I bought it. I felt surprised at how easy it had been to find something, then realised that nothing could be *too* over the top for an event like this.

I got changed at the hotel, doing my makeup and practising my walk backstage. I met some other contestants. I couldn't always tell whether they were transvestite, transgender or transsexual women, or whatever else, and I didn't ask – I was more interested in where they were from, what they did for work, who they were 'out' to, and how people had responded. Emily was the same height as me, with long fair hair and a striking black dress with a white stripe, giving off an air of defiance with every step in her heels, every stroke of mascara. I loved how assertive Naomi was, bold in black PVC boots and a top with a hologram-style eye on it. She told me about leaving her family in Germany and coming to Brighton because, like me, she thought it would be a safe place to explore herself and find a community. Then we were ushered into the hallway for a photo shoot.

I'd always hated being photographed, but I disliked it less as Juliet and nobody seemed to be taking themselves too seriously, so I let myself be pictured in the Paganini Ballroom. We marvelled, half ironically, at the red carpets and opulent chandeliers, before Brighton and Hove mayor

Carol Theobald spoke about how proud she was to support the city's transgender population. Next came Lyn Daniels, a performer at a burlesque night called Sirens. She wore a red bra and knickers with matching stilettos, garlands of flowers on each wrist, dancing with a white veil. The audience was captivated as she put burning sticks in her mouth and ate the fire and clapped as she held up the charred wands and then strutted off stage.

We watched the Miss Mature contest before a Tina Turner impersonator warbled through 'Simply the Best'. Then the men came on. *Imagine only being able to choose between suits and ties*, I thought, soon realising that I was missing the point: the opportunity for them to display their maleness. They didn't seem to be taking themselves any more seriously than we had backstage; I clapped as Lee, with his bleached hair and beard, topless in white trousers, wowed the judges with his quick wit and big smile, before he held up the little silver trophy for the winner.

I kept drinking as Emily and Naomi took their turns in the main pageant. Tara-Mae, small, beautiful, her hair in a bun, told the compere that she was from the Philippines, smiling as she gave vital statistics far more plausible than mine.

'Would Juliet please come to the stage!' yelled the compere. I strode up to cheers and whistles. Then I froze, anxious that my ignorance of Bond or *EastEnders* would make me look even more ridiculous than I felt. Luckily, the first question covered neither: 'If you were queen for a day, what would you do?'

'Abolish the monarchy,' I said, laughing.

I got a muted reception and no follow-up questions, and I was relieved to step down.

Next Rani walked on in a trench coat over a white frock, saying in a Borat-style accent that the person she would most like to meet was Vladimir Putin, and that if she were queen, she would talk to George W. Bush 'about his relations with Russia'. I clapped her off before Amy stepped up, telling the audience that she would 'get the troops out of Iraq' to another mixed reception.

The judges chose their top three on looks, personality and audience reaction. Rani was third, Amy second. The winner was announced – Tara-Mae, who posed for photos, smiling with a bouquet. Then she came over to me.

'Are you on hormones?' she asked. 'You look amazing!'

'No,' I replied, 'but I'd like to be.'

I'd like to be ... Those words rattled through my mind as Tara-Mae told me how she'd had to leave her family and the Philippines in order to transition, working in Croydon and eventually settling down with a boyfriend who supported her.

'I haven't had any trouble, but I *pass*,' she said. As another photographer whisked her away, she called out: 'Good luck with the hormones!'

On the next day – my twenty-sixth birthday – I was on the cover of the *Argus* with the other contestants. Owing to the newspaper's habit of juxtaposing their main headline with a picture story, we appeared under the words 'MAN, 79, IS SUSPECT IN BOMB HOAX.'

Feeling that we deserved a better report, I wrote something for the NCTJ course and then sent it to Cliff James, who edited *one80news*, a free weekly LGBT newspaper given out in Brighton's clubs. He loved it, publishing it and asking me to write a regular column called Trans Eye View. As well as reviewing events of interest at the Brighton Festival and elsewhere, I wrote about Kellie Telesford, a trans woman of colour born in Trinidad in 1967 who had been murdered in Thornton Heath. I noted that the *Sun*'s headline – 'Trannie

Killed in Sex Mix-Up' – both demeaned Telesford's identity and anticipated the 'transsexual panic' defence, suggesting that a violent response from a man who hadn't realised that she was 'a transvestite' (their words) was her fault for not disclosing her gender. The following August, an eighteen-year-old man was found not guilty of her murder; no one was ever convicted.

As part of my NCTJ course, I arranged work experience at the *London Magazine*, a literary journal founded in 1732.

'But it's *so* conservative!' said my friend Alex.

'The latest issue had a transgender woman on the cover,' I replied, referring to Peter Hujar's photograph 'Candy Darling on Her Deathbed', taken in 1974 as Darling was dying of cancer. 'I'm sure it'll be alright.'

I took my book, as Heppenstall had written for the publication in the 1960s, and showed it to Steven, the London Magazine Group's managing editor. He read the back cover.

'Currently "working on a volume of short stories about transgender lives", eh?'

'Yeah,' I murmured. I'd regretted including that in my author biography as soon as I saw it in print. This was partly because I'd since decided that 'experimental' short fiction wasn't a priority right now, as the *Guardian* and the BBC, two of Britain's supposedly 'liberal' media institutions, routinely ran transphobic content. I'd shifted my focus to a transgender equivalent of *Queer as Folk* that I was working on with a friend. But also, I worried about what my parents would think when they saw it, and how other people might react. *Wasn't I basically outing myself?*

'I had a friend once who went from "he" to "she",' Steven said. 'Rather amusingly, as he was a six-foot-five rugby player.' I smiled weakly, wondering what life might have been like for the 'friend' who'd become his punch line. 'I don't think they should do gender reassignment on the NHS,' he continued. 'I worked for the NHS, and for every sex change we could have done fourteen prostate cancer operations.'

Before I could ask about how these operations might have saved trans lives, let alone improved them, or even where I might verify his statistic, Steven got me researching contacts for a new publication called *Military Book Review*. As I glared at lists of generals and barracks, a woman entered and introduced herself as Sara-Mae. I asked what she did.

'I edit our new magazine, *Trespass*.'

'What's that?'

'Contemporary art and literature,' she replied. 'Quite experimental.'

'Interesting,' I replied. Steven showed my book to Sara-Mae.

'Great!' she said. 'Want to interview a transsexual performance artist called Pia?'

'I'd love to,' I said. I drafted some questions and emailed Pia. I'd not seen any footage or even photographs of her performances at London club nights such as NYC Downlow or Horse Meat Disco, but recognised her even before she walked through the ticket barriers at Brighton station. She was tall, wearing boots and jeans with a black top and denim jacket, and had long brown hair. Her lifetime's worth of experience handling transphobia was written into her expressions and body language as she glanced around, protecting her space.

Back at my flat, I asked what her transition had involved.

'My last twenty-five years,' said Pia, 'and a lot of pain. I lost money, security and many friends. Some people were fine, but initially others were hostile because I was doing something that made everything else seem a bit inane.'

'Is it a continuous process?'

'You express yourself more,' she said. 'You become free to find your place between feminine and masculine values, which, because of people's social conditioning, can be very confusing.'

I loved how clearly she thought and spoke. 'Transitioning demands willingness to throw yourself off a mountain,' she continued. 'You have to say, "This is me and if you accept me, great, but if you don't, so be it." You need belief that you'll survive.'

I felt nervous. I'd written in my diary that I was thinking about transition but wasn't sure where to start. Now, thanks to Pia, I knew, and it was terrifying. But she *had* survived, turning all that uncertainty into creativity, using her body to confront preconceptions.

'I do a performance to "O Superman" by Laurie Anderson,' said Pia as I asked about her work.

'I only just discovered that song,' I said. 'I love it so much!' I'd read a book on post-punk, which explained how Anderson's epic, eight-minute mixture of vocoder 'ha, ha' sounds and oblique poetry became a surprise hit in 1982 after John Peel played it on BBC Radio. I'd bought the album, *Big Science*, and become obsessed with it.

'I come on as a bastardised Clark Kent,' said Pia, 'in a rubber fuck-doll face mask, and strip in a nasty, *Friday the 13th* fashion. When I shed the Clark Kent suit, you see I'm Superman, and then I take off the Superman suit and I'm a muscleman. As I remove that you see I'm a woman, but between that and my skin there's a thick layer of fake blood, as though I'm peeling off the exterior to reveal the inner heart of Superman. As I peel the chest down, people don't see my breasts and with my mask they don't see my face – when I had my suit on, they thought I was a male stripper. Then I peel off my bottom half at the end to once again confuse the issue – first they thought I was a man, then a woman, then I'm trans.'

With the interview done, Pia and I went for a drink, sitting in a lesbian bar. As we talked quietly, I realised that Pia was showing me a way to be myself without having to avoid doing things that seemed 'unfeminine'. I walked her to the station and went home, feeling a little better about the conflicts and contradictions that I'd discussed with my counsellor.

———

I was still writing for *Filmwaves*. Tim, who ran Brighton's *CineCity* festival, asked if I'd cover two Austrian avant-garde directors and suggested another film that might interest me: 'Ian McDonald's documentary *Brighton Bandits*, about the club who won the National Gay Football Supporters' League last season'. I'd loved football since England's run to the 1990 World Cup semi-finals. I'd been captivated by the simple drama and tension, those memorable moments of skill, that sense of belonging that came with supporting a team. I'd watched the West Germany game and cried when my favourite player, Chris Waddle, missed the decisive penalty in the shoot-out. I played little games against my brother, the two of us shooting at each other with our garage as a goal. In summer 1993, I decided to train with Horley Town Football Club.

I wasn't good enough for the first XI, who had just beaten Manchester United's under-twelves in a friendly match, so I joined the reserves. I'd never been part of a team, always put with the geeks in PE and having to do everything myself, dribbling past the more popular boys who got angry because the weird kid had scored. I tried the same during a practice match and came unstuck: after running into yet another defender, a lad called Rob just screamed: 'Why don't you *pass?*' I had no answer, saying sorry and resolving to give the ball to my teammates more often. I never knew what to say at training, feeling awkward and looking absurd in my cycle shorts and tight T-shirts, but the manager promised I would be part of his side, so I stuck it out. In my first game, against Godstone, I scored from a twenty-five-yard shot and went to celebrate, turning to see I was alone. Nobody passed to me during matches: I was soon dropped and quit after half a season, sick of standing on the sidelines every week as the in crowd lost yet another match. Three years later, I played twice for Oakwood's B team at left-back, but it was clear that I was only picked to make up the numbers. Any display of skill in PE lessons or on the playground was met with snarls of 'you jammy cunt'. Frustrated, I gave up.

After my counselling, I'd made a point of visiting my GP whenever I felt anything was wrong with my body. We'd also discussed my mental health. He'd prescribed beta-blockers for my anxiety, which I never took, and told me to treat my depression with exercise. As I left the cinema, I thought the Brighton Bandits might be the right place to play competitively again.

The first few players interviewed in the documentary emphasised how 'normal' they were – ordinary blokes who loved football and just happened to be gay. I understood, having seen how hard it was to fit in with the lads at school, that urge to repress any action, any *word* seen as too feminine, or 'gay'. Even though I'd never got on well with men who might be described as 'camp', I struggled with how some players accused such men of 'a put-on'. Couldn't camp be radical, as Susan Sontag or Kate Bornstein had argued, challenging ideas of what it meant to be male or masculine, female or feminine? It didn't *have* to be like the ridiculous, sexless caricatures in 1970s sitcoms, did it?

My favourite person in *Brighton Bandits* was Jason. He was an artist who'd designed the club badge, and who liked the way the club's name reclaimed a homophobic insult ('arse bandit'). Unlike the others, he identified as bisexual, making me feel that I didn't *have* to be gay to play.

I went to training and asked if I could join, despite not identifying as gay. 'Of course,' they insisted. 'We're gay-friendly, but open to anyone.' After scoring a few goals in five-a-side, I was picked for my first match – at home to London Falcons, who were top of the GFSN League.

That Sunday, I met the team in Preston Park. A figure loomed wearily into view, carrying a heavy-looking bag, making a show of dropping it and picking it up again. 'Here comes Steve,' said Jason.

'You alright?' asked Alan.

'I'm sick of this,' said Steve, reaching the clubhouse and throwing down the bag. 'Every time I take the kit, wash it, iron it and bring it back. We should have a rota. Week one – I do it. Week two – Ben does it. Week three – Paul does it. That's the only way it's fair.'

'No, that's too complicated,' replied Jason, grinning. 'You keep doing it.'

We laughed as Steve chased Jason across the park, swinging at him and missing, until the manager told us to get changed. I proudly put on the dark blue-and-black kit, wearing number fourteen like Johan Cruyff, and joined the pre-match huddle.

'We've got a new player today,' said Aidie, the captain, pointing me out. 'I hope you'll make him welcome.' After a round of applause, I took my place on the right wing. I was soon exhausted and substituted, and we lost 6–0 to a younger, faster, better side. But the International Gay & Lesbian Football Association World Cup was being held in London that summer, and I was determined to get fit enough to take part.

———

In February 2008, I finished the journalism course and needed work. *Trespass* never got Arts Council funding and *Filmwaves* lost its grant and closed, but I got an interview for a film journalist post at *TimeOut*.

'You were never going to get that,' Phil said, after I told him how I'd frozen in the interview and been declined. 'How many people applied – two hundred? You did well to get that far.'

'I know,' I replied. 'Doesn't pay the bills though, does it?'

Disappointed, I registered with an agency specialising in temporary public sector jobs. I took a position in Mill View mental health hospital in Hove, and then another as a council administrator, working in a Portakabin in a depot surrounded by barbed wire. The salaries barely covered my rent and bills and I made no inroads into my overdraft, which the bank kept offering to extend.

I kept writing for Brighton's LGBT publications and playing for the Bandits. That month, Paul drove Jason and me to a game near Nottingham Forest's stadium. Jason, a Forest supporter from Nottingham, looked at the Brian Clough Stand.

'The tenth anniversary of Justin Fashanu's death is coming up. No one's talking about it.'

'It's complicated, isn't it?' I replied, thinking back to my bedroom as a teenager. By then I knew I'd never be a footballer, and concentrated on watching games – a few times a season when my dad took me, or on television. For my thirteenth birthday, my parents gave me a video of classic Norwich matches. My favourite moment came against

Liverpool in 1980, as Norwich, 3–2 down, passed the ball in Liverpool's half. John Ryan gave it to Justin Fashanu, who had his back to goal. Ryan ran on to the wing, expecting a return pass. Instead, Fashanu flicked it over his head, turned and hit a twenty-five-yard volley, into the tiny space between the goalkeeper's hand and the post. 'Oh, *what* a goal!' screamed the commentator as Fashanu, just eighteen, raised a single finger to announce his genius and the stadium erupted with cheers.

By 1994, however, Justin's younger brother John was more famous, starring for Wimbledon and hosting *Gladiators* on TV. I only heard of Justin from sly innuendos in football magazines, and gradually realised he was gay. *Was that why I never heard about him?* I'd almost forgotten about him when I was about to leave school, thinking about how I might come out to my new friends in Horsham. The morning before Norwich's final game of the season, the news broke that Justin had killed himself in a lockup garage in Shoreditch, believing that he was wanted by police after being accused of sexual assault in the United States.

The nationwide mourning for Princess Diana months earlier had baffled me, but Justin's death hit me hard. I talked about how he'd spent his childhood in a Barnardo's home and then with a foster family in rural Norfolk. He starred for Norwich in a time when the National Front encouraged fans to hurl abuse at any footballer who wasn't white, and moved to Forest in 1981, becoming the world's first black £1 million player. In Nottingham, at age twenty, he'd realised he was attracted to men and started going out on the scene. Legendary Forest manager Brian Clough found out, blaming this for Fashanu's disastrous performances, asking in front of the whole squad why he kept going to 'those bloody poofs' clubs'. Justin had joined Notts County the next year, returning to form before a serious knee injury. After several years in North America, he returned to England, unable to find a club until he came out via the *Sun* in 1990 – which led to his brother John disowning him. He joined Torquay and then Airdrie and Hearts in Scotland, but his career ended in 1994 after he tried to sell stories about sex with Conservative MPs to the tabloids.

'That *is* complicated,' said Paul.

'We've all experienced homophobia in football though, haven't we?' said Jason.

'I went to Brighton–Norwich in 2005,' I said, 'with the Brighton fans because the away end was sold out. The Norwich fans spent the whole game singing 'Does your boyfriend know you're here?' It annoyed the fuck out of me, I just wanted to watch the game.'

'We should start a campaign named after Fashanu,' said Jason. 'You in?'

'Sure, why not?' I said.

We held our first campaign meeting at Jason's house soon after. Quickly, the dynamic emerged: Jason would float extravagant ideas; I would ask if they were politically sound or practically feasible; and Paul would ask if we could afford them. We launched at the Amsterdam, a gay bar that sponsored the Bandits, and Jason persuaded Justin's friend Peter Tatchell to speak. I felt uncomfortable when someone yelled at us, suggesting it was wrong to use Justin's name like this. Raw passion had sparked us into action, but now we needed a little more thought.

At work, I got a text message from Jason: 'Imagine if all this led to a book.' *On Justin Fashanu?* Why not? My TV script had stalled, and I was looking for a new project.

I went to London for Joe's book launch, as *Friction* had just been published. Laura from Performance had suggested

I go as Juliet, so I brought the dress from Miss Transgender and changed at the venue. I was starting to feel like I could be myself in venues other than LGBT bars and clubs: I'd been as Juliet to a few electronic music nights that Clare had put on, finding that as I felt more relaxed, people seemed far more interested in talking to me. I had a funny conversation with Clare's friend who asked about my gender. When I said, 'I'm not sure,' she replied: 'I like things to be black and white, but you're the greyest person I've ever met.' Here, with old friends, there were no such questions. Instead, Joe said he'd finished a second novel, *Wild Side,* and introduced me to a literary agent.

'Nobody's done Fashanu already?' said the agent.

'No. I checked.'

'Perfect,' he replied.

I returned to work, spending every possible moment researching, writing to old teammates to ask for interviews. Soon, I was obsessed, talking at length about Fashanu to anyone who would listen. I stopped looking for a permanent job, certain we'd soon sell a proposal to a publisher and that this would clear my debts. Meanwhile, I carried on with the Justin campaign.

Jason's next idea was to show *Brighton Bandits* at the Odeon, followed by a Q&A with several players. Jason often argued with Steve during games, fed up with Steve yelling at him for any mistakes, which made me glad that I played up front, far away enough to pretend I'd not heard. Steve and some others worried about us using the club for our events, and when Jason came round to design some flyers, I asked him about it.

'They're just scared,' he said. 'They play for a gay team, they can't say that's not political.'

'I agree,' I replied. 'Can we say the screening's on the

International Day against Homophobia, Biphobia and Transphobia, rather than just homophobia? Then it's more inclusive.'

'Sure.'

'You know I'm transgender, right?'

'Some of the guys saw you in the *Argus*. They were giggling about it. I just said, "So what?"'

'Oh yeah, I was in that pageant. I do drag.'

'Why do you call it drag?' asked Jason. 'Does it feel like drag?'

'No,' I replied, pointing at my second-hand T-shirt and jeans. 'These do.'

'Not drag then, is it?'

———

I couldn't afford a week off work unpaid, but when else was I going to play in a World Cup? I arranged to sleep at a friend's place and travelled to London with Paul, Jason and Ian. I'd scored once in the League and twice in pre-tournament friendlies: this had impressed Brian, our manager, who put me in the starting XI. I played behind Abdullah, who had been stationed in England to learn engineering by the Kuwaiti Army. Brilliant with the ball, Abdullah drew defenders to him: I would run into the space he made, only to find he hardly ever passed. In our first match, he took on three Sydney players; I ran alongside, knowing that if he gave me the ball, I'd have our first World Cup goal. '*Abdullah!*' I screamed as he ran into their goalkeeper, dived and demanded a penalty. I slammed the ground.

'I think you scared him,' said Steve.

As the games went on – five in three days – I found that Abdullah's style took some pressure off me. Having missed a few chances to score, I concentrated on winning the ball and giving it to him once we'd made some space, and we struck up a partnership. Against the London Titans, I beat three players and hit a long ball to Abdullah. He chested it down to Jason, who smashed it into the net, helping us win 2–1. *I can do this,* I thought, no longer feeling sick after twenty minutes of running, able to mentally immerse myself in the games. Growing in confidence, I made two goals for Abdullah in our 4–2 win over the London Leftfooters, but we lost our next two games and went out.

We had a day off before we entered the Plate – a consolation tournament for teams beaten in the first round. I went to the team hotel in Swiss Cottage and Ian filmed my conversation with Jason and Paul about Fashanu's life and its relationship to our campaign, as we'd often been challenged about the ethics of using his name.

'Fashanu didn't *like* campaigning – he didn't want to feel he *had* to be an activist just because he was "out",' I said. 'Lots of his problems came from his conversion to evangelical Christianity – Clough kicked him out because he hated that, more than his sexuality.'

Jason sighed, frustrated. 'On the most basic level,' he said, 'he suffered from homophobia in football. He said he only came out in the *Sun* because they would have hammered him if he did it elsewhere.'

'Okay, that's our line,' replied Paul.

'Agreed,' I said, and started thinking about our next games.

I came on during the second half of our Plate semi-final against the Leftfooters, not managing to score in our 4–0 win but chasing down defenders and holding the ball up to good effect. I started on the right wing in the final against Birmingham. The opening goal came from the left: Abdullah beat several defenders, let out a piercing yell, slotted the ball past the goalkeeper and collapsed.

'Is he alright?' asked a Birmingham player.

'He does this all the time,' I replied. But Abdullah had dislocated his shoulder, and the game was delayed while we called an ambulance. I moved up front and nearly scored, but there were no more goals and the final whistle came – we'd won a trophy! I hugged my teammates, and that evening, we all went for dinner: Abdullah came from the hospital and sat with me, and I got a chance to tell him we'd never have got anywhere without him. He gave me a knowing smile, and the next day, we went on the pitch at Leyton Orient, where former England star Trevor Brooking gave us the Plate. I danced in celebration, arm in arm with Jason and Steve, holding up the prize, thinking about nothing else apart from how wonderful that moment felt.

'I am going to talk about what it's like to use a men's changing room when you don't have a penis,' declared Jason Barker at the third Transfabulous festival.

I'd found out about the 2007 event a week too late, looking wistfully at the website, seeing that I'd missed the trans activism, body image and sexual empowerment workshops, the film about Leslie Feinberg and Kate Bornstein's performances. I didn't recognise anyone featured in the 2008 programme, but that didn't matter. I was sure they'd be great, and anyway, I wasn't just going for the acts. I wanted to meet some new people.

I stayed with a friend in Balham, shaving and putting on underwear there, getting changed at the venue – Oxford House in Bethnal Green. I loved doing my makeup in the mirror: the toilets weren't gendered, and for the first time since that night at the Harlequin with Corinne, I felt free from assumptions about who I was, returning the smiles of the people I encountered. More than Miss Transgender, even more than Chicks on Speed and Performance at Pride, this felt like home.

On the first evening, I didn't meet anyone. Instead, I watched the two performances. The first was by Barker, who had co-founded Transfabulous with Serge Nicholson in response to the Gender Recognition Act, which allowed people to self-define as 'male' or 'female' but nothing else. As Sandy Stone had suggested twenty years earlier, the artists here explored spaces between themselves – life was never as simple as ticking one box or the other.

Barker's piece was called *Menstrual Cycle*. He came on riding a bike and dressed as a uterus and stopped at the microphone to huge cheers. He paused. 'I wanted to have children, so I stopped taking testosterone and my periods started again.' As I laughed with the crowd, I thought about Thomas Beatie, a trans man who had done the same when his wife was unable to conceive, and who recently made global headlines after writing on his pregnancy in the *Advocate*, a Los Angeles LGBT magazine. I'd written about the furore that followed in the 'straight' media, but Barker showed us that Beatie wasn't as 'miraculous' or unique as the newspapers and chat shows made out. Like many of us in that hall, I imagined, they were balancing their bodies and identities with their other desires and dreams.

Next came Ignacio Rivera's *Dancer* about a 'butch dyke' stuck in Hawaii who danced for tourists for money. 'Am I a person born a girl struggling to be a boy pretending to be a girly girl trying hard not to get the boy inside of me?' asked Rivera, wearing jeans and a sweater, recounting a conversation with a trans woman called Lola about performing a certain type of femininity while trying to work out how masculine to be. There were so many labels: 'Lola told me about female-to-male, male-to-female, pre-op, post-op, no-op, genderqueer … She told me about being Mahu – that means female and male. Mahu are indigenous transgender Hawaiians, but Christian missionaries and colonialists changed all that shit. Lola opened up a new language for me.' Plenty of this was new to me, too, but I loved the way Rivera refused to pick one label, instead closing with all those options open, and I went home to think about them.

The next morning, I met Pia. 'I wish I'd had something like this when I was a kid,' I said after the Queer Youth Theatre performers shared their stories about how they'd come to understand their genders and sexualities, and how they'd come out. Pia nodded, and we walked to a café on Bethnal Green Road.

'How were things with your family?' I asked.

'It took a while,' she replied. 'Once they realised it was either this or death, it got easier.'

'You felt like that?'

'Sometimes,' she said. 'It's better now. You know that obsession with doing everything *now* – that "death drive"?'

'Yeah,' I said, smiling and sighing.

'That calmed down with transition, I found.'

Reassured, I returned to the festival. I tried on male and female clothes at the radical drag workshop, drawing a moustache and beard over my foundation, using black eyeliner to match my dress. I went to the picnic in Weavers Fields and joined in the football match, using jumpers and cardigans for goalposts, where I scored the only three goals. Then we watched the closing performance: the Border Fuckers' Cabaret, presented by the Queer Belgrade Collective, and written and directed by Jet Moon.

Jet came on stage with co-presenter Majda to introduce the show. I loved the way they parodied the slightly camp

male-and-female duos that I'd seen host so many TV programmes and award ceremonies: Majda in a suit with a bright
orange tie, Jet in a glittery see-through top. Majda's performance was about going to an anti-fascist demonstration after
the Serbian far right attacked Belgrade's first Pride parade
in 2001. But immediately, the queer activists got told to put
away their rainbow flags: some men feared that the football
hooligans they'd invited for 'protection' would object. *Your
struggle comes next* was the message – gender and sexuality
could not be the main issues even as the fascists chanted, 'Kill
the faggots.'

What kind of 'progressive' politics was that? I wondered
as Marija came on in her underwear, waving a box of
Marlborough cigarettes – 'a currency of exchange, when
money fails'. She talked about pretending to be a boy on Brick
Lane in the early 1990s because the hyper-macho traders
wouldn't let girls sell anything there, part of a journey in
which she was constantly crossing borders, between nations,
between genders.

Despite opening with someone dancing to the *Hawaii
Five-O* theme, the next piece was even more serious. 'Most
people know me as D. ... but I also go by Dylan or Dijana,
depending on the crowd I hang out with.' Wearing a
'Forensic' shirt and rubber gloves, D. discussed gender first:
'For me, trans is being able to transgress the definition of it
being from point A to point B, but more like point A to point
B to point A to point B ... That's reflected in my life, I guess.'
D. moved on to work – digging up mass graves from the
Srebrenica massacre of 1995, struggling to make sense of the
bodies. Ninety-eight per cent of the time it's possible to iden-
tify which sex you were born as by the bones of the pelvis
... But it's not possible to tell what gender you lived as or
what religion you believed in or what nationality you called

yourself.' D.'s piece made me think – I'd never heard the idea that *biology is not destiny* put in such stark terms.

The next act made me laugh – a parody of 1980s therapist Louise Hay performed by Milan, bearded, wearing a blonde wig, black dress and feather boa. 'If you live in Serbia and you want to change your sex and you receive an average Serbian monthly salary, which is two hundred euros, and you need seven thousand euros for sex reassignment surgery, just affirm: "Money is my friend! The whole medical establishment loves and supports me!" ' Jo and I cheered. We both knew that no 'positive thinking' could ever fix that – and it felt strangely affirmative to hear it.

The stage went dark, the room silent. Gradually, I realised that one of my favourite pieces of music was playing: the first track on *Lift Your Skinny Fists Like Antennas to Heaven* by post-rock group Godspeed You! Black Emperor, with its slowly rising cellos and violins. In walked Josephine and Andjela, only their silhouettes visible. They danced as recordings of their voices played. I didn't know which words were whose, but it didn't matter. 'You are born. You breathe in air. Still a baby, you don't realise anything is the matter … You grow older, and slowly you become aware that it's different for you, that your life is a black and white film …' *Someone's finally put that into words,* I thought, my hand on my heart. 'I first began to learn what I was through daytime television. A horrendous talk show gave me my first hints. But in the world of mass media television, "transsexuals" were hidden behind screens and their voices changed to keep their anonymity … No image to welcome me, and no information that didn't allude to a terrifying future.'

The lights came up, and Josephine and Andjela stood before us on stage. They talked about coming out, finding love, having children, no longer wanting to die, being rejected by some family and friends but embraced by others. 'Transition is something wonderful, magical, and at the same time it's terribly complicated, hard, emotionally exhausting.' The piece, and the festival, ended optimistically: 'I have every respect for those who enjoy their films in black and white,' said Andjela. 'But still, my film is in colour.'

The trumpets and drums reached their climax, and then the entire Collective joined Josephine and Andjela onstage. They bowed and curtsied, and I joined the standing ovation. Then I got changed and went home. *If only life could be like this all the time,* I thought, travelling back to Brighton alone in my drab T-shirt and jeans. I got home, sent Facebook friend requests to Jet and a few others I'd met, and went to sleep.

———

Transfabulous and the World Cup had been brief escapes. Once they were over, 'reality' reasserted itself. My temporary contract had ended in July 2008, and soon I was back at my overdraft limit. I took out a big bank loan to clear it, feeling like a one-person credit crunch as the global economy collapsed. *Those were the boom times?* I thought, looking back at my boring, badly paid jobs. Desperate to stop my debts from getting worse, I veered in and out of short-term work, in clothes that were falling apart.

In October, I turned twenty-seven. Unemployed again, I got £37 in royalties for my Heppenstall book. I listed my unpublished works, from the ambitious TV scripts and plays to the shortest stories, angry with regret for never being able to finish anything. *Everything depends on Fashanu,* I told myself. I'd sent three drafts to my agent, rushing each one, frustrated at how long he took to respond. Then the email came: the book proposal wasn't working, and he wasn't prepared to consider another version.

Deep down, I knew he was right. Fashanu's life, especially his childhood, had been so traumatic that few people wanted to talk about it, and consequently, my sample chapters felt flat, colourless. I lay down and wept.

That's it, I thought. That night, I would go to the beach and march into the sea. I wrote a note. I'd never been happy, but since my teens, I'd tried to give some meaning to my life through writing, hoping to leave the world even a little better than when I found it. It hadn't worked, and I couldn't take any more of the instability, disappointment and loneliness of my adult life. I didn't mention my gender: that would no longer matter at the bottom of the ocean.

Your friends will know, though, won't they? What will they think when they see the male name on your headstone? Remembered briefly by that, and then forgotten as a failure? I pictured my funeral, trying to predict who might come, who would speak, who would cry, who would just stare into space. I was tired of living as male for other people, but I couldn't hurt my friends or family by killing myself. I thought back to my ten-year-old self who had repressed that transsexual desire and lived in fear. No more: as Josephine and Andjela had put it, 'I could kill myself, I could die inside and try my hardest to be "normal", or I could work through all the opposition and try to be true to myself.'

I couldn't go to my grave knowing I hadn't done that. I tore up the note and threw it away, telling nobody. The next day, I played football with friends at the University of Sussex. I felt strangely liberated, taking joy in every tackle, every pass and every goal – nothing mattered besides the fact that I'd made it through the night. My new life began with a ball leaving my foot and hitting the net, a pleasure as simple and beautiful as it had ever been, even though nobody was even keeping the score.

———

I started to get my life in order. The agency offered me another council job, at £7 per hour. After tax, and payments towards my bank loans, I'd have £875 per month. I would have to stop living with Phil – his girlfriend was about to move in, and it felt like time to go. I found a cheap room in a five-person house near Preston Park, which seemed like a quiet place to write. I didn't care that there was no communal atmosphere, with people constantly moving in and out: the one thing I *did* have was friends. If I was really disciplined, I estimated, I'd have £50 a week for food and another £50 for going out. I gave away my bass guitar, my Commodore 64 and plenty of records, sending many of my books back to Horley. I moved into the box room, covering the peeling paintwork with posters.

Suddenly, things turned my way. A flatmate moved out, allowing me to take a room big enough for a desk. My parents offered to pay off my most recent loan. I wanted to decline: *didn't being a writer mean refusing such privilege? Why should I be bailed out like a multinational bank?* I looked at my balance and told myself not to be so stupid, counting my blessings instead. Then the temp agency called. Forget the other job, they said, we've got a six-month contract in the Health Promotion team at the Primary Care Trust, which commissioned NHS services across Brighton and Hove, at £9 per hour.

Tim, the Public Health administrator, laughed at the big collars on my shirts. 'I've meant to replace them for ages,' I said, 'but I can't find any I like.' He laughed and showed me around the office. My manager, Doreen, seemed friendly, as did the rest of our team. I took minutes in meetings on everything from smoking cessation to sexual health services, genuinely interested in the work. I soon made friends – West Ham fan Jon, who helped run a hip-hop festival; Olumide, from Nigeria, who talked to me about football and African literature; Beth, who wrote short stories; Tom, who shared my love of post-punk; Cat, who swapped newspaper stories with me about the absurdities of small-town Britain. For the first time I felt like I fitted in, and was happy to go drinking with them on Friday evenings.

An email from Human Resources invited those who were interested to join an LGBT staff group run by the equality and diversity manager. I met Andrea from the patient advice and support team. She was open about being transsexual and seemed comfortable, but I decided not to ask her about how people had reacted to her transsexual identity. For now, just seeing her go about her days without snide remarks like the ones I'd heard at Legal & General, was enough to make me feel that, if I managed to keep things stable, this might be the place to transition. *Once the time's right...*

———

Travelling for League games with the Bandits during the 2008–9 season, my old physical anxieties kicked back in. I remembered an interview with Fashanu asking how he'd scored *that* goal. He didn't know: 'I just hit it and it flew in.' Far from banal, this was the perfect statement on that symbiotic, sublime relationship between body and mind needed to succeed in sport: it is so difficult to reach that point, after years of practice, when the body does what the mind desires without having to be told.

I was nowhere near that. After a night at Bar Wotever where I swapped numbers with Jet Moon and went to a pub

until 3 a.m., I threw up the first time I ran on to the pitch
for a game against the London Titans and missed two easy
chances, still drunk. Against the Leftfooters, I ran towards a
cross, outpacing the defender and leaping towards the ball.
It hit the top of my head and bounced over the open goal, to
laughs from my opponents, groans from my teammates and
my own astonishment. They took the goal kick and attacked:
Steve hacked down their centre-forward and got booked.

'*Thanks* for that,' he yelled.

It's not my fault you were too fucking slow to catch their centre-forward, I thought but didn't say anything, turning to see that
I was being substituted. *You're not letting me make up for that?*
I thought as I sat down, frustrated and furious.

'Talk us through the header,' said Steve after the game.
Jason led me to the car, preventing me from picking up a ball
and throwing it at Steve.

'I'd have missed anyway,' I told Jason.

'If this is what it's going to be like when we win, I can't be
fucked with losing,' he replied.

'It's not worth it, is it?'

I didn't start another game until a friendly in April. I tried
to control a pass, under no pressure. I kicked the ball against
my face and out for a throw-in. I asked to be taken off.

'Are you alright?' asked Alan, our manager.

'No,' I said, changing into my jeans and trying not to cry.

After the match, Simon drove Jason, Paul and me into
town.

'You're depressed,' said Jason. 'What's up?'

I paused.

'I'm transsexual. I'm going to see my doctor about it.'

'Good for you!' replied Simon. 'If that's what you need to
do, then go for it.'

'Absolutely,' said Jason. 'We're behind you all the way.'

'Are you going to stick with the team?' asked Paul.

'I'm not sure,' I replied.

'We'll understand if you don't want to play, but if you do, we'll back you.'

———

The next day, I entered the waiting room at the Charter Medical Centre and sat alone, trembling. As Pia had put it, everything felt banal: the walls were covered with posters telling people to keep hydrated in summer and the tables stacked with *Top Gear* and *Cosmopolitan* magazines. I heard over the speakers the name that I was about to discard, and then:

'Go to Room 8, please.'

My regular GP, Paul, was there.

'What can I do for you?' he asked, smiling.

I took a deep breath.

It's an appointment like any other. Just say the words …

'I want to have gender reassignment.'

You've thrown yourself off that mountain, YOU'VE SAID IT—

'Oh yes,' he replied. 'We spoke about this before.'

6

'Did you want to go privately, or via the NHS?' asked my GP.

'NHS. I can't afford private.'

'I've not had any training on this, and I don't know much about it,' he said. 'All I can do is refer you to specialist services.'

'That's what I'd expected.'

'You know it'll be slow, right?'

'I don't know *how* slow, but yeah.'

'This is all done through mental health, so I'll refer you for a psychiatric assessment at Hove Polyclinic. Don't worry, it's just screening to make sure you're suitable for the Gender Identity Clinic in London.' He paused. 'There's a waiting list. Three to four months.'

'That *is* slow.'

'Spend the time thinking about how you might tell people. It sounds like you've done your research, so if you know any support services, I'd get in touch.'

I left, full of questions. *What if the psychiatrist says no? If he says yes, how will I tell my friends? What if they disapprove? What about my family – what if they disown me? What about work? How am I going to pay for all those new clothes? How long will this take? What will the clinic want me to do? What's going to happen to my body? Where do I even start?*

Calm down, I told myself as I got home. *At least you know* what *you're going to tell everyone: I'm transsexual. They'll understand that – changing your name and appearance, hormones, maybe surgery. At least you've got* time. *There'll be more questions, but they can wait.* For now, I was glad to have picked a path through all those options I'd encountered in Feinberg and Bornstein, online and at Transfabulous.

I emailed the Gender Trust to say I was considering reassignment and wanted to speak to a qualified therapist. They suggested I visit the Clare Project's drop-in centre, held on Tuesday afternoons at the Dorset Gardens Methodist Church in Kemp Town. I arranged some time off work, put on a little makeup and walked over in a pink shirt and black trousers, wishing I'd brought a friend.

It didn't look like a church. Instead, it was a modern mix of red brick and glass with no curves, one corner resting on a stone wall that I guessed was a relic from an older building. I pushed through the door, surprised at how heavy it was and exhausted as it slammed behind me.

'Hello,' said the facilitator. 'How can I help?'

'Well …' I caught my breath. 'I'm thinking about gender reassignment, and I was told this was a good place to come.'

'We think so,' she replied, smiling. 'Have some handouts. There's tea and biscuits in the common room if you want to go and read them, or chat with anyone.'

I sat and looked at the Frequently Asked Questions sheet, produced by the Gender Trust.

How Many Transsexual People Are There?

The rate of occurrence of transsexualism is not accurately known. Because of the social stigma attached, arising from widespread lack of awareness of the true nature of the condition, it is often kept hidden. Therefore it is only possible to collect statistics on the numbers of declared transsexual people, and such figures undoubtedly represent only a proportion. Estimates vary widely between one in four thousand and one in ten thousand.

What Is the Medical Treatment for Gender Dysphoria?

The currently accepted and effective model of treatment utilises hormone therapy and surgical reconstruction and may include counselling and other psychotherapeutic approaches.

Speech therapy and facial surgery may be appropriate for some trans women, and most will need electrolysis to remove beard growth and other body hair. In all cases, the length and kind of treatment provided will depend on individual needs. The male to female person will take a course of female hormones (oestrogen) similar to those used in the contraceptive pill and HRT; the female to male individual will take testosterone. At this time trans people will also be required to carry out the Real Life Experience, during which they will be required to change their name and all documents, including passport, driving licence, medical card, legally, to be consistent with their new gender role. During this, they will also be expected to live, work and socialise full time in the new gender role, to deal with any problems which may arise for example at work or within the family, and generally become familiar with the reality of living this way. After a minimum of a year (or two in some NHS gender clinics), if the Experience has been successful and the psychiatrist in charge is satisfied with the progress made, they can be referred for surgery. After surgery trans people will continue to take hormones for the rest of their lives, but probably at a reduced dosage.

No wonder friends had said 'Do you really want to go through all that?' when we'd talked about transition in the past. I put the leaflets on hormone therapy, hair removal and name changes in my bag, and made some tea. There were a couple of trans women, older than me, quietly drinking. One of them smiled at me, and I thought we'd get on.

'Hi, I'm Juliet.' I said. 'Nice T-shirt – I love *Unknown pleasures.*'

'Thanks. I'm Steph.'

Naomi walked in. I recognised her from Miss Transgender, and we talked about music, sharing our love of the 1970s Krautrock bands. Then a woman called Alice entered, with long white hair and a flowing skirt, gloating to Steph about that weekend's Arsenal match.

'You like football?' I asked. Steph and Alice nodded. 'Who's your team?'

'Stoke City,' said Steph, proudly. 'Season ticket holder.'

'Really?' I replied. 'Do you get any hassle?'

'No, my friends there have known me for years. Who do you support?'

'Norwich.' They laughed. 'I know. Someone's got to.'

Lynne, the counsellor, came in. 'We're going for drinks if you want to come.'

'Sure,' I said.

I sat in the pub with Ryan, a trans man, and asked where he was from.

'Horsham,' he said.

'Oh, right. I went to Collyer's.'

'How did you find it?'

'Best two years of my life,' I replied. 'I came out as a cross-dresser, and my friends were really supportive. Several of them moved to Brighton and we're still in touch.'

'You didn't try to transition there, did you?'

I shook my head. He told me how the teachers hadn't backed him or used his chosen name, and how his classmates had shunned him. I'd always been cautious about who I told out of fear, but I realised how lucky I'd been as a teenager to find people who had always backed me, and that I hadn't needed to make such a leap at such a vulnerable age. Now, though, I couldn't compartmentalise in that way, and Lynne asked how I thought coming out to *everyone* would be.

'My friends should be fine. I think work will be okay. My contract's up in a few weeks anyway,' I said. 'No idea about my family.'

My phone lit up. 'Matt', it said: a text message from my brother. He never wrote unless we had a family event to organise. *What did he want?*

'I'm getting married next summer and we'd like you to be an usher. All the guys are going to wear matching suits, so we'll need your measurements.'

I stared at the text, head in hand, laughing.

'What's up?' asked Lynne.

'Twenty-seven years.' I explained. 'He couldn't have picked a worse day.'

'You'll work it out,' replied Steph. 'You've got ages.'

'You're right,' I said, smiling. 'Shall I tell him I'm a size fourteen?'

We laughed, and I put my phone away. Walking home, drunk, I just wrote: 'We'll talk about this soon.'

———

I invited Clare round for dinner. Since I'd left Legal & General, we'd not seen as much of each other, but I often recalled how our conversations had helped me through hard times. It wasn't that I'd planned to tell her first – just that she was the first person I saw after going to the doctor.

'I'm going to transition,' I said, taking the potatoes out of the oven. 'From male to female.'

'This changes everything I thought about you.'

'Does it?' I replied. 'You've seen me as a woman before, haven't you?'

'Well, yes, but … you'll have a different name, you'll look different, you'll speak differently. You just won't be the person I met.'

'Most of the changes will take ages, we'll barely notice them,' I said. 'I'm not going to stop listening to Chicks on Speed, or taking the piss out of people like our boss at work for being twats.' She laughed. 'Why would I?'

'I guess you're right,' she replied, and we ate, talking about what we might want to see in the forthcoming Brighton Festival.

Days later I went to London for the launch of Joe's second novel, in the café at Foyles bookshop. I sat at the back, looking at the microphone and chair on the empty stage. Joe walked on in a suit and bow tie, carrying a guitar. He sat down.

'People tell me I look nice,' he began. 'I say, "I know, I made a *special effort*." ' Then he played and sang an absurd song about his sister's phone getting broken. I laughed, alone, aware that the confusion and irritation of the audience was central to his performance. After the song, he stepped down to silence, and nobody followed us out.

'How are things?' he asked. We'd spoken so much about my gender, its different incarnations, what I read and how I wrote about it, but beyond feeling certain that he wouldn't be disgusted, I couldn't predict his reaction.

'I went to the doctor about gender reassignment,' I said. 'I'm finally doing it.'

He lit a cigarette.

'Will you still support Norwich?'

'No, *Ipswich*,' I replied. 'Of course I'll still support Norwich. Why wouldn't I?'

'Because you're shit?'

'Hasn't stopped me so far.'

Joe paused.

'Do you think you'll get relegated?'

'Half the squad is on loan, the players we own are useless and the manager is on his first job and totally out of his depth,' I said. 'We're fucked.'

'Have you told many people?' he asked.

'Hardly anyone.'

'Your friends all know anyway, right?'

'Most of them have seen me as Juliet. It's a big jump from there to "I'm transsexual", though.'

'How do you think they'll respond?'

'I don't know. I'll just have to find out.'

———

I'd quit the Justin campaign and the Bandits, knowing I wouldn't be able to give them the time they needed. I was throwing my life in the air, and I would be busy trying to ensure that everything landed where I wanted, however long that took. Then a letter arrived from Hove Polyclinic: my appointment would be in two weeks. *You'll have to start living as Juliet sooner or later,* I thought. *Why not now?*

I told my housemates. They were fine, but we'd only just met. *What about people who've known me for years?* I put on a black dress and went with Clare to see Diamanda Galás, finding that after our chat, nothing had changed – we talked about the same things in the same way. We tried to go to a pub near the Brighton Dome, but the doorman wouldn't let us in.

'Why not?' I asked.

'You just can't.'

We stood for a moment, stunned.

'I know why he won't let us in,' I told Clare.

'It's a shit pub anyway,' she replied. 'Let's go somewhere else.'

I woke the next day and reflected. *A better pub let us in, nobody even glanced at you at the gig, and your friend supported you. You've started coming out – it's best people find out from you, rather than someone else, or seeing you in the street.*

I had no idea what to expect. I'd thought Clare would be casual about it and that Joe would have lots of questions. I had been wrong, but ultimately, both of them had worried that I'd change beyond recognition, so I decided to write to everyone, focusing on that. Then, I was in control. Wasn't this too serious for a round-robin message? Would people be upset that I'd not told them face-to-face? But I was already exhausted with saying 'I'm transsexual' and there were so many people to tell. *You'll soon talk to your closest friends about it*, I thought. *Just do it.*

I made a cup of tea, sat at my desk and spent two hours writing.

As you know, I've identified as transgender for many years and it's come to the point where I feel I have to live as a woman far more often – in fact, all the time when it's possible, which will hopefully become 'all the time' in the not-too-distant future.

My long-term aim is gender reassignment, but I'm not rushing – I'll be discussing my feelings with specialists, and friends, should they want to (although I don't want to overburden, or just bore, any of you with it – that's what the professionals are for), and the whole process will take at least a couple of years.

Anyone who transitions feels 'out on a limb' at times, and for all my resolve, I'm no different. I've always chosen my friends carefully, and since I moved to Brighton, I've made a point of forming close friendships only with people I could share my female persona with – I consider myself charmed to know such tolerant, intelligent, kindhearted and open-minded people, and I'm sure you'll support me.

I'd love to say 'I'll still be the same person' but that isn't quite true. I'll have a new name, and my body will change, but you've seen me as Juliet before, in photos or real life, and you know I will still be essentially the same character, with the same tastes and interests and the same qualities that make us friends – the major change is that I'll be calmer and happier because after two decades of struggling, I will finally be comfortable in my body, and will be perceived (and treated) as I have always wished.

I understand that a lot of my friends have never met someone who is undergoing, or has undergone, gender reassignment, and may not be sure of how to react – what words to use, how to treat them, etc. From this point, I would prefer to be called Juliet and referred to as 'she' and 'her', but I will understand if it's hard. I'm a forgiving person (at least, I like to think so) and I'm not going to hold any slips or difficulty adjusting against anyone – the reason I've sent you this is because I value you and hope we remain friends for a very long time.

I should point out here that although I am currently pursuing this – I have a psychiatric assessment soon, and then hope to be referred to the Gender Identity Clinic in London – it's not definite yet, and if I'm going through the process and find it's not right for me, I can opt out at any time.

I can understand that you might have worries about this – I've told a few friends already and they've expressed concerns that I may be rushing into this, or see it as a panacea for other problems, or get into trouble socially, but I can assure you that I've given this a lot of thought, and that I've made a point of living in Brighton because it's the safest place in the South of England, probably the whole of the UK, to be openly transgender. I am in contact with local support groups, and I like to think I know how to handle myself – I know there will be difficulties, both with things inside my head, and with intolerant people in the outside world, so I hope you'll be there to help me through it.

I moved the cursor over the button, shut my eyes, pressed Send and then closed my laptop.

Now, I had to go shopping. I needed lots of new clothes. *What to wear?*

This isn't like dressing up for Miss Transgender or Transfabulous, I thought. Remembering all the abuse I'd taken walking around Brighton, I decided to try to 'pass'. I straightened my hair, putting on foundation with a little mascara and lip gloss. My old friend Laura from Avatar Jewels had been thrilled when I'd told her I was transitioning, giving me skirts, tops, cardigans and necklaces that she didn't want. I wore her old white T-shirt with a knee-length black skirt, tights and flat shoes, packed a handbag and left.

I walked towards Lacies. It was hot, and the shop was a long way from my house. I put on my headphones to stop myself worrying about people pointing me out. My trip was peaceful, but I was still nervous as I entered.

'I'd … like to buy some breast forms,' I said, faltering. 'My old ones are falling apart.'

'Do you want the same size as the ones you've got?' asked the assistant.

'Please.'

A friend had given me some bras that she thought might fit, and I didn't want to spend more money replacing them.

The assistant took me into a room full of wigs and boxes. I took off my top, removed the old inserts and threw them away. She handed me several silicone forms, all surprisingly heavy. I tried them on in front of the mirror, seeing how they looked under my T-shirt. I spent £110 on a pair and left. I worried that they were too big and altered my appearance too radically, but 'authenticity' wasn't my main concern: all I could think was *pass, or you'll get beaten up.*

The more banal my task, the more fraught it felt. *What if I got hassle on the bus? Could I never use public transport again? What if transphobia stopped me buying groceries?* After leaving Lacies, I rode into town, head down, trying to look confident yet inconspicuous. I went to the Co-op. A friendly woman who often served me put my bread and milk through the till, asking how I was. 'Not bad, thanks,' I said, bagging everything. Reassured, I got home and collapsed, relieved that I'd got through my afternoon. Then I remembered the email.

Just a handful of responses had come: all supportive. I stayed in that night, exhausted, telling myself not to force the issue any further.

I got up the next morning and went online, finding a few more replies. Several people were pleased that I'd thought they were worth telling. Some apologised in advance for getting my name or pronouns wrong, asking that I return their good faith with forgiveness. 'I'm not able to understand this, but perhaps I don't need to,' one told me, saying that he hadn't realised this was so important to me, appreciating my sincerity and trusting that I'd thought it through. A few guys said they knew it was slightly selfish to be sorry to 'lose' the male me, and I appreciated their honesty.

My friend Amanda simply wrote: 'Welcome to the dark side!' It seemed that while certain male friends felt like I was leaving them, some female ones felt I was joining them.

Some were 'proud', or called me 'brave'. I didn't feel courageous – I was just trying to *live* – but took their comments in the kind spirit offered. Some mentioned other transsexual people they'd known, saying it had taken time to adjust, but that this time it would be easier. Someone mentioned a transsexual woman in his office who seemed calmer since transitioning, but whose father also worked there, refusing to use her chosen name or pronouns, making life awkward for everyone.

It felt like *anything* could happen. No one yet had said they never wanted to see me again, but still, I panicked. Who *hadn't* replied? *Why?* I tried to think about something else.

It was the final day of the season, and Norwich had a big match away at Charlton. Lose and we'd be relegated; win and we might not. *I could go,* I thought. *As Juliet?* There'd be so many angry people if we went down, looking for *any* target for their rage. But having made the leap, I didn't want to go in male clothes – especially as I'd already started giving those away to friends.

I listened online as Norwich went 3–0 behind after thirty minutes, the commentators discussing the visible fury of my fellow supporters. *I'm so glad I didn't bother with that,* I thought. Instead, I went to see Jon, celebrating his birthday with some other friends from the PCT. I put on the same clothes as the day before, trying to remember which of my colleagues I'd told. It didn't matter: they'd spoken before I arrived. Ailsa asked if I would come out at work.

'Probably not,' I said. 'My contract's up soon, it's a lot of trouble for a fortnight.'

'Everyone wants you to stay, though,' she replied. 'What if you get another role?'

'Then I'll have to, I guess.'

'We'll support you,' said Jon.

'I know you will,' I replied, getting up. 'Now – who wants a drink?'

I went to the bar. A man followed, tapping my shoulder.

'Excuse me,' he said. 'Are you a bird or a bloke?'

What to do? Demand a third option? Say 'woman' in my untrained male voice, or some camp-sounding high-pitched tone?

'Bloke,' I replied, crestfallen. It seemed the safest option, yet the least comfortable.

'I *thought* so!' he said. 'Nice tits!'

As I wondered how many people in the tiny bar had been speculating about my gender, he squeezed the contents of my bra and ran off. I sat down, feeling simultaneously violated and relieved that it hadn't been worse, resigning myself to hearing that question a lot more in future.

———

Two days later, I went back to the PCT. *It's just for two weeks,* I told myself, but going to work in my old shirt and trousers after coming out as transsexual proved to be one of the most dysphoric experiences of my life. I got to my desk, feeling colourless. Kevin, the head of security, cheerfully greeted me by my old name – as did the rest of the team. *This is too weird,* I thought.

I emailed Doreen.

'Can we talk about finding another job here?'

We went into a meeting room. Once again, I wondered about who could see through the glass walls, and what they might think we were discussing.

'There's an admin job coming up with the Adults & Older People team,' she said. 'I'll happily give a reference to Wendy, the team manager. Just tell her you're interested.'

'I will, thanks.' I gulped. 'There's one more thing.'

'Yes?'

'I'm transsexual,' I said. 'I'm about to start the process. I've come out to a few friends here, but I don't know how to handle it in the office.'

She paused. 'Speak to Phil, the equality and diversity manager, and Sarah from HR. They'll be able to help.'

'I will,' I replied.

'How have your friends been?'

'Mostly fine. Some of my older ones are struggling a bit, perhaps because they're so used to me as a guy. But we'll get there.'

'I think people here will be alright,' said Doreen. 'Nobody has a problem with Andrea – except that she votes Conservative.'

'*I* find that disgusting,' I said, laughing. 'I was at Pride last year, behind a float that said, "I've come out – I'm a Tory!" I just thought: "Go back in!"'

'Have you spoken to your parents yet?'

'No. I'm still trying to work out the best way. I'm terrified.'

'My son told me he was gay a few years ago,' she replied. 'I hadn't expected it, so it took me a while to come to terms with it, but he's still the same person and I still love him. Anyway – I'm sure you'll sort it out.'

I thanked Doreen, and arranged a meeting with Phil and Sarah. I felt confident they'd support me – the Sex Discrimination Act in 1999 had made it unlawful for employers to discriminate on grounds of gender reassignment, the same year that the right to access these services via the NHS had been secured – and I was lucky enough that our conversation was mostly about the right way to tell people, rather than to discourage me from taking another job.

'We'll support you if anyone makes things difficult,' said Phil.

'I don't think it's fair that you should have to tell *everyone*,' continued Sarah. 'Why don't you tell Wendy before joining her team, and she can let them know if necessary? You can finish with Health Promotion next Friday, letting them know you'll be staying, as Juliet.'

'That makes sense,' I replied. 'Thanks so much.'

I returned to my desk. Andrea had emailed me.

I've heard you're transitioning. Congratulations! Happy to chat if you've got any questions.

We went outside.

'I lost friends and family,' she told me. 'My mum died, I wasn't allowed to go to the funeral.'

'That's awful,' I replied. 'I'm so sorry.'

'That's the price. Sometimes.'

'Was it worth it?' I asked.

'Definitely,' she said, her eyes lighting up. 'I'm so much happier. No regrets.'

I met with Wendy. She told me what the job involved, and I assured her I could do it.

'I'm sure it's not a problem, but there aren't many men on the team,' she said.

'Funny you say that …'

Feeling confident, almost blasé, I explained. She thought nobody would have a problem with my gender identity, and agreed to take me on. Time to write another email.

I'm finishing in Health Promotion this Friday. I've had a marvellous six months – it's been a pleasure to see the positive side of the NHS, gaining insight into the innovative projects you're devising, and how you're promoting them.

Some of you have touchingly signed emails with 'What will

I do without you?' The good news is that you won't have to just yet, although things may be slightly different, at least on the outside. Thanks to some kind words from the team, I had no trouble securing another job, and I'll be working for Adults & Older People from Monday.

What may (or may not) surprise you is that I will be doing so as a woman. I have always lived with gender dysphoria and have reached the point where I feel it's time to act, so I began the process of reassignment two months ago, and I am now living as a woman everywhere except work. Having spoken to HR and Wendy, I'll be working as female there.

The reason I've been so keen to stay, besides my friends here, is that it is a welcoming environment full of open-minded people, and I feel confident that you'll welcome me back without fuss – nonetheless, I wanted to let you know so it doesn't come as a surprise.

My new name will be Juliet, and I would like to be addressed accordingly (and referred to as 'she' and 'her'). I'll understand and forgive any slips – I know the difference between malicious comment and force of habit, and adapting to any name/ identity change is always difficult. (Ten years on, I still refer to 'Starburst' as 'Opal Fruits'. It's never easy.) So don't worry that you'll offend me if you call me the wrong thing – it's cool. Anyway – feel free to chat about this if you want, but don't feel you have to, and I'm glad that I'll still get to see you.

Kevin turned around. I'd always hated the way he kept referring to Tim and me as 'the lads', and I wondered how he'd respond.

'Great email, Juliet!' he said, and went back to his work. I talked the team through my decision in the office and at my leaving drinks.

'You talked a few weeks ago about writing on transgender

issues,' said David. 'We wondered if you were a man who used to be a woman.'

'Ha, really?' I replied. 'I love the idea of that. But now you know ...' Liz and David laughed. 'Seriously, though, I'm so glad I'm staying – I didn't like the idea of trying to get another job, I've got enough on my plate already.'

I came back on Monday, wearing a short dress with some trousers. Immediately, I regretted the decision not to tell everyone, however much I resented the obligation.

'What on earth are you doing dressed like that?' asked Marilyn, who did a double take as I opened a door for her. I'd met her during my last job even though she hadn't been on my team. She reacted calmly once I explained, congratulating me on my decision, and I soon found that only a few people shied away from me. Others seemed keener to chat, telling me they'd sensed I was holding something back and that I seemed more approachable now. I discovered that in a healthcare organisation, my colleagues were a little *too* keen to discuss things.

'Maybe in a few weeks,' I would reply. 'Right now, I'd rather talk about *anything* else.'

They respected that, and I realised how lucky I was to have such a problem. People wanted to help, telling me when my posture was too slouched or my skirts were too short, but this made me more anxious. Luckily, nobody made an issue of which toilets I used, and I was constantly in the bathroom, worrying about how visible my facial hair was, especially in the afternoons.

'Have you read *Conundrum* by Jan Morris?' asked Jenny, as we did our hair in the mirror.

'Yes, a few years ago.'

'I really enjoyed it,' she said. 'I wondered what you thought of it.'

'It was interesting but it's pretty old now,' I replied, surprised that this was still her reference point, thirty-five years after its publication. 'She kept everything secret while she joined the army, had kids and all that. My journey has been quite different, partly because I've never tried to be a "straight" man, and I think a lot's changed.'

Sunanda, from my new team, invited me for a chat.

'You know we fund gender reassignment for people in Brighton and Hove, don't you?' I nodded. 'I was on the Transgender Working Group that designed the local pathway.'

'There isn't a national one?' I asked.

'No, each PCT makes its own decisions about what to fund. Like most places, we follow the World Professional Association for Transgender Health's Standards of Care, so there are at least three months of Real Life Experience before hormone prescription, and a year or maybe two before surgery. We pay for those, but we don't fund hair removal because it's not fair on anyone else who needs it.'

'Right,' I said, wondering how much it would cost to get electrolysis or laser treatment.

'We don't fund surgical reversals either, so you need to be sure you're doing the right thing.'

'I've got three years,' I said, looking at the local pathway document that she'd brought.

'I used to work for West London Mental Health Trust, who run the clinic at Charing Cross,' she said. 'The Clare Project are right to tell you to expect a six-month wait for appointments. But I'll email them and ask if they can acknowledge that you've already started the Real Life Experience – that should speed things up.'

The lead clinician at Charing Cross replied to Sunanda's message to say that there was 'nothing to stop this patient working in the female role in advance of hormone treatment and any such commencement would be taken into account at the first assessment.' Sunanda told me to keep the email 'as a record of agreement' and I did. But now, I had the local assessment to worry about.

––––

The Clare Project recommended that anyone beginning transition undergo counselling using their low-cost service, at £10 per hour. Lynne, the counsellor, told me to expect discrimination, to be patient with my friends as they adapted, and to keep putting on makeup because it would help me to 'pass'.

'What if the psychiatrist rules me unfit to transition?' I asked.

'He won't,' said Lynne. 'There's a raft of psychiatrists to go through – this just checks for any obvious mental health problems, and that you're transsexual rather than an effeminate gay man.' In the past, apparently, GIC appointments had been wasted by referrals for people who did not fit conventional gender expectations but had no desire to transition. 'Explain everything calmly and you'll be fine.'

I went to Hove Polyclinic and sat nervously in the waiting room. Roy, the psychiatrist, called me into his office. He gave me a disarming smile, seeing that my shoulders were hunched.

'Relax, Juliet. It's just a few simple questions.'

He asked about when I'd first realised that I wanted to be a woman, and what I'd told my family. Then school: I said I'd gone to a private school, Reigate Grammar, left at age twelve because my parents couldn't afford the fees and gone to Oakwood. I'd struggled with my awareness that I'd missed out on a better education, I said, but I didn't think being transgender would have been any easier at Reigate Grammar than at Oakwood.

I told him I'd begun the Real Life Experience, and was employed in a supportive environment. I said I was in touch with support services and had met with Spectrum, the LGBT Community Forum, to discuss the needs of local transgender people. I told him about my counselling for depression and anxiety, that I didn't drink too much and only smoked dope occasionally.

'Okay, great. I don't think I'll have any problem referring you to Charing Cross,' he said. *You've crossed the first barrier,* I thought, smiling. 'Come back in two months for a follow-up appointment, just to make sure you're suitable.'

I sighed and left. Clearly, getting this appointment so quickly was an anomaly. But right now, I had more pressing concerns. I had to tell my parents. *But how?*

———

I discussed it with friends, people at the Clare Project and transgender forums. Telling them face-to-face, or over the phone, seemed too difficult. The last time I'd seen them, I'd left on my nail varnish from a night at Bar Wotever. Clearly they'd dismissed my college cross-dressing as 'a phase': my mum kept asking why I was wearing it and I just laughed, awkwardly, when she asked, 'You're not planning any operations, are you?' I read the 'Coming Out Tips' on the Transsexual Road Map website:

> *You might consider writing a letter that they can read when you aren't around. Tell them that you love them and you understand that this is all very difficult. Tell them how you feel, and share some moments from your childhood that made you realize there was something going on.*

Writing was the best option. I could think carefully about what to say, and they could respond at their own pace. An email felt too casual, so I found a fountain pen and some nice paper and sat down to write.

No blank page had ever felt so terrifying. I put it aside and opened Facebook. The site had helped me come out, as I'd changed my picture to one of me as Juliet before I'd even seen my GP, and my first name shortly after emailing everyone, letting me hint at what was happening without using the words 'I am transsexual'. Now, I *had* to use them: under 'People You May Know' was my mum. *Has she opened an account? What will she say when she sees my profile?*

I was due to see my parents that weekend. *You've got to do this now,* I told myself. *Where to start?* I remembered the News Writing section of my journalism course: open with Who, What and When, before moving on to How and Why.

Dear Mum and Dad,
I'm writing because I have to tell you: I'm transsexual. I've felt like this since I was ten, and for the last seventeen years I've tried to find ways to live without going through gender reassignment, but I can't any more.

I wrote three pages, explaining how keeping things secret had been disastrous for my mental health as a teenager. I referred to an evening during my first year at Oakwood when I'd screamed and cried for hours because I couldn't face another day at that school – or in that body. I talked about my disappointing postgraduate trajectory: it wasn't that my studies were a waste of time, but that doing a degree hadn't opened the same opportunities for my generation as theirs. Making a living from writing was tough, I said, and doing so with anxiety, depression and gender dysphoria was almost impossible. I closed by saying that I'd given this plenty of consideration, and that I was certain it was right for me.

I hope this makes sense and that we can talk about it soon.

Trembling, I signed the name they'd given me and the one I'd chosen myself. Then I wrote the address of my childhood home in Horley, sealed the envelope, walked up the road, took a huge breath, closed my eyes and dropped it into the postbox.

I spent several days contemplating their response. *Would they think it was their 'fault'? Fear for my future? Be ashamed of me?*

Then an email arrived:

Mum and I have read your letter. Although we are having difficulty coming to terms with the direction your lifestyle is taking we respect the choices you feel you have to make. However we would ask that you respect our feelings in this matter and that, for the foreseeable future, you remain 'male' when you attend family occasions or when Mum and I visit you in Brighton. We will always be here for you and hope that with time and understanding we can continue to be a part of each other's lives.

I wrote back the same day.

Hi Dad,
I'd planned to stay 'male' around the family for a while yet: nothing is finalised, so we can manage things at the right pace. I'm glad you'll always be here for me: I've worried about breaking this to you because I've never wanted to lose you.

I talked to friends at work. 'I think it'll be okay,' I said. 'They haven't told me never to contact them again, so that's a start.'

A text message arrived from Mum: 'Do you still want us to visit this weekend?'

'I think it's for the best,' I replied. 'See you on Sunday.'

Their car pulled up outside my house. I put on a T-shirt and jeans and went outside. Dad said he'd found a pub in Hove where we could have lunch; my mum didn't speak.

I thought about why my father might be finding this less difficult. He'd been seriously ill as a toddler, spending months in hospital with nephritis, a kidney problem that was not such a big deal now but grave in the 1950s. He was the oldest of three brothers; the second, Robin (or Robbo, as he liked to be called), had been an extremely bright boy until one day when he ran into the road to escape some bullies and was hit by a lorry. He'd suffered severe brain damage, freezing much of his development at the age of eight. As a child, I'd been close to Robbo, listening to him sing or play the harmonium at my grandmother's house when we drove up from Horley, and he came from his care home to see us. My grandfather had been bipolar, and sick for much of his life – I only ever knew him as a doddery old man, shuffling down the stairs to ask my grandmother for a drink. The kindness and patience with which she cared for him and Robbo always amazed me.

So I thought Dad might be seeing my transition as just one more challenge – something to be dealt with pragmatically. He tended to laugh his way through everything. He'd spent his teens going to see Jimi Hendrix, the Who and other bands; the two of us and Robbo had always bonded over music.

Even though Mum's parents had spent more time in other countries – her father in Argentina, her mother in India during the colonial period – they were quite Victorian, and politically more conservative than Dad's family, and she hadn't grown up with the same kind of countercultural interests. She'd always said she didn't understand the books I read or the films I watched, let alone the music I liked. As a teenager, she'd always stopped me from growing my hair long, and never liked seeing transvestite comedian Eddie Izzard on TV in his lipstick and nail varnish. I worried more about her reaction to my transition.

We found a table and ordered food. Then there was silence.

'We're going to have to talk about this eventually,' I said.

Mum looked at me, angrily.

'What if you regret it?' she asked.

'The whole thing takes ages,' I replied. 'At least three years, and I have to talk to loads of specialists. They'll make sure I'm doing what's right.'

'You're more likely to regret not doing it,' my father said.

'*Right!*' I replied. When I was young, he'd nearly always taken my mum's side in arguments, and it had often driven me crazy. Now, in the biggest one of all, he'd taken mine. I felt more confident as the questions kept coming, knowing he would support me.

'Most transsexuals don't look like women,' said Mum.

'It's not about that,' I replied. 'It's about being comfortable in myself.'

'You might get beaten up.'

'You might get beaten up anywhere, for anything,' said my father.

'That's what I thought every time I went out in Crawley,' I said, 'but I never was.'

'I had a transsexual patient once,' she told me. 'It was all really difficult, and the operation was incredibly painful.'

'I'm sure it was,' I said, 'but it would be more painful not to do it. When was that, anyway?'

'Late seventies.'

'That's a long time ago,' I said. 'Things have changed now. Physically and socially.'

'I'm sorry,' she told me, 'but I'll always think of you as my little boy.'

'We'll see,' I said, shrugging.

The conversation fell flat. I tried to ask how things were with them – whether Dad could find another job in the plastics industry at his age, how Mum was getting on at work, how their pet dogs were – but they didn't want to talk.

We went for a long, awkward walk in Hove Park. After protracted silence, Mum said she worried that I wouldn't be the same person.

'Maybe that's not so bad,' I said, glancing at Legal & General's office on the far side of the park. 'It's been a tough few years. I need something to change.'

'Who am I going to talk to about football?' she asked.

'Me!' I replied. 'You're a woman and you like it, right?'

She laughed, and there was a little light. She opened up about how hard she would find it to adapt, and especially to stop using the name she'd chosen for me. As for Matt's wedding, we agreed that I wouldn't be an usher, and they promised to let him know. Otherwise, we had time to think about how to handle it. We decided not to tell either of my grandmothers, both in their nineties. It made me sad, especially as my dad's mother had always seemed quite open-minded, once telling me that she didn't understand how people could be racist or homophobic. But I knew it would be a huge adjustment for them, with their memories failing, so it seemed easier to remain 'male' whenever we met. The important thing was that we loved each other – I'd already accepted that this journey wouldn't be as simple as moving from A to B.

'I've been trying to find some support services for families, but I haven't seen much,' she said.

'Try the Gender Trust,' I told her. 'Or Depend – they help families where someone's transitioning. Otherwise, I'm not sure. There's Mermaids but that's for under-eighteens, I think.'

I worried about how my parents might counter the *Daily Mail* stereotypes that they must have seen so many times, but now would *have* to question. I said I'd look for other people or groups who might help them, but that the best thing would be for us to keep talking. The time came to say goodbye, and I walked them back to their car. My father's embrace, and then my mother's, made me think that however long it took, we'd find an understanding – just as my dad had promised.

7

I waited eight weeks, and then returned to Hove Polyclinic for my follow-up assessment.

'How's it going?' asked the psychiatrist.

'Fine,' I said. 'I told my parents. It'll take time but we're still talking. Work have been great, as have my friends. I'm a lot happier.'

'Great, then I can refer you to Charing Cross,' he replied, and I left after five minutes.

Days later, a letter arrived: my first Gender Identity Clinic appointment would be in seven months. Then another letter postponed it ten days further.

Crestfallen, I told people at the Clare Project, who said I wouldn't even notice the time pass. I wasn't sure about that, but knew dwelling on it would only make it go slower.

They also said the clinic preferred a legal name change before they would prescribe hormones, which were what I wanted most.

'That's a big step,' said several friends. 'Are you sure you're happy with Juliet?'

'I'll just change it again if I get bored,' I joked.

Nobody had refused to use my new name, but everyone was struggling to adapt, and the longer I'd known someone, the harder they found it. *Some people just aren't great with names,* I thought, wondering when to start correcting them.

Perhaps it's not a matter of time but how often you see someone,
I realised: it felt hypocritical to get angry at friends who used
my old name when it was always on the tip of my tongue.
Whenever anyone did, I tended to let it pass – we both knew
it had happened, and I thought getting angry would make
them nervous and more likely to do it again. The one exception was when people were annoyed with me and used my
old name, which infuriated me: the slightest transgression
and my identity was revoked.

You'll just have to be patient, I thought, finding the UK
Deed Poll Service online. The 'Advice for Transsexuals'
section said that although it would not legally change my
gender, I could change my title, and would need to before I
could get a Gender Recognition Certificate. I ordered one for
£30 and texted my old friend Lindsey from Collyer's.

'I need a witness for my deed poll. Up for it? I'll get pizza
xxx'

She came to the studio flat near Brighton station, where I'd
just moved.

'Are you enjoying living alone?' she asked.

'It's expensive, but worth it to not feel judged,' I replied.
'Right now I feel uncomfortable if people see me without
makeup, in my pyjamas or whatever.'

I opened the Deed Poll folder. There was a list titled 'Who
to Advise after Changing Your Name': I'd ticked Employer,
Inland Revenue, Passport Office, Bank, National Insurance
Contributions Office, Register of Electors, health services
and utilities. I signed the document twice, once to abandon
my old name and again to legally adopt the new one. Lindsey
added her name and address, giving her occupation as 'filmmaker'. She put the pen down and we grinned.

'How are you doing?'

'Fine,' I replied. 'It's just a bit of paper, isn't it?'

I sat at my mirror, combing and re-combing my hair as she set up a video camera. We had talked about making a film together, and now felt like a good moment to start.

'I know you're not keen on being photographed, but a film might be different,' she said. 'It could be like a love letter to your body and its gradual changes. How about you record yourself whenever you feel like it, or when there's a milestone in your transition, and at the end let's see what we've got.'

She asked me to talk about how signing the Deed Poll felt. I spoke about how I'd always been Juliet, and how this just made it official, but that I was worried about how my parents would react as I'd renounced the name they'd chosen. She finished shooting and left the camera.

Then I called Joe. We hadn't spoken for a while: he was busy recording the second Performance album and writing another novel, as well as making a movie with some friends in Manchester and teaching Creative Writing at Keele University.

'How's it going?' he asked.

'It's getting there,' I replied. 'A friend wants to make a film about my transition.'

'You sound reluctant.'

'I'm just not confident in how I look,' I said. 'I've had so much shit from strangers. I expected it, but now it's con-stant. It's not quite the same – when I went out in wigs I got people yelling "tranny" and wolf-whistling, now I'm trying to "pass" they shout "geezer" or throw things.'

'How do you react?'

'I keep quiet and walk off, quickly. The other day I was near Churchill Square in some new lipstick with a T-shirt and skirt. These six lads went, "Look at that man!" I thought they were going to chase me home. It's better if I wear jeans and less makeup but I'm still on edge all the time. Just going to the launderette is a nightmare.'

'Pitch a blog to the *Guardian*,' said Joe. 'They'll bite your hand off.'

'Have you seen what they publish about trans issues?'

'No,' he replied.

'There's a brand of feminism that's really transphobic, and they write most of it.'

'All the more reason to do it then,' he told me.

The *Guardian*'s coverage of trans issues was deadlocked in arguments around freedom of speech, especially after Stonewall nominated Bindel for their Journalist of the Year award in 2008 and 150 activists went to protest, which Bindel cast as an attempt to shut down debate. I didn't see how people sending threats to her helped, but Bindel's protestations about attacks on her 'freedom of speech' seemed to invalidate the collective response. More than anything, it seemed that she wanted to set the terms for 'debate' about trans people and politics without being challenged. I thought those terms were uninformed and unfair, forcing us to constantly defend our right to exist at the expense of any discussion about the realities of our lives. I also thought they did real damage to trans people, especially when governments consulted these feminists about provision for sex reassignment services or access to refuges for those who experienced rape or violence. I'd been told that editors thought readers wouldn't be interested in transgender politics, and that they would only accept autobiographical narratives. I had my reservations, but thought that a regular column might let me get beyond the 'wrong body' clichés I'd always seen in newspaper articles, as well as attack the stereotypes on which transphobic feminism and conservatism relied.

My writing was deadlocked, too. I'd abandoned Fashanu, not wanting to add another complication to my transition by worrying about how the ex-footballers and evangelical Christians I'd asked for interviews would respond. My transgender short stories had felt too 'underground'. A television script hadn't worked either – the breathless pace of most comedy-dramas was too far from the Fassbinder and Almodóvar films I loved, let alone the 'experimental' writers who inspired me. A broadsheet blog seemed the right middle ground for what I wanted to say.

I emailed Chris Borg, a sub-editor at the *Guardian* who often watched Norwich matches with me, asking if he knew anyone I could contact. 'I think transgender people are practically invisible, not just underrepresented, in the mainstream media,' he replied. 'There's no reason why, so I'll ask Rachel on the Life and Style site. I'd be amazed if they weren't interested.'

'I think this could be a good resource for the transgender community, and will raise awareness,' replied Rachel, asking for three pieces. If she liked them, they would go ahead. If not, I imagined, I'd get a small kill fee – maybe £200. I wrote the first on my adolescence, the second on moving from 'transgender' to 'transsexual', and the third on my first week of living as a woman. 'I like the first and third, but the second article is weighed down with too much politics. Can you make it less theoretical and more personal?'

I'm not some 'confessional' journalist, I thought. I wanted to write like Julia Serano. I'd just read her *Whipping Girl: A Transsexual Woman on Sexism and the Scapegoating of Femininity* (2007), on the difference between gender identity and gender roles, and attitudes towards trans people in feminism, psychology and the media. Still, I redrafted. *The personal is political,* I thought as I described my journey through counselling, Pride and gay football, Miss Transgender and Transfabulous, and sent it all to Rachel.

'Great,' she said. 'We'll run fortnightly, starting ASAP.'

After a long email exchange, the *Guardian* commissioned me to write a rolling blog. They didn't know when it would start, though, so I decided to focus on getting my life in order.

———

I was trying to calm things down, but I'd become so used to chaos. I thought back to Mattilda Bernstein Sycamore's anthology *Nobody Passes* (2006), which 'examine[d] passing as a means through which the violence of assimilation takes place', not just with regards to a transsexual past but also efforts to elevate the 'right' race, class, sexuality, age, ability or body type. I didn't want to be 'normal' and hated the idea of going 'stealth' – it felt like a holdover from when Gender Identity Clinics told people to move away from their families, friends and jobs and start a 'new' life where nobody knew their history. *Imagine being cut off from all support networks like that*, I thought. *It must be heartbreaking.*

Still, I worried that friends thought my transition was an act of conforming and relinquishing my opposition to character-ising *anything* as 'male' or 'female', 'masculine' or 'feminine'. My main concern was my body, I told them, but all the com-ments and challenges I got from people were about the name I attached to it, the movements and sounds I made with it and the clothes I put on it. Staying in a position where everyone knew I was transsexual soon felt as unsustainable as finding (yet alone maintaining) one where no one did, as the barrage of harassment and intrusive questions ground me down.

I'd thought changing my name had been too easy, and so it proved. I still got incorrect correspondence months after I thought I'd covered everyone, and became irritated with different official policies on whether they'd accept photocopies of deed polls, and what evidence of transition they demanded. The local supermarket asked for two utility bills and a letter from my GP before they would replace my loyalty card.

'There's £2.40 on it,' I said. 'I'll just get a new one.'

Soon my transition stopped dominating conversations with friends. With strangers, it was different. I got to a small house party at midnight, chatting to a few women who had invited me to a clothes swap. 'Don't worry if you haven't got anything to give away,' they said. 'Everyone knows you need some new stuff.'

I thanked them. A guy, hearing my voice, asked:

'Excuse me – are you a man or a woman?'

I thought back to Jon's birthday, and how much I'd hated myself for saying 'bloke'.

'I'm transsexual,' I replied, hoping to close down any further discussion.

'What does that mean?'

I asked him to leave me alone. He looked offended. My old friend Paul, from Horsham, took me aside.

'English isn't his first language,' Paul told me.

'Sure, but I'm sick of all these questions. Why am I always asked to explain everything?'

'I don't think he meant any harm.'

'No, probably not. I'm tired, I'm going home.'

I walked back, exhausted, and went online to watch Calpernia Addams's video *Bad Questions to Ask a Transsexual*. I'd seen it before, but her mixture of frustration and fury was so righteous and hilarious, the perfect tonic after such an exasperating encounter.

'I'm an actress in Hollywood,' she said, 'and I thought I'd share with you some of the stupidest questions I've ever been asked.' I recognised nearly all of them. *What's your real name?* Anything about our sex lives, or genitals. *Do you date straight men or gay men? Are you a 'tranny'? Can I see a picture of you from 'before'?* I loved the way she turned the questions around, her smile never quite concealing her contempt. 'Can I see a picture of *you* at your most depressed, your loneliest, your most self-hating?'

That seemed like a good tactic for when I was feeling more confident, but I liked her point-blank refusal to answer *Are you a man or a woman?* 'If you can't tell, you don't need to know,' she said firmly, and I understood how she'd become so fed up. But I couldn't find it in me to be so assertive. As the interrogations got worse, my body language became more defensive – my shoulders hunched, arms folded, eyes narrowed. Still, the questions kept coming. At another party, my friend Emily introduced me to someone.

'I'm Jeremy,' he said.

'Hi, I'm Juliet.'

'You're not like the other Juliets I've met.' My heart sank. 'Can I ask a question?'

'Tell you what – ask whatever you like, and I'll reserve the right not to answer. How's that?'

'Fair enough,' he replied. Then: 'Do you not think you're mad?'

I started to explain how many psychiatrists and therapists I'd seen already, with several more to come, but he wasn't listening. I pretended I needed the toilet and walked off.

Even my flat wasn't a refuge. I got a knock on the door: *there's that book I ordered,* I thought.

'Are you Juliet?' asked the postman. I said yes. Incredulous, he looked at me, unshaven in my dressing gown. *Do I have to do my makeup and everything else even at home?* I wondered, signing for the parcel.

Most questions boiled down to: *Why?* I had no answer to this question, any more than I could convey to people why I was left-handed, and I didn't think it was fair that I was constantly being obliged to answer it. It wasn't my main concern: I didn't think too much about nature and nurture when I was worrying about the possibility of having my head kicked in if I answered back to any of the people who yelled at me in the street. *The scientists and the sexologists can argue about that*, I thought.

———

I met Laura from Avatar outside Churchill Square. I was carrying an old charity shop handbag and wearing cheap flat shoes that were worn to pieces.

'We're getting rid of *those*,' she said, grinning. 'What else do you need?'

'Some new tops, maybe a couple of dresses. Definitely a coat, a bag and a purse. Ideally stuff I can wear to work or the pub, I can't afford two wardrobes.'

'Then I'm afraid it'll be the high street rather than the trendy boutiques,' she said. 'We'll find some nice stuff.'

She took me to H&M and started rooting through the sale rail. 'This is nice,' she said, handing me a purple-and-white T-shirt. 'And this.' She gave me a black top with silver decorations, and another with a blue arrow down its front. 'This is *perfect!*' she continued, picking out a black dress with brown polka dots. I threw them in a basket as we found the coats.

'You need something that gives you hips,' said Laura. 'Try this.'

She handed me a double-breasted black coat that flared out at the waist.

'Try them,' she insisted. 'I'll tell you if they work.'

Laura smiled at the assistant as I asked to use the changing

room. Sweating nervously, I tried to relax, carefully checking how to put everything on, terrified of breaking anything.
Laura didn't think the blue top worked – 'too teenage'.
Another reminded me that most of my fat went to my stomach
– but I liked the dress and T-shirts. Then I tried the coat.

'That's *amazing*!' said Laura. 'And only £10!'

We found a purse and a black handbag. I tried on some
pumps, relieved to squeeze into a size seven, and bought some
blue patterned tights to go with a black dress from Dorothy
Perkins.

'Now you need some makeup,' said Laura, taking me to
Boots. 'You can't keep wearing that Superdrug stuff.' She led
me around the stalls. I recognised some of the brands from
my old job at World Duty Free, trying to remember which
ones targeted women older than me and which younger,
which went for people more traditional in their style and
which were trendier.

'Let's try the Benefit counter,' said Laura. 'The woman
there looks young and friendly, I'm sure she'll be fine with
you.'

'Hi, how can I help?' asked the assistant as we approached.

'My friend would like a makeover,' said Laura.

'No problem, just sit here,' said the assistant, putting me
in front of a mirror. I smiled as she wiped the makeup off my
face and then looked sadly at my five o'clock shadow. She
said nothing as she put some moisturiser and foundation over
my skin, and I started to relax.

'You've got lovely cheekbones,' she said. 'You're lucky
with your features – nothing too big or strong. Try some soft
blusher and emphasise your eyes. Pink and black are good for
you, and brown as it matches your hair. Now look up.' She
put some black eyeliner on me, and then mascara and smoky
eye shadow, with shiny lip gloss.

'That's great – thank you!' I said. I took the eyeliner and some eye shadow and went to the till. Laura stopped at the perfume stand, testing a few sample fragrances.

'This is nice. Hold out your wrist,' she said. She sprayed something by Clinique on to it. 'No, it doesn't work on you – too musty. Maybe this one.' She tried a DKNY.

'I like that,' I replied, smelling my wrist.

'Great! Get it,' she told me, and I paid for everything.

'Now throw those away,' insisted Laura, pointing at the old bag and shoes. I chucked them in the nearest bin, hugged her and went home.

The street harassment didn't stop, but it became less frequent as I became more confident, and I held up my head, slouching less. After a while, getting hassle felt like a surprise rather than an inevitability, and I felt angry at people for being so gutless, rather than depressed. They always heckled me in packs, or from passing cars, and the only single guy on the street to laugh at me had an angry-looking dog, which stopped me from head-butting him Zidane-style.

As summer turned into autumn, 'passing' became easier: my makeup stayed on for longer, not running in the heat, and I felt less exposed as my coat and thick tights covered my flesh. One September evening, going home alone, I was jolted by a group of lads driving past.

'Alright darling!' they shouted. 'Get your tits out!' They cheered and whistled as I carried on walking, trying to ignore them. *Christ, I get shit if I don't pass* and *if I do?* I suddenly remembered just how many times I'd seen or heard of female friends being propositioned in the street or grabbed in nightclubs.

One afternoon I went to the Clare Project, and decided

to go for dinner afterwards. As we walked down St James's Street, a group of mostly trans women with a couple of trans men, I became conscious of just how many people were staring and shouting at us. I'd recently been to an old friend's wedding in Storrington, a village in West Sussex. That had been the first time I'd left Brighton as Juliet, and I'd been nervous, expecting to feel more conspicuous in a smaller, more conservative place. Nobody commented on my gender – perhaps people didn't notice, or just didn't care. Maybe it was faux middle-class politeness, and they'd just laugh behind my back. Or, possibly, those I encountered were so unused to meeting a trans person that they had no idea how to react. Here, in the queerest part of a city known for its LGBT population, people were looking for us. Spotting us was a game, and the prize was a chance to take out some aggression on a community that few would be prepared to protect.

We got halfway down the hill. Convinced I was more easily 'read' with the group, I walked on ahead. In particular, I thought Kelly, in her big hoop earrings, high heels and leather miniskirt, was making us stand out, and I tried to distance myself from her.

I heard a smash. I turned: someone had thrown a bottle at Kelly. It had shattered by her feet. She was shaken; the others were holding her. I knew all too well how I would have felt if someone had left me exposed like that, and realised the abuse wasn't her fault for how she dressed. I walked back up the street, and checked that Kelly was okay. Perhaps we *were* more obvious together, but we were also stronger.

Later, I reflected: I would try to 'pass' when alone on the street, and my gender didn't need to be an issue during small tasks like buying a newspaper, but otherwise I wouldn't try to hide who I was. After all, the whole point of coming out was to stop doing that, I explained to my friend Karin at a Queer Mutiny disco at the Cowley Club. We stood at the bar in 1980s-style dresses with lots of makeup: we thought we would catch a few eyes and make some new friends, but no one seemed to be saying hello to us.

'I think we're too straight for this place,' she said. I remembered what Jet had told me at Bar Wotever: not to be too hung up on having trans or queer friends, but just to have friends. It wasn't realistic to expect to get on with everyone I met in 'the community', however much I craved it. 'Passing' in so many different spaces was a constant balancing act, and I accepted that I couldn't always get it right. Keeping myself safe and staying proud of who I was without being too desperate to please others seemed like a good start, even if I knew that maintaining such self-respect and composure under such intense provocation wouldn't be easy.

———

In September 2009, my contract at the NHS Primary Care Trust expired. I had mixed feelings: the work was dull, but the people were supportive. I didn't have much money and worried about how difficult it might be to get another job. The Sex Discrimination Act stopped employers from sacking people for transitioning but offered little protection against them deciding I'd be too much trouble to take on, as long as my gender wasn't the stated reason. I'd read that the Count Me In Too survey, conducted in 2007, had found that 26 per cent of trans people in Brighton and Hove were unemployed, with another 60 per cent earning under £10,000 a year.

You're twenty-eight years old and you've only ever had admin jobs, I thought as I walked to the Jobcentre. *What will you say when people ask what you've done with your education? No one will employ you – you couldn't get a job in a university library as a man during the boom years. There were seventy applications then. You're fucked. Imagine turning up for an interview, your makeup running, stubble showing, hair thinning …*

I signed on, relieved that housing and unemployment benefits covered my rent and bills, leaving a little for food, and that the staff made no issue of my gender. I applied for numerous jobs, some in journalism but mostly clerical positions, becoming ever more depressed as I wondered just how long I'd be doing such menial work. I emailed the *Guardian* asking when they would run my blog. They weren't sure, and I started to think it wouldn't happen.

Suddenly, I understood why, historically, so many trans people had done sex work, and why the transsexual characters I'd seen in TV programmes and films did it. I'd been on transgender forums and chat sites, staggered by the number of married guys who would message me, sometimes asking for a date but usually just telling me they were wanking over my photos. Given how hard it might be to find stable employment in a friendly environment, and how few of the men who contacted me seemed prepared to be public about their attraction to trans women, let alone form a meaningful relationship, I started to wonder if sex work might be the only place where people like me were actually *wanted*.

Then, another temporary job came up at the PCT. In January 2010, I was made permanent, scraping through an interview ahead of 110 other applicants as I was already familiar with their questions, having prepared similar tests for other employees. Even if I had no job satisfaction, at least I had some security. Whenever I complained about the boredom and people told me I 'should be grateful just to have a job', I just shrugged.

Back in work, I wrote to the Royal Sussex County Hospital, asking about speech and language therapy for transsexual women. They had a nine-month waiting list, and I wondered what else I might do before my first Charing Cross appointment. I looked into facial hair removal, sick of shaving twice a day. I discussed it at the Clare Project: people said it was best to do it before starting to present as female – not massively helpful by then – and that my chest hair would become easier to epilate once I started hormones. Nobody could recommend good or reasonably priced services, though, so I made an appointment at a clinic in Hove, where Emma, the consultant, examined my skin.

'Laser surgery would be better than electrolysis, darling, as your hair is so dark,' she said. 'We do it once a month, and you don't shave for two days beforehand. I can do your face for £110 for the first six sessions, then it gets cheaper.'

'How long will it take?'

'I don't know, your hair is very thick. It will be a lot. Hopefully we can shift 10 to 15 per cent each time.'

I took a deep breath and agreed to part with hundreds of pounds for the privilege of being repeatedly shot in the face, every four weeks, until every hair was gone. Or nearly every hair, she said, as no amount of treatment would shift it all.

The clinic resembled a dentist's surgery as imagined by Stanley Kubrick: an imposing white box labelled 'GentleLase Plus' with a black top and a digital dial sat next to a reclining chair, which was covered in blue paper. Above this was the laser, with a metal rod to maintain the right distance from my face. After washing off thick makeup covering the required stubble, I lay back and Emma covered my eyes.

'Now this *does* hurt …' she said. 'Let me know whenever you need a break.'

She flicked a switch. I saw a red light through my blindfold and felt something like a wasp stinging my cheek, over and over, accompanied by a bleep.

'What do you do for a living?' she asked over the whirring.

'Nnnurgh!' I cried as the laser zapped my top lip. 'Stop for a moment,' I said.

'You're doing well. Lots of my patients scream at me.' I breathed heavily. 'You should hear the things they say!'

'That's not very grateful.'

'It's just because it hurts so much. They don't mean it.' She sprayed cold air on to my face to cool it down. 'You ready?' I nodded. 'I get lots of transsexual women here,' she continued, 'and I try to give them money off if I can. It's not fair that you have to pay for this, it's hard enough already and it's not like you can go without it. Turn over and I'll do your other cheek.' She handed me an ice pack to put on the area she'd just done. I saw flash after flash, the cold on one side of my face offset by the searing heat on the other. 'Now lie on your back,' she ordered. 'This is the worst bit. Pull your top lip down.'

I pursed my lips together and she started on my moustache. Each strike was more painful than the last, but I managed not to scream or cry, let alone hurl abuse at her.

'All done!' she said, turning off the laser. 'How did it feel?'

'It hurt less than I expected,' I replied as she handed me a wipe.

'Good! Now go and clean up.'

I looked in the mirror.

'It's still *there*!'

'The hair isn't burned off immediately,' she said. 'It's killed at the root. Soon, some of them will go white and fall out.'

Sure enough, by the time I got home, this had started to happen. I shaved the next morning, put on makeup, went to work, came home and went to bed. At 2 a.m. I woke, feeling like my face was on fire. In agony, I looked at my reflection: I was bright red and covered in spots. I practically bathed in the aloe vera she'd sold me but it hurt too much to sleep, and I feared that for the next few days, 'passing' would be harder. Gradually, my skin calmed down. My facial hair looked less strident, and after each appointment, I noticed myself walking a little less anxiously, and getting a little less hassle.

———

'Bloody hell, you're *going*!' said Lindsey, hugging me at Brighton station.

'Yeah, I've only waited seven fucking months,' I replied.

'How're you doing?'

'Nervous,' I said, sighing. 'There are all these rumours about how you have to dress ultra-feminine, give them the story that they want to hear.'

'What sort of story?'

'Oh, the old "I knew I was different as a child" routine …'

'And you did, right?' she asked.

'Well … yes, I suppose I did. It's just that people on forums say they make it harder than it needs to be.'

'So what are you expecting?'

'My friends at the Clare Project said the horror stories about trans women being chucked out for wearing trousers come from people who've never been. Most of it goes back to that BBC documentary from the eighties. Someone said to downplay my depression, but if I work with the clinicians then I should be alright.'

'Why would you need to downplay your depression?'

'Apparently they don't like it if you have mental health problems,' I replied. 'But you'd think they'd understand that this isn't that easy. I don't know, I'm just sick of waiting.'

'You're shaking, lovely,' said Lindsey.

'I know, it's freezing.' I took off my gloves, then my hat, and checked my hair in a mirror.

'You were always shaky, though. I remember in English class you'd put your hand up to speak and I could see your fingers wobbling.'

'That's anxiety. It got too much for my brain and ran right through my body.' I paused. 'I remember that time being very happy, though.'

'Me too,' said Lindsey. 'It was so bloody refreshing to go from school and uniform to actually being able to express ourselves a bit. We were lucky to find that weird pack of people just like it, I didn't expect that in Horsham.'

Lindsey looked at the lapel on my coat.

'Is that a Morrissey badge?' she asked. I nodded. 'How *old* are you?'

'Twenty-eight.' She laughed. 'Shut up! This is basically a second puberty. Even before I get the hormones. Who else would I listen to right now?' She smiled at me. 'When I was a teenager, I liked the ones about how shit school was, or being lonely in nightclubs, or not wanting a job. Now I like the ones about broken relationships, or disappointment with things. You know "Paint a Vulgar Picture"? About a singer who's been chewed up by the music industry. The way he sings, "You could have said no, if you wanted to / You could have walked away, couldn't you" knowing that he couldn't – it's heartbreaking.'

Lindsey grinned. 'You haven't changed a bit, have you?'

We left the Tube at Hammersmith. I checked my watch.

'We've got ages,' said Lindsey.

'I left plenty of time. Imagine if I'd missed it and had to wait another six months. Let's find the clinic first, then get lunch.'

We walked up Fulham Palace Road. There was ice on the pavement, and it was busy with cars, buses and ambulances. We passed a few pubs, kebab shops and restaurants, some tower blocks and the Pizza Express opposite Charing Cross Hospital, Sainsbury's Local on the corner of Greyhound Road.

We looked down the street, seeing a newsagent, a launderette and the Hammersmith & Fulham Conservative Club. There was an anonymous-looking brown door with a buzzer, and a plaque saying WEST LONDON MENTAL HEALTH TRUST.

'That's it,' I said. 'Let's go to the pub.'

We entered the Southern Belle, between the hospital and the clinic. Although it was empty at midday, they were playing loud music.

We sat on a bench by the road. Without speaking, I took a mirror, did up my makeup and checked my hair again.

'It's not a job interview,' Lindsey said, smiling.

'I know, I just thought it was best to wear a dress today ...' She took my hand.

'It's nice. Where did you get it?'

'A friend gave it to me.'

'You'll be fine,' she said. 'Trust me.'

We finished our lunch and went back to the clinic. I pressed the buzzer.

'I'm here for my appointment,' I told the receptionist. The door opened and we climbed the stairs to the waiting room.

'You okay?' asked Lindsey. I nodded, and we sat quietly. I thumbed through the magazines, looking at the Arts section in *Time Out* and wondering if I'd find more to do in London than I had in Brighton lately. There were two other women in the waiting room talking loudly and confidently. I picked up

a pamphlet advertising the independent Charing Cross GIC
User Support Group, but decided I would get my support
from my friends at home instead.

My name came over the intercom, right on time.

'Good luck,' said Lindsey. I thanked her as the doctor
beckoned me to Room 7.

I sat opposite him in the office, trying not to stare out of
the window.

'Are you living full-time already?' he asked.

'Yes. I'm out everywhere.'

'How's it going?'

'I work for a Primary Care Trust. They've been supportive – they have processes to ensure that. All my friends
know – it was difficult to tell some of them, but everyone I
care about has stuck with me, and everything's settled down.
My parents have found it hard, especially to use my preferred
name, but I'm trying to be patient.'

The doctor nodded. 'Do you have any brothers or sisters?'

'One brother, who's three years older. My parents told
him, but we've not talked about it.'

'Okay.' He made some notes. 'When did you realise you
had gender dysphoria?'

'When I was ten.'

'And how does it relate to your sexuality?'

'I don't know. I'm attracted to men and women but I've
only slept with guys.'

'Was there any sexual element to your cross-dressing?'

'Maybe in my teens, but then there's a sexual element to
everything. Now – no.'

'And your mental health – what's that been like?'

I paused. 'Up and down. I had depression in my teens but
it's never been as bad since I left school. I had some counselling three years ago and again when I started this. I know

transition won't fix everything but coming out has been a huge relief.'

'And how have you found living as a woman?'

'Mostly it's much better – it feels more comfortable, more colourful. I'm getting tired of the hassle I get when I'm out.'

'What sort of hassle?'

'Usually people yelling at me for being a "tranny". Sometimes they ask rude questions, occasionally they hit on me in bars. It's less frequent in winter, but I'm constantly anticipating it.'

'How do you deal with it?'

'I talk to friends, or trans people at the Clare Project and elsewhere. It makes it easier to know it doesn't just happen to me.'

'Have you looked into hair removal?'

'I've started it. I've changed my name and I'm on a waiting list for speech therapy.'

He looked surprised and made more notes – I guessed that he was ticking boxes.

'I've been getting frustrated at how slow this is,' I said. 'I just want the hormones.'

'Bear in mind that for you, this is the end of a process,' he replied. 'For us, it's the beginning, and there are lots of people wanting to use the service. We can speed it up a little as you're doing so well – you'll only need half an hour next time. If things are still fine then we should be able to pre-scribe hormones. Hand in this slip of paper at the front desk and they'll give you a date for your next appointment.'

I looked at my watch: forty-five minutes had passed. I returned to reception.

'How did it go?' asked Lindsey.

'Fine,' I replied, handing in the slip.

'The next slot is in seven months,' said the receptionist.

'Really?' I asked. 'The doctor said it would be sooner because it's only thirty minutes.'

'Oh, right,' she replied, tapping her keyboard. 'We've got one in five months. Would you like me to print your letter now?'

'Yes please.'

'We'll have to address it to your male name as we don't have your deed poll.'

'I sent it,' I replied.

'It's not here.'

'Oh ... whatever. I'll bring it next time.'

The receptionist handed me the letter, telling me to return in mid-July. Lindsey and I walked out and past the Southern Belle, then the black railings, the garden and the silver sculpture by Henry Moore outside the hospital. We stared at the fifteen-storey blocks that towered over the reception – the 'Charing Cross' – and then went through the revolving doors.

'This blood test is just to work out which hormones I should get, and make sure I don't have any other health problems I don't know about,' I told Lindsey. I left her at the café and went upstairs, where the nurse put a syringe into my upper left arm. The last task finished, Lindsey and I set out to take a walk in nearby Margravine Cemetery.

'What questions did they ask you?'

'Same as Hove Polyclinic, more or less,' I replied. 'Nothing about how I dressed, or anything like that.'

'Are you going to write about it in the *Guardian*?'

'I think I'd have to.'

'Aren't you worried that it might get you in trouble with the clinic?'

'I've no idea,' I said. 'Chances are I'll be done by the time they start publishing, anyway.'

We laughed and headed back to the tube, reflecting on how low-key and uneventful the appointment had felt. In a sense, the clinicians were gatekeepers, but their main role was not to lead the changes to my body and my life but instead to slowly guide me through them.

———

I returned to work, feeling more patient. Now, I couldn't see any real obstacles to my transition. For the first time since graduation, I had some sense of stability – from here, life might go where I wanted. As the long, bitter winter finally melted into spring, I spent less time at the Clare Project talking about the probable effects of taking oestrogen, and started to think about how to move beyond my dull administration job. *Perhaps I could move up through the PCT into Healthcare Commissioning*, I thought. *They'll probably let me go part-time and I can write for a couple of days a week.* Between arranging meetings and printing papers, I looked at Project Management training courses and read about the impending general election.

On the day in May 2010 when David Cameron became prime minister of the Conservative-led coalition, I wore black to work. Andrea, who kept a picture of Margaret Thatcher on her desk, laughed at me.

'Your entire existence depends on a liberal society and a functioning state health service,' I snarled. 'How can you vote for *them*?'

Before Andrea could reply, the equality and diversity officer butted in. 'Don't worry,' he said. 'There'll be plenty of time for this in the dole queue.'

The conventional wisdom after the economic crash had been that public sector jobs were safe under Labour but not the Tories. I didn't believe Cameron's promises that his party would not touch the NHS, and feared for my future – at the PCT, and as a transsexual woman.

I may need a way out, I thought. I emailed the *Guardian* again, asking, would my series run soon? They still didn't know. I called Jet Moon, frustrated.

'Are you sure you want to play everything out in public like that?' she said. 'You don't know what's going to happen with the hormones, or how writing about it on that sort of platform will affect your mental health.'

'My mental health isn't great anyway,' I replied, 'This can't make it any *worse.*'

'We spoke before about the problem of becoming a professional trans person,' said Jet. 'Do you want to make this the main thing you talk about?'

'I mentioned this to a trans guy and he just said it was all anyone ever asks about. If I wrote about anything else and then came out as trans, then I'd just feel obliged to discuss it. Someone needs to, it can't just be left to the old-school feminists. I'll be in control of everything.'

'If you're sure,' said Jet, 'I'm doing a show at the Arcola Theatre in Dalston in July. I'd like to get some people who don't usually perform to tell their stories. Are you up for it?'

'Absolutely,' I replied.

'Great! We'll co-write a script. I'll be in touch to arrange some rehearsals.'

Summer came around, and the street harassment kicked back in. Again, I tried to ignore it, internalising the rage it inspired. My depression returned, with suicidal thoughts racing through my mind at work when I was supposed to be greeting people and taking minutes in a meeting. *I can't take much more of this,* I thought on my way home. *I've taken so many blows, and for what?*

I opened my laptop. There was an email from Rachel at the *Guardian*: 'The series will start next Wednesday.' *Let's give this a chance.* The next day, I asked my line manager for a chat: she had been on the PCT's Trans Health and Wellbeing Strategy Group to discuss concerns about housing, employment, relations with local GPs, police and the council, as well as physical, sexual and mental health, so I knew she'd be sympathetic.

'Have you tried anti-depressants?' she asked.

'No, it's the one thing I've not done. I got prescribed some a couple of years ago but I didn't take them because I was worried about the side effects. My doctor said to treat it with exercise, but I've stopped playing football now because I can't use male or female changing rooms.'

'I know people who've found them transformative. Try it and change them if they're not right.'

I went to my GP and filled out a Hospital Anxiety and Depression scale, stunned at how much worse my results had become since 2008.

'I'm going to prescribe Citalopram. It's the most common,' he said. 'It'll raise your serotonin levels. Take one a day for six months at least, a year if possible.'

'Will this affect my hormone treatment?'

'Absolutely not,' he said, 'but you must tell Charing Cross.'

I looked at the side effects: 'May cause suicidal thoughts.' *I'm having them already,* I thought, *what's to lose?* I started taking the pills, soon noticing the worst of my depression subsiding, but being replaced with minor headaches and slight nausea. I thought about asking for time off, then worried that my colleagues might think I'd requested it because the World Cup was about to start.

A few days later, I had something else to think about. My

editor at the *Guardian* wrote to say the series would launch 'tomorrow'.

'Do you want the comments enabled?' she asked. There was no time to think about it. It seemed churlish to block reader responses out of fear. Besides, what could anonymous people on the Internet say that the hecklers on the street, let alone my friends and family, hadn't? *They can't beat me up from behind their keyboards*, I thought. I emailed Rachel: 'Yes, let's have comments.'

At 11:15 the next morning, it went online. 'Juliet Jacques was born a boy, but always knew that something wasn't quite right,' ran the subheading, under the words *A Transgender Journey: Part One*. Several comments appeared minutes after. The first was supportive; the second, less so: it had been deleted, but I gathered that it was along the lines of 'Is this all you have to do to get a *Guardian* column now? I might put on a dress and see if I can get one – it's political correctness gone mad.' *Thank you*, I thought, reading through the responses that said things like 'What a ridiculous and backwards attitude to have to such an important blog.' There were debates on a range of issues, but particularly gender stereotypes and how trans people relate to them, and the merits of providing reassignment services on the NHS.

Satisfied by the positive feedback that my column wasn't completely shit, I sent the link to a few colleagues. At 5 p.m. Anna looked up from her screen and stopped me on my way out.

'Juliet,' she said. 'Are you famous now?'

'I don't know,' I replied, laughing, and made my way home.

Conundrum: The Politics of Life Writing

Ever since the publication of *Man Into Woman* in 1933, which documented the life of Lili Elbe, autobiographical narratives have been the means by which transsexual people have explained their transitions to a 'curious' public. *Man Into Woman* was a strange text, written under a pseudonym and then edited by Niels Hoyer (also an assumed name.)

In Britain, the most famous of these works remains *Conundrum* by Jan Morris. Morris differed from many similar authors in that she was not famous solely, or even primarily, for being transsexual. She was already a well-known writer as she began transition, having covered John Hunt's successful expedition to Everest in 1953 and published a cultural history of Venice seven years later. Continuing to write as James Morris after starting hormone therapy in 1964, she had little choice but to make public her tansition and sex reassignment surgery eight years later, knowing it would be impossible to keep secret as transsexuality remained of great intrigue to the mainstream media. By writing a book, Morris could at least remain in control of her story.

Conundrum was the first book she published as Jan Morris. In the narrative, she presents her realisation of the transsexual impulse as the conclusion to an internal psychological dilemma. As a result, her work codified many of the conventions of the transsexual autobiography, not least that a description of being in the 'wrong body' features early in the narrative.

Although *The Empire Strikes Back* (1987) was a response to Janice Raymond's *Transsexual Empire*, it opened not with Raymond's assault on transsexual women and the Gender Identity Clinics, but with *Conundrum*'s 'Oriental', an almost religious narrative of transformation, peaking with Morris's visit to Dr Burou's clinic in Casablanca where she (and April Ashley) underwent surgery.

Its author, Sandy Stone, examines with suspicion how the accounts of Morris, Lili Elbe and others provided little continuity between being male and becoming female, failing to explore the space between them. Instead, the genre frames each subject's operation as the instant at which she ceased to be a man. Questioning these writers' conflation of socialised gender roles with physical sex – in one instance, *Man Into Woman* implausibly describes how Elbe's handwriting becomes 'a woman's script' after surgery – Stone asked who these narratives were *for*, given that the Gender Identity Clinics did not view them as reliable insights into the transsexual condition (for which, in turn, no diagnostic criteria had yet been found).

'No wonder feminist theorists have been suspicious,' wrote Stone. 'Hell, *I'm* suspicious.' Subsequent writers shared Stone's distrust and attempted to abandon the transition memoir genre, or at least take a more theoretical approach to it, as her text found an audience amongst early adopters of the Internet. Certainly, digital communications changed the dynamics that had previously silenced and separated trans people. Now, we could talk, find resources and organise far more easily. It also meant that hostile editorials in left-leaning papers could be shared more widely, becoming lightning rods for activists and exposing their exclusionary logic to a wider audience. Anti-trans writing had already leapt from the relatively closed circuits of feminist conferences and publications to the mainstream media, but now people could leave counterarguments in comments sections and campaign in larger numbers.

I'd never written for the Internet, but it seemed the most exciting form of cultural communication. When I'd published short stories or arts criticism in magazines, I'd been certain that only the people already interested in the topic read them, and very few at that. Recalling how often I saw colleagues at Legal & General or the NHS browsing the *Guardian* site, I felt like *anyone* could be reading, or commenting, or talking about my writing on Twitter, which I soon joined – it seemed that *every* journalist was there, having dialogues about their editorials and airing their 140-character opinions.

When I began thinking about putting together the blog, I was hesitant about the autobiographical framing of the series. I was concerned I might struggle to avoid perpetuating a stereotype of trans people as concerned mainly with themselves rather than their communities, and the problem of one person's thoughts and feelings being taken as representative of the whole. The important thing was to secure enough space to get beyond the 'wrong body' narrative, and a blog would allow me far more leeway than traditional publications. It seemed like the best way to change the terms being set for discussion: once I'd accepted the compromise of documenting a 'personal journey', I would have to sneak theory and politics past only a single editor. Then I could bring it to the Internet's potentially limitless audience, who might not even know they needed it, let alone where to look for it.

To my relief, the paper didn't request photos of me but instead illustrated every piece with stock images: someone putting on lipstick when I discussed 'passing', or women at a water cooler when I wrote about my job. This let me retain some anonymity and kept the focus on my writing. I was encouraged to respond 'below the line' in the comments section, but I didn't often need to – a community soon formed around the articles, with regular visitors taking up recurring arguments about the validity of trans identities on my behalf, some calmly, some furiously.

People unfamiliar with the *Guardian*'s trans coverage assumed this was just another example of the paper's 'politically correct' agenda, and always thought they were first to smash some imaginary liberal consensus by asking: 'Why is this funded on the NHS?' Eventually, journalist Jane Fae wrote about how much gender reassignment actually cost, sick of seeing dubiously sourced figures of up to £80,000 in the tabloid headlines. With the help of clinicians and activists, she found that for male-to-female transsexual people who didn't have surgery, the overall cost was unlikely to exceed £1,000 over a lifetime; for those who did, it would not top £15,000. For female-to-male people who had more complicated phalloplasty, it would be closer to £20,000.

The series exposed some interesting fault lines: criticism for trans people in general came from straight and cisgender (non-trans) men and women, who said they didn't understand why someone might need to transition; conservatives who thought we went against traditional values; socialists who complained that 'identity politics' distracted from the class struggle; gay men who felt we divided the equal rights movement; lesbians who repeated the old radical feminist arguments. I worried about how I might get all of these people onside. But support came from all of these quarters too, usually with the same approach: that prejudice and discrimination made life for trans people far harder than it should.

As it turned out, challenging both conservative and feminist stereotypes simultaneously proved easier than I expected, especially the one about trans women blindly conforming to gender expectations. All I had to do was mention my admiration for the footballing skills of Norwich City's centre-forward (Grant Holt) and that theory just collapsed. I was surprised, though, that the articles on trans-specific issues such as 'passing' attracted far more comment than on how transition complicated more universal experiences, such as finding work.

This took me back to Sandy Stone's question about Lili Elbe and others: who was my account *for*? I took up Joe's idea after thinking back to my ten-year-old self in Horley, not knowing where to begin in the search for literature about (let alone by) people like me. Seventeen years later, there was plenty of information online but no obvious starting point, either for people beginning to explore their own gender issues or for those around them. The ability to hyperlink to other resources proved invaluable, as did the comments. These further developed the discussion, meaning that although the series wasn't meant primarily for trans people who'd already figured out their identities, other trans people could back me in certain arguments, correct me on other points, share their own stories and point people towards other useful websites.

The blog was also aimed at newspaper editors and TV/ film commissioners, trying to encourage them to think differently about what terms were set for discussion of trans lives and politics. I wanted to foreground our perspectives, and perhaps to show that audiences were more interested in these issues than they thought.

I never imagined that my writing alone would change that, and there have been plenty of setbacks in the liberal press since the series started. Refusing to operate in those spaces never felt viable, though. No publication had a *good* record, and given widespread transphobia across left- and right-wing politics, their coverage could not be left in the hands of trans-exclusionary radical feminists, reactionary conservatives or faux-alternative comedians any longer. I had made so many compromises in managing my gender identity: really, how much could *just one more* complicate my life?

8

On the first Saturday after my *Guardian* series started, I woke at 7 a.m. and glanced at the mirror. *You need a shave,* I thought: so far, the laser sessions had barely removed any facial hair. I ran my electric razor over my skin, and then took off my pyjamas and looked at my body.

Ignoring my efforts to keep it hairless in summer, it was exactly the same as when I'd begun the process thirteen months earlier. I sighed, wondering when I'd get my hormones. Then I pulled a suitcase from under my bed and opened it. I'd given most of my male clothes to friends, but kept a few in case I needed them: a couple of shirts, one pair of black trousers and one pair of loafers, as I'd always hated shoelaces.

I put on the old, itchy trousers over a simple, comfortable pair of black briefs, and matching socks. I ironed a pink shirt and wore it with no tie or jacket. I rubbed moisturiser and foundation over my face and neck, and then stared at my long, straightened hair, pierced ears and plucked eyebrows. I thought back to 2004, when I'd worn these clothes and revelled in what I thought was androgyny. Looking back, I saw that time as a step towards transition, but returning to it felt like regression, even though I knew it was just for a day.

I'd spoken with friends about how to handle my brother's wedding ever since he'd asked me to be an usher. The closer it came, the more I discussed it.

'What do you normally wear when you see your parents?' Alice asked one evening.

'A women's T-shirt, jeans and jumper, with trainers,' I replied.

'Will this be so different?'

'I guess not.'

'And it's not the only time you've been a guy in the last year, is it?'

She was right. Just weeks after I had told my parents, my uncle Robin had died of a heart attack and I'd been distraught. We'd agreed I would write something to read at his funeral, which I did. I hadn't informed any of my wider family at that point, and hadn't wanted to do it there.

'I can't think of a worse place to come out,' said Alice. 'Sometimes you need to compromise. My parents are atheists but they had to go to Catholic weddings to keep their families happy.'

'Yeah. I don't even believe in marriage, but I go for my friends. I'll think of it as a drag king performance, that'll make it more fun.'

I took a handbag with my purse, phone, keys and a book, and left. *You'll feel the dysphoria more when you see everyone,* I thought, trying to work out how to minimise it. I made sure I used the toilet on the train, not wanting to go to the Gents in the pub where we would meet, but otherwise, I didn't have any ideas.

I arrived, and everyone greeted me by my old name. I could see strangers staring at me: I tried to ignore them, sticking with my parents, barely speaking. I felt relieved when we left for the church. Dad parked the car, and we entered. There were 350 people in the building, all talking loudly, competing with the Christian rock music playing through the speakers with the lyrics projected on to a big screen. I saw John 3:16 on the wall, and then met Matt's best men and his new in-laws, awkwardly trying not to give my name. I felt glad when the ushers, in their matching suits, showed us to our pew, thinking about how conflicted I'd have felt if I'd joined them. As the vicar talked about marriage being 'God's way', Mum put her hand on my knee.

'Thanks for coming,' she whispered. I smiled, and forgot everything else as Matt and Claire walked down the aisle. They exchanged their vows and kissed, then walked out of the church together in a shower of confetti. After the service ended, I joined my family for a few photos and then the reception.

'Congratulations,' I said to my brother. 'You guys look great.'

'We really appreciate you coming,' replied Claire. 'We know it's not your thing.'

'I'll skip the barn dance, if you don't mind, but I'm glad I made it.'

When I rejoined my parents, Mum told me she had read my piece in the *Guardian*. 'I thought you explained things very well.'

'I know we've not spoken about it,' said her brother, Keith, 'but it makes sense in hindsight.'

'Keep reading,' I replied. 'Hopefully it'll help. I'm going to head off, but let's speak soon.'

I headed back to Brighton. At home, I changed into a turquoise T-shirt, black jeans and pumps and went to meet Phil, Paul and Mark at the pub, calmly telling them about my day.

A few weeks later, Dad called me Juliet for the first time. The compromise had been worthwhile.

———

Proudly wearing the Norwich City badge over my chest, I held a ball under my arm and walked out before the crowd as if I were leading a team out for a Cup final. I put the ball down, and then flicked it up with my toes. I chested it down and then did kick-ups, like I used to in our garden as a teenager. The Arcola Theatre audience whistled, cheered and clapped – even when I smashed the ball at the fire exit. It bounced back: I trapped it under one of my wedges, worn with black leggings and a miniskirt, and began reciting *Justin and Juliet*, the script Jet and I had co-written about my relationships with football, gender, sexuality and the media.

I was about twelve years old when my mum bought me a video: the one with Justin Fashanu's Goal of the Season. That was around the same time that I realised I was a 'cross-dresser' – that's what I called it back then. I didn't have the word 'trans': I just knew that I liked dressing up in my mum's clothes and that somehow this made me 'different'.

The main reason I wanted to play football was because I loved it. The second was because it was a way to fit in. But I just wasn't a team player. I wanted to get the ball and light up the game. But even when I scored with a twenty-five-yard shot, I wasn't one of the lads. I didn't relate to football like my teammates. I liked the art of it. Heaven forbid I'd sound pretentious but when football is played well there's a real geometry to it: visionary movements in space, that sublime pass that splits a defence or the long-range shot that nobody saw coming.

The other boys didn't care about that: they just wanted to win. They were more bothered about the camaraderie of the team, and that the girls thought they were fit. Nobody spoke about the homoeroticism. They just called anyone who didn't tackle hard enough 'gay'.

Jet had visited my flat, sat down with a notebook and asked: 'What story do you want to tell?'

'Well, I've tried to make football more welcoming to LGBT people,' I said. 'Perhaps it'd be nice to turn that around?'

'That's a good hook,' she replied. 'I've never seen anyone at queer events talking about sport. Have you been to a game since you came out?'

'Yes, but I femmed down,' I said. 'Took out my chest, didn't wear much makeup, wore jeans and trainers with my City shirt. I wasn't sure how to tell my friends there, but the *Guardian* blog got posted on the forum I use, so they all know now.'

'How did that go?'

'Well. Once I confirmed it *was* me, everyone was supportive. One guy replied with "Good luck, fella" and my friend Rich just wrote "For fuck's sake" underneath it. Then some of them started posting about what their female names would be, before asking themselves what they were doing. It was pretty funny.'

'Will you go as Juliet now?'

'When the new season starts, yeah.'

'Lovely! Let's try something that ends positively,' said Jet. 'With reconciliation.'

We constructed a narrative about how I understood myself as transsexual, and how Fashanu's death made me feel that football could never be for me. We explored how I'd found the Bandits and started writing my transition blog for the *Guardian*, motivated by never having seen anyone in the mainstream who reflected my reality.

'Now, I've become the media,' I concluded. 'As *The Rocky Horror Picture Show* says: don't dream it, be it.' There was applause as I picked up the ball, bowed and walked off. Back in the audience, I watched Natacha's piece on the complexities of being a non-transitioning trans woman, and Iris's story of moving across Europe, her Arabic heritage denigrated in Belgrade and her Serbian parentage attracting scorn elsewhere. I laughed at Jason Barker's monologue on being a pregnant man after the Thomas Beatie story broke, and Greg Renegado's story about growing up queer on a Dublin estate and learning to masturbate from a Mary Whitehouse text. I returned to Brighton electrified: finally, I'd found a relationship with 'masculinity' and 'femininity' that felt comfortable, and somewhere fun to explore it.

———

After my laser surgery started to take effect, I felt I 'passed' well enough to keep out of trouble, most of the time – as long as I didn't have to speak. I'd long been insecure about how I sounded: I'd tried to face it head-on by singing in bands, hoping I'd learn to accept it, but practice rooms and stages were safe spaces – the wider world was different. On one of my first nights at the Harlequin, someone had said: 'You're pretty, but you ain't half got a deep voice.' People would try to 'read' me by getting me to say something: one morning, while I was walking to the office, a man asked me the time. I sensed something more, and silently showed him my watch. He paused, grudgingly thanked me and walked off.

I soon came to dread using the phone. An unknown number would flash up, and I'd answer:

JULIET: Hello?
CALLER: Hi, can I speak to Juliet please?
JULIET: Speaking.
CALLER: *(Pause)* You're not Juliet, are you?
JULIET: *(sigh)* I'm transsexual.

CALLER: Right …
JULIET: What's this about, please?
CALLER: Would you be interested in BT mobile broadband?

At work, I'd have awkward conversations with my line manager:

MANAGER: 'Juliet, can you ring Andrew's personal assistant to sort out a meeting?'
JULIET: 'Can't I email?'
MANAGER: 'No, it's urgent. Phone them now please.'

I would sigh like a sulky teenager, my heart sinking every time I got a hesitant reaction to the words 'It's Juliet.' I started announcing my name immediately, emphasising the final syllable as much as possible, but when someone replied with 'Don't you mean Julian?' I struggled to hold my temper. I was glad, then, when the nine-month wait finally ended, and I went to the Speech and Language Therapy unit at the Royal Sussex County Hospital for my appointment.

'How authentic a voice do you hope to achieve?' asked Duncan, the therapist.

What does that even mean? I thought. *Surely my current voice was 'natural' and any work on it was artifice?* Then I remembered that just as the way I dressed and moved had been policed throughout my life, so had the way I spoke: boys at school making fun of the lads with high voices, or calling me queer for using words like 'fabulous' and admitting to liking poetry.

So I replied, cautiously: 'Sixty to eighty per cent? I want to "pass" when I'm talking to strangers, but I'm not going to pressure myself to do it all the time.'

'Good, that's realistic,' he replied. 'First we're going to

measure your lung capacity. Take deep breaths and make *s* and *ʒ* sounds.'

'Zzzzzzzzzzzzzzzzzzzzzzzzzzz ...'

'You lasted twenty-six seconds. That's promising – you should be able to project your voice at a different pitch without sounding too quiet.'

'This is a Laryngograph,' he continued, strapping a sensor around my neck. 'It measures vocal fold activity. It should tell us how your voice is likely to be perceived.'

He asked me to make a number of sounds, and then printed some graphs.

'You're at 133 Hz,' he said. 'Ninety to 130 is usually considered male, so you're at the very highest end of that.'

'Doesn't that make it androgynous?'

'No, that's 160 Hz at the lowest. Try again.' I did. 'Better, but you're hitting falsetto at times. Try to relax. You're getting there on certain sounds – that's good. I'm going to give you a short story to read, called *The Tale of Arthur the Rat*. It contains all known English phonemes, so we can test for fluctuations in pitch, or difficulties with particular sounds.'

Once upon a time there was a rat who couldn't make up his mind. Whenever the other rats asked him if he would like to come out hunting with them, he would answer in a hoarse voice, 'I don't know.' And when they said, 'Would you rather stay inside?' he wouldn't say yes, or no either. He'd always shirk making a choice ...'

'You did well,' said Duncan. 'Your silences and speech are well balanced, and there aren't any irregularities, so that's a solid basis for retraining your voice. You can either stop now, carry on with individual sessions, or join my group for transsexual women.'

'I'll try the group – sounds interesting.'

At the first session I attended, at Hove Polyclinic, I introduced myself to Duncan's assistant Karen and the rest of the group.

'Here are a hundred adjectives that might describe a voice,' said Duncan, handing us a sheet. 'I want you to label them "M" or "F", according to your perceptions.'

We glanced at it, stopping on several key words.

' "Feminine" makes me think "female", but "effeminate" feels male,' said Katy.

'It's interesting that we have a word for a man being *too* feminine, but not the opposite,' I replied.

'Perhaps "manly",' came another response. I noticed that I'd marked that with 'M'.

'It might help to think about this visually,' Duncan told us. 'I want you to draw your voice as it sounds now, and as you'd like it.'

I drew a monochrome image of a faceless office worker as 'male' and a singer, in colour, for 'female'. Duncan looked at it.

'Good,' he said. 'Who's your favourite female vocalist, Juliet?'

'Laurie Anderson.'

'I don't know her.'

'I remember her,' said Katy. 'She had that hit – "O Superman".'

'That's right.'

'If you want to sound "feminine" rather than "effeminate", or at least not masculine, it's good to give some musicality to your voice,' said Duncan. We tried 'ha, ha' sounds at different pitches, trying to match ours with Karen's, before spontaneous vocal utterances: coughing, sneezing and laughing.

'That gut laugh that people do when they're laughing *at*

someone. That's male, isn't it?' I said. 'Women are taught not to do that.'

Everyone nodded, and then someone replied: 'I know a woman who does that all the time.'

We smiled, and agreed that we couldn't fix any boundaries between 'female', 'feminine' and 'effeminate', and that no generalisations about how men and women talked would work. Over time, I adjusted my tone as much as I could without feeling like I was acting, trying to find the same kind of balance in how I spoke as in how I dressed, and to relax a little.

———

I went back to the Gender Identity Clinic, this time alone. I was still nervous: I would have to convince a second clinician that I was suitable for transition, and in particular a hormone prescription. My main worry was about telling them I was taking anti-depressants. In some ways, the Citalopram had helped. My suicidal thoughts had faded and my mind felt clearer, though not free, of internal chatter. My energy levels had dropped dramatically, though – just getting up to watch the World Cup was a struggle – and my dreams had become terrifying. In one, I had elephantiasis; in another, my hair fell out. One night, I was chased by Frankenstein's monster. I'd tried not to question myself too often while living as female – that way lay madness – but I couldn't fend off self-doubt in my sleep.

'Eighty per cent of people prescribed 20mg of Citalopram don't need that much,' said my GP. 'Take half just before bed so the fatigue hits you at night.'

Meeting the second clinician for the first time, I was asked again about when I had realised I was transsexual, and how I had handled it before transition; about my sexuality and

relationships; when my Real Life Experience started, and
how I could verify this; and about my family and friends, and
whether I knew many trans people.

'You're rare in sorting all of these things so early,' she told
me. 'What do you for a living?'

'I work for the NHS, but I do some journalism as well.'

'Who for?'

'Whoever will have me. Mostly film magazines, but sometimes the *Guardian*.'

'Do you write the column?'

'Yes ...'

'You sound surprised to be asked.'

'It's under a pen name.'

'I know, but we don't get many people through here who
write for national newspapers,' she told me. Suddenly, I felt
cold. *If you write* anything *they don't like, they might throw you
off the pathway*, I thought. *Yes, but if they do, you'll document
it in* the Guardian, *so it wouldn't reflect well on them.*

The clinician broke through my introspection: 'Do you have
any lesbian, gay, bisexual or transgender family members?'

'Not to my knowledge.'

'What kind of child were you?' she asked.

'An unbearably precocious one.'

She smiled, and I retold the well-rehearsed narrative of my
gender-variant youth.

'Have you ever self-harmed?'

'No.'

'Are you taking any medication?'

'I'm on anti-depressants,' I said, deciding not to mention
the dreams, which had become less intense. 'Will that affect
my treatment?'

'Absolutely not,' she replied. 'You know we offer ten sessions of one-to-one counselling?'

'Yes, but I don't think I need that right now.'

'Do you smoke, or take recreational drugs? Don't worry, it's just to explain any irregularities in your blood test results.'

'I don't smoke cigarettes. Dope very occasionally.'

'It won't affect your treatment, but you've got high cholesterol, so try to avoid fatty foods,' she said. 'Your testosterone level is 19.9 nanomoles per litre.'

'What does that mean?'

'It's average for someone born male-bodied,' she replied. 'We need to reduce it to 3. Actually your oestrogen is above average – 125 picomoles per litre, but you need it between 400 and 600. I'm going to prescribe 2mg of estradiol a day. You can double the dose after a few months if you're doing well.'

I'm finally *getting them,* I thought as the clinician made her notes.

'One more thing,' she told me. 'You should think about whether you want to save some sperm, because the oestrogen will make you infertile, possibly within six months. The prescription may take a month to reach your GP, but you can't have it until you've made a decision.'

A friend at work had asked if I planned to do this, and I'd said I wasn't sure. When I was young, I'd said I never wanted children, ignoring family members who insisted I'd change my mind. On my way home, I wondered if I ever would. As the train passed through Horley, I called my surgery and made an appointment.

———

'Your regular doctor is away,' said the receptionist at the Charter Medical Centre. 'Would you like to see the senior partner instead?'

'Well … okay,' I replied. I felt nervous as the loudspeaker called me to Room Six, thinking about what I'd have to explain to a total stranger.

'How can I help?' asked the doctor.

'I've been to the gender clinic at Charing Cross and they said that before I start on hormones, I should talk to someone about saving sperm.' Silence. 'Is that okay?'

'Yes, absolutely,' he replied. 'It's just not something I've dealt with before.'

'I can imagine.'

'Do you want children? Or expect to have them?'

'Not desperately, but I feel I should keep the option open.'

'The number of donors has dropped, because they can no longer remain anonymous,' he said. 'So if you donate, it's quite likely that someone will want to use your sperm, and maybe trace you. It's also quite expensive. Call the Human Fertilisation and Embryology Authority, and the Agora Clinic in Hove, and decide from there.'

I thanked him. To my surprise, he shook my hand as I left.

I telephoned the Agora Clinic. Before I went any further, they said, I needed a blood test. I returned to my surgery for that, and then rang back.

'I'm a transsexual woman who's about to start on oestrogen. Can I ask about saving sperm?'

'Have you checked for HIV, syphilis, hepatitis B and C?'

'Yes – all clear.'

'Okay, you'll need to book an appointment for a freeze.'

'How much is it?'

'It's £165 if you come in for the initial consultation, or £55 for fifteen minutes on the phone. Then £395 for freezing with annual storage fees after that.'

'I'll have to think about it …'

'If you reconsider after starting on hormones, you'll have

to come off them for six months before your sperm might be fertile again.'

I discussed it with friends at work.

'It's worth the money,' they said. 'I can't think of anything about this that you're more likely to regret than not being able to have your own children.'

'But it's *so* expensive, and I really don't want any,' I replied. 'The most painful thing I've seen in all this were the older women at the Clare Project, in floods of tears because their kids had disowned them.'

'Yeah, but that's different. Yours would have known nothing else. They're so accepting when they're young, too, you could explain before anyone else does.'

'Sure, but imagine how much shit they'd get at school.'

'You'd cope,' they insisted. But I didn't want to get a credit card or sink deeper into my overdraft, and I didn't want to delay my hormone treatment any further.

'If I ever change my mind,' I said, 'I'll adopt.'

———

I called the Gender Identity Clinic.

'Have you sent the hormone prescription to my GP? They've not heard anything.'

They said they had, so I made an appointment at the Charter Medical Centre. To my relief, my regular doctor was back. He clicked through a wave of blue screens.

'I can't find it,' he said. 'Can you remember your prescription?'

'Only that it's oestrogen.'

'You don't know which one?'

'How many are there?'

'Let's see.'

He took out a book the size of a telephone directory and

read out a bewildering list of medications. *You're not going to get these until the clinic sends him another copy, are you,* I thought to myself.

'Are you *sure* you don't have the letter?' I asked.

He went back to the computer. After what felt like forever, he found a recommendation for estradiol, starting on 2mg.

'Will I need an anti-androgen shot?'

'To suppress your testosterone? Did the clinic mention it?'

'I don't think so.'

'There's nothing about it here. Try these and see how you get on.'

He handed me a prescription. I thanked him and left.

'You mean I can just get these *here?*' I said to the pharmacist.

'Sure, why wouldn't you?'

'It's just ... nothing,' I replied, thinking about how hard it had been to get something held five minutes from my flat, and how we'd talked at the PCT about the possibility of local GPs administering them.

The pharmacist found two small, pink boxes and put them in a paper bag. I signed a form and paid my prescription charge, taking the pills out of their packaging before I even got home.

ELLESTE SOLO™ 1mg and 2mg (estradiol hemihydrate)
Elleste Solo treats the symptoms of menopause (change of life). It is usually given to women who have had a hysterectomy (had their womb removed).

Not knowing if the side effects that might trouble menopausal women would bother me – weight gain, genital itching, headaches, stomach or back pains – I took out a sachet with four rows of seven orange tablets, arrows between the days of the week on the foil that contained them. Resisting the temptation to up my dose, I popped out WED and swallowed it.

I didn't expect any visible changes for weeks, but warned acquaintances about my second puberty. Several colleagues, I suspected, were hoping for tears and tantrums – I half-expected one in particular to install a hidden camera at my desk – but with the low dose, I noticed little initial effect, and attributed my rising irritability to ditching my anti-depressants.

Julia Serano wrote in *Whipping Girl*, 'Sex hormones have become horribly politicised in our culture, evident in the way that people blatantly blame testosterone for nearly all instances of male aggression, or the way that women who legitimately become angry or upset often have their opinions dismissed as mere symptoms of their body chemistry.' I kept this in mind and soon realised I only felt angrier in the office – not surprisingly, as the Conservatives had broken their pre-election promise not to reorganise the NHS and had announced the abolition of the PCTs. We were being forced to reapply for our jobs, knowing that many of us would be made redundant with the workloads divided among those who remained. I resented having to take on more work, especially as the government had frozen public sector pay. But I had no other outlet for my fury besides commiserating with colleagues over email about our hatred for the management consultants who were taking over the organisation.

So I had plenty to be furious about, as I explained to Joe when Performance came to Brighton to promote their second album, *Red Brick Heart*. The band went through the motions, playing to nine people at the Hope on a wet November evening.

'We're splitting up after this tour,' said Joe after the gig.

'It's a shame,' I replied. 'You deserved so much better.'

'We're supporting the Human League for our final show at the Royal Festival Hall, so it's not all bad. How are the hormones?'

'People tell me they can see changes – one or two colleagues said my skin was looking good, or that my hair looks thicker. I haven't really noticed it. I think my body hair is growing a bit slower but I still have to shave every day.'

'Have they changed you mentally?'

'I don't think so – I've become more feminist but that's largely to do with the amount of shit I've had off dickhead men. Weirdly I think I'm more the same than ever. I suppose the main change is it's harder to *ignore* my feelings now. Julia Serano talks about testosterone draping a curtain over her emotions – I felt that too, but it's shifting now. That said, everyone told me I'd cry more, but it hasn't happened yet.'

On Christmas Day, back in Horley, the catharsis finally came. I was reading *How I Came to Know Fish* by Czech author Ota Pavel, a book about how Pavel bonded with his father and uncle Prosek through fishing, and his father's attempts to look after their family before, during and after the Nazi occupation. The father breeds carp for sale and then becomes a travelling salesman, but his vacuum cleaner business is destroyed when he is taken to the Terezin concentration camp. He survives and tries to rebuild by breeding rabbits for sale. He invests all his hope in them, particularly one called Michael, but Ota just sees sadness in their eyes. He takes them to a show, where the judges say that as he has not manicured or pedicured them, or washed their privates, he cannot enter them in the contest, and nobody will buy them.

'You bastards!' he shouts. 'You don't like Jews!' He sits, defeated, waiting for something to save him. Nothing does, and by evening he is alone with the rabbits. He takes them to a field and lets them out of their cages, but having never known freedom, they will not leave. 'In the end', wrote Pavel, 'he ran away from them. His beloved Michael kept up with him the longest, but Papa finally outran him, too.'

I burst into tears. I closed the door, hoping nobody would disturb me. I kept rereading the paragraphs, letting out all the tension that had built up since I'd slipped that first tablet down my throat, since I'd first been told that 'boys don't cry'. The next day, Dad drove me back to Brighton. I talked him through *The Rabbits with Wise Eyes* and wept again. For the next week, I cried every time I thought about Pavel's story. It was terribly sad, but I was always reading melancholic or tragic stories, or writing them, and nothing had ever brought on such a reaction. Seeing that the estradiol had fundamentally changed the way I physically processed my emotions, I began to relax. At last, my body was catching up with my mind, and I felt they might finally develop a healthy relationship.

———

My third GIC appointment was in November. There, we briefly discussed my family, social life and job, and then spent most of the half-hour session talking through the physical changes. Recently, I had felt my bras becoming tighter as my breasts rose beneath the inserts, which I wasn't yet ready to discard. I regretted buying such large forms: a woman at the Clare Project said she'd got the smallest available so nothing appeared to change when her breast growth started. 'I wish someone had told me that,' I replied. Now, my colleagues said my hips and backside were getting larger, and my hair thicker, but I wasn't yet feeling happier in my body. Getting the hormone dose doubled, I hoped, would bring that closer.

When I finally got a new prescription, the mood swings kicked in. At work, I felt a fatigue I'd never known, walking slower than usual, my eyes narrowing to slits through which light barely came. Often, I put my head in my hands and tried not to collapse on to my keyboard. I stopped reading or watching films, too drained to do anything after work, and found that almost everything made me angry. I still wasn't sure how much of this was hormonal, but I knew that having the anti-androgen injection was now essential.

I got the Decapeptyl jabbed into my stomach at my surgery, surprised at how much more painful it was than most other injections I'd had. Nonetheless, I soon had far more energy, feeling able to socialise, read, write, and play football again, buying some sports bras and turning up for games at the University of Sussex in my kit to avoid using the changing rooms. Nearly two years after I'd thrown everything up in the air by coming out, I'd managed to land it all, almost exactly where I wanted.

———

By spring 2011, I had published twenty *Transgender Journey* pieces on the *Guardian* site. Commissions to write about transsexual living started coming in, and a television company asked whether I'd be willing to co-write a drama with them, postponing our meeting when the producer went on leave. My favourite response, however, came from Dad: 'It's amazing how much work you have to do to become an overnight success, isn't it?'

I tried to write about my transition as if doing so hadn't affected my life, but even before it started running, the series added a layer of complexity to every social challenge. Occasionally, I found myself wishing the street abuse would escalate, or that the medics would block my path, or that someone close to me would cut me off, just so I'd have more 'colour' in my articles.

Soon, however, I realised what a terrible attitude this was. On Twitter, I opened a link shared by Trans Media Watch, a pressure group aiming to improve print and broadcast representations of trans people. The group had formed online in 2009 in response to ITV sitcom *Moving Wallpaper*, where a character was referred to as 'it' and 'a walking GM crop', with jokes about her 'hairy hands, stubbly face and Adam's apple'. Their post linked to an *LA Weekly* feature, headed 'Mike Penner, Christine Daniels: A Tragic Love Story,' covering a chain of events I'd somehow missed. Penner and Daniels were the same person: Penner had joined the *LA Times* in 1983, becoming an acclaimed sports writer before publishing an article headed 'Old Mike, New Christine' in 2007. This described how it had taken 'more than forty years, a million tears and hundreds of hours of soul-wrenching therapy' to come out in 'a world whose knowledge of transsexuals usually begins and ends with *Jerry Springer*'s exploitation circus.' The article prompted thousands of positive emails, so the *Times* persuaded Daniels to blog her transition as *Woman in Progress*.

Then everything fell apart. On Daniels's first day back at the *Times*, her wife, who also worked there, filed for divorce. Another sports writer attacked her 'dress-up role playing'; trans activists criticised her blog for focusing too much on appearances, believing it reinforced negative stereotypes, which would not have been such a problem on one of the numerous transition diaries that people kept on their own, less high-profile blogs. Daniels emailed one: 'I'm a real woman ... not a trans-anything who needs to "represent" some undefined community. For the first time, I'm being true to myself, and my true self loves makeup, clothes and shoes.'

Feeling 'used', Daniels withdrew from public appearances at LGBT events. Her final *Times* byline appeared in

April 2008: she was hospitalised in June, doctors suggesting that the stresses of public transition, the death of her mother and her ex-wife's distance were manifesting themselves as abdominal pain. *Woman in Progress* – which never mentioned family issues – was deleted from the *Times* archives. Daniels stopped taking hormones and asked to be addressed as Penner again, pulling out of scheduled sex reassignment surgery. Penner returned to work in October, but the desired reconciliation with his wife did not materialise. A year later, he committed suicide.

I was terrified. I'd been prepared for hostility from commenters, even other writers, but even though I'd talked often about the issue of becoming a 'professional trans person', I'd not thought enough about how the series might increase the pressure to act as an advocate. I drew on Bornstein, Stone, Feinberg and others, but my main inspiration was Heppenstall: what excited me most about the project was the idea of creatively exploring my own subjectivity. Like Justin Fashanu, I felt uneasy about being drawn into activism just because I was visible; but unlike him and Penner/Daniels, I *was* prepared to see what I did, and who I was, as inherently political.

Now, I felt thankful that my previous projects had failed so unspectacularly, and that I had no public persona to shake off. I was grateful, too, that I knew trans theory, politics and *people*, so that none of the comments generated by my writing came as a shock. I thought about quitting but it felt too late – I'd done seven entries already. It didn't feel like the right thing to do anyway: transsexual people and their family members had started writing to say how the series was helping them to understand each other. They needed to read the column, and I needed to write it. It was a cruel set of circumstances that had broken Penner/Daniels, but they were very different to mine: I had dealt with most of the social challenges of transitioning before the first piece had been published, so I wouldn't be playing out such painful rejections before a crowd. So I decided to continue, but had to ask myself: *how trans did I want to be?*

I pitched articles to various publications about literature, film, art, football, music and LGBT politics, but kept getting knocked back, though more kindly than before. Now, people bothered to reply, at least, but I still struggled to persuade editors to commission anything other than pieces about being transsexual. Able to track Facebook and Twitter shares, Likes and retweets, I became obsessed with how many people were reading, who they were and what they thought, spending every other Wednesday at work clicking 'refresh' on my posts to see any new comments. I made an exception for the tenth part of the series, which covered my mental health, asking my friend Lisa to join me for lunch when it went up so the moderators could delete the most unpleasant replies while we ate.

I tried to get other trans and queer writers into the *Guardian*, with limited success: they ran a brief political history by Stephen Whittle of Press for Change, Bethany Black on her life as a transsexual comedian, and poet, journalist and activist Roz Kaveney, who had contributed to the *Guardian* for years, about trans people and respectful language. But proposed pieces by Julia Serano, Ignacio Rivera and Jason Barker never made the site – something I regretted later when a tabloid newspaper tried to identify a pregnant trans man. I thought that if Barker's monologue from *Jet Moon's Speakeasy* had been posted on such a mainstream space, it may have been a useful counterpoint to gutter press muckraking.

One lunchtime in October 2010, I got a phone call: 'Hi, this is the *Guardian* readers' editor. Have you heard about this Sonia Burgess story?' Burgess was a prominent immigration lawyer, known professionally as David but to everyone else as Sonia – including to me, on a transgender forum I used, where we'd spoken in passing. That week, Burgess had been murdered; the tabloid coverage had been horrific, with initial headlines using phrases such as 'man in a dress pushed under a train at King's Cross'.

'Yes, of course,' I replied.

'Obviously we're going to cover it. Did you see our story on Mikki Nicholson, the transsexual woman who won the national Scrabble competition recently?'

'I did.'

'We got the pronouns wrong – we've corrected that but we mustn't do it again here.'

'The Nicholson thing wasn't that complicated – ask if you're not sure, but if someone uses a female name and wears women's clothes, it's probably best to go with "she" and "her".'

'Sure – it was wrong on the press release and our reporter went with that. This one is trickier. Could you look at our editorial on trans people and language, particularly the bit on Burgess, and let us know if anything needs correcting?'

'Have you contacted Trans Media Watch?'

'There isn't time – we wanted to ask someone we knew. It's only two pages.'

I didn't feel I could say no. I opened the document – if anyone at work asked, I would tell them I was proofreading some NHS policy. I read it twice, took out every gendered pronoun relating to Burgess, emailed it back and rushed off to minute a meeting.

At the same time, I started being asked to discuss my experiences at events. I thought back to my time at Reigate Grammar, aged eleven, when I'd tried the Debating Society, thinking I was being a good feminist in supporting the motion that 'This House believes that *In Bed with Madonna* is degrading to women'. But I knew nothing of 'feminism', except as a pejorative to belittle humourless, unreasonably angry women. I couldn't see any women in the room, and I was jeered as my side lost by 110 votes to 3, called 'queer' by the older boys. Those arguments presumed a level playing field: I didn't have the confidence that the swaggering sixth formers or the more established opinionators managed to project, and I preferred events where issues that affected the trans community might be talked through rather than shouted down.

I spoke in Newport and Cardiff, on panels held by the European Human Rights Commission to discuss media portrayals of four groups: asylum seekers, gypsies and travellers, people with mental health problems and trans people.

'We're forced to walk a difficult line by this insistence that we only write about our personal journeys,' I told the audience. 'We end up in this position of only being allowed to represent ourselves, but having to make sure we don't *misrepresent* anyone. This creates some division in our communities – everyone has their own opinion about what's good representation and what isn't, and you can't please them all. I hope more space will open up for people with different backgrounds – at the moment, there are so few trans people in the media, and they're nearly all white, middle-class trans women. There's far more to do besides telling individual stories, but I think that's a good start.'

I'd felt out on a limb at times, and by spring 2011, I was thinking about stepping down. It looked like I could find more writing work elsewhere, even if it wasn't exactly what I wanted to do, so I went part-time at the NHS. I decided that a second winter in my studio flat with no central heating was enough, and moved to a one-bedroom place in Embassy Court, a Modernist tower on the seafront.

'Everything looks like it's going well,' said Phil.

'That's what I thought about a month ago,' I replied. 'I'm not sure where the next commission is coming from, though.'

'Are you still doing the series?'

'Yes, occasionally rather than fortnightly because I've said most of what I want about the social side, and I've still got no idea when I'll start seeing the surgical team. I'm not sure if I want to write about that anyway. None of my pitches are getting commissioned, people have stopped coming to me for trans stuff and I've got no idea what to do next.'

Trans Media Watch had supported me from the start of *A Transgender Journey*. The group was growing fast, and its organisers invited me to London to celebrate Channel 4 becoming the first broadcaster to sign their Memorandum of Understanding about how trans people were treated in and by the media. Stuart Cosgrove, the channel's director of creative diversity, was there, as was the minister for equalities, Lynne Featherstone. 'There will be campaigners here who, like me, will know what a struggle it has been to ensure trans issues even got a look in. A few years ago, this would have been unimaginable, but here we are today with one of the biggest public service broadcasters, with a reach of millions, making a commitment to improve their coverage of transgender people.'

Meeting Trans Media Watch's team – journalists such as Jennie Kermode and Paris Lees, as well as others who helped to organise their campaigns – I could see how such collective activity could bring confidence to our community. I struggled to assess how much impact my work was having, but as Featherstone spoke about the gains being made for transgender equality, I thought about how important it was that our achievements be visible. I came away from the event with the energy to write my next article, a simple, gentle piece bringing readers up to speed on my clinical appointments.

———

At my fourth GIC appointment in March 2011, we discussed the operation for the first time; my oestrogen levels hadn't been high enough to do so before. After a short discussion about how I was coping with the hormones, they wrote to my GP:

> *She is keen to move forward for genital reconstruction surgery. We have discussed this procedure, she is aware that it is of course irreversible and invasive. She wishes to have a neo-vagina created, she knows that she would need to dilate this on an ongoing basis to prevent loss of depth or potential site infection should the patency of the vagina be lost. In terms of benefits, she spoke of an inherent sense of dislike towards her male genitalia ... It would seem this level of dysphoria has only increased in the past few years with self-identification as being transsexual and a growing sense of incongruence now she is living in the female gender role.*

I made a fifth visit in August, when my secondary clinician confirmed I would be recommended for surgery. 'You won't see us again until after the operation,' she said, before I walked back to the Tube. Oddly, given how significant this was, I can't find any correspondence about the appointment or even remember it, and the words quoted here are the ones I published in the *Guardian* about the end of the Real Life

Experience. 'I thought I'd be jubilant,' I wrote, 'but I'm strangely indifferent' – perhaps because, although an end was finally in sight after twenty-seven months, I still didn't know when it would come.

Despite the uncertainty, I started to think about other aspects of my life. One reason I'd stayed in Brighton, despite most of the venues and club nights I liked disappearing after the credit crunch, was that I'd had so many support networks to get me through the early stages of transition. Now, it felt like London was the place for me – if I was going to build on the *Guardian* series, I would have to do it there. I handed in my notice on my job and my flat, and found a place to live.

9

I got on the Central Line at Bethnal Green and checked my watch. Liverpool Street, Bank, St Paul's ... *You're going to be late.* Chancery Lane. Holborn, Tottenham Court Road ... *It's still miles away, you fucking idiot.* Oxford Circus, Bond Street, Marble Arch ... *Well done, you're actually going to miss it.* Finally, I got to Notting Hill Gate, jumped off the Tube and ran for the District Line. Seeing that none of the trains went to Hammersmith, I raced up the escalator and flagged down a taxi.

'Charing Cross Hospital?'

'£12.'

'Fine, let's go.'

The cab dropped me outside the clinic with two minutes to spare. I'd already missed this appointment once as I'd forgotten to tell them I'd moved and they'd sent the letter to my old address in Brighton. As I rushed up the stairs, I panicked. *What if I've missed this one too? Won't I have to be re-referred? How long will that take?*

'We're running a little late,' the receptionist told me.

'Really? Thanks so much.'

'Take a seat and we'll call you.'

I flicked through a magazine until the loudspeaker called me to Room 1, where a man and a woman were waiting for me.

'Hi, I'm the surgeon,' he said, 'and this is the clinical nurse specialist. She's an important part of the team, she'll be responsible for your care while you're in hospital. Just try to relax – we're going to talk to you about the operation, and how you need to prepare.'

I took deep breaths, trying not to look flustered. The surgeon looked through a file.

'You've just moved to London?'

'Yes.'

'Who do you live with?'

'My friend Helen,' I replied, confused. 'Why?'

'Is she close enough to take care of you after your surgery?'

'I mentioned this when I moved in. She just smiled and said, "I'll look after you!" So I think it'll be fine.'

The surgeon ticked a box.

'Okay, good,' he said. 'How much do you drink?'

'I don't know. Not that much, usually.'

'Do you smoke?'

'No.'

'Any heart problems or diabetes?'

'No.'

'Have you had any operations?'

'Never.'

'Right,' he said, 'we're going to run through the procedure. Are you ready?'

'Okay.'

'We're going to remove the erectile tissue of your penis, along with your testicles. We'll turn the remaining skin into a vagina, making a clitoris from the glans. The depth and width of the vagina can vary, and orgasm may or may not be possible. Very occasionally there can be rectal injury or deep vein thrombosis, or unexpected reactions to drugs, but this is extremely rare.' He paused. 'Any questions?'

I felt like I'd been punched in the gut. Perhaps in reaction against TV shows like *Sex Change Hospital* or *My Transsexual Summer* that took a prurient interest in the mechanics, I'd read little beyond a brief outline of the penile inversion technique, pioneered by Sir Harold Gillies in 1951, and certainly hadn't been directly confronted with its realities like this. I collected myself, and tried to think practically.

'I'm temping, with no holiday or sick pay. How will I support myself?'

'You'll be on benefits. It won't be much.'

'When do you think it'll be?'

'We can't give you an exact date today, but six months' time. Probably June or July.'

I had no more questions: after waiting for so long, the summer seemed terrifyingly soon, and I didn't feel at all ready. As I left, they gave me documentation on the operation and how to prepare for my pre-admission appointment and eight-day hospital stay.

Anxious about losing money, I'd only taken three hours off from my job as a project officer at NHS London. I got the Tube to Victoria, walked into the office and took my seat. Then I just started shaking.

'Are you okay?' asked Sharon, who sat next to me.

'No.'

'What's up?'

'I'll email you.'

I sent her a brief explanation of my morning, and how anxious I felt. She told me to speak to Lizzie, my line manager.

'Go for a walk and see how you are,' said Lizzie. 'If you don't feel like coming back, just text me, and we'll see you tomorrow.'

I thanked her, got my belongings and went to St James's Park. I called my parents.

'Hi Mum, it's me.'

'You sound flustered. Is everything okay?'

'I've just seen the surgeon at Charing Cross. He says I'm going to need two months off work. I'm really scared.'

'We'll make sure you don't run out of money,' she replied.

'Okay, thanks – that's a big weight off my mind.'

'Who's going to look after you?'

'Helen said she would.'

'That's a lot of pressure on her,' said Mum. 'Why don't you come and stay with us?'

'Really? You mean that?'

'We'd rather you didn't do this, but we know you're going to. So we'll look after you, so we know you're alright. You can stay in your old room for however long you need.'

'Oh my god … That's amazing … Thank you so much …'

'It's no problem at all. We're looking forward to it.'

———

Helen and I sat in our living room with a bottle of wine. We'd met several times in Brighton at gigs or parties and always enjoyed talking, but we'd barely got to know each other. I'd committed to moving to London in mid-October, but the first two flats I'd looked at had fallen through. Stressed, I'd gone on Facebook one evening and caught her post about needing a housemate. I said I was interested and she replied:

It's a 2-bedroom place close to Bethnal Green tube and rail. Both bedrooms are the same size, not huge but good size doubles. The house is part of this square which you access by gates and opens out onto this beautiful communal garden. Rent is £715pcm plus bills. I know that seems a lot but in this area it was one of the cheapest, crazy I know.

Let me know what you think – it'd be nice to have someone

around who has vaguely similar tastes x

It sounded perfect – the only drawback was I didn't have a job. She said that was alright, so I came to look around. The bedroom *wasn't* huge, but it was just big enough for a desk and chair, bed, wardrobe and chest of drawers. From the window, I could see the Gherkin and the Heron Tower, two of the dystopian, phallic towers that symbolised the twenty-first-century City, dwarfing the nearby 1970s Brutalist-style block of social housing, and I thought this would be a stimulating environment. After an evening drinking and laughing, talking about her band, Shrag, recording their third album, our favourite bands and writers, our memories of Brighton and why we'd both moved from there to London, we agreed to live together.

'I paid the deposit and rent this afternoon,' I said as Helen poured me a glass. 'I knew it'd be expensive, but *fucking hell.*'

'Calm down,' she told me. 'What are you going to do tomorrow?'

'I'll start signing on, and call the temp agencies that someone at NHS Brighton and Hove suggested. If I get something within the next few weeks, I should be alright.'

I started pitching articles, only to find that plenty of people wanted my work but nobody could or would pay for it. I got an interview for an NHS admin job but it wasn't offered to me. I looked through old emails, desperate, and found the message from the TV producer about co-writing a transgender script. *She should be back from leave now,* I thought.

'Is this still something you'd like to pursue?' I asked.

The reply came fifteen minutes later:

'It's on the back burner as Sky have a drama coming up

about a pre-op transsexual hit woman which means I won't be able to get this away for a while.'

Joe invited me to Soho for the premiere of *Wizard's Way*, the comedy he'd made with some friends in Manchester. I laughed at his portrayal of an exploitative documentary maker, trying and failing to manipulate his subjects to give 'colour' to his film, and then explained my liaison with the TV industry.

'I put *everything* into fighting these stupid stereotypes, and this is what I get,' I said, half-smiling, half-scowling. 'They were even advertising for a "male-to-female pre-op trans-sexual" actor. Why would they do that if they weren't going to obsess over people's bits?'

'You can't get too worked up about these things,' he replied. 'They're out of your control. Just take it as confirmation that what you do is necessary.'

I guess he's right, I thought as I got a taxi to Channel 4 studios, where I'd been invited for the launch of *My Transsexual Summer*. Trans Media Watch had been consultants on the reality show about seven people sharing a house, made after the Memorandum of Understanding was signed, so I expected it to be better than anything I'd seen on television before.

It wasn't perfect: I got frustrated with the repeated shots of people putting on makeup, Before and After pictures, and the graphic, gratuitous surgery scene. However, I liked the way it showed a community, talking about 'passing' and coming out to their families, referring to testosterone as 'T' like the trans men I knew. And it featured an interesting range of identities, with some transsexual men and women and some non-binary people. Even though not all the cast members were happy with how they had been represented, or edited, I left feeling a little more optimistic. It was weird to see community concerns push up against commercial interests in the same show, but slowly, with considerable compromise, I could see progress being made.

———

An invitation dropped through my door.

Diversity Role Models requests the
pleasure of the company of

Juliet Jacques

in the State Rooms, Speaker's House
by kind permission of Mr Speaker,
Rt Hon John Bercow MP

We will be celebrating the official launch of Diversity Role Models with guest speaker Rt Hon Theresa May MP, Home Secretary and Minister for Women and Equalities

Diversity Role Models was a new charity that took LGBT people into schools, talking to pupils about their lives and achievements as a counter to homophobia, biphobia and transphobia. *I wish we'd had that at Oakwood,* I thought – but could I go to an event fronted by the Conservative home secretary?

Under Blair and Brown, I'd usually felt angry and disappointed; now, I was desperate and defeated. Working at the PCT as it was dismembered and downsized, watching as arts funding, unemployment and disability benefits, mental health services and support networks for women and LGBT people were ruthlessly cut, I'd often told friends that one problem I had with the coalition was I could never decide which MP to despise the most. Arguing in favour of abolishing the Human Rights Act, Theresa May had spoken of 'the illegal immigrant who cannot be deported because – and I am not making this up – he had a pet cat', and she was always near the top of my Hate List.

'Are you going to go?' asked Helen.

'I hate the Tories and everything they stand for, but if this sort of work stops them passing another Section 28 then I guess it's positive. It'll be an experience, anyway, and I might meet some interesting people.'

'What if you have to shake Theresa May's hand?'

'I'll try to avoid her. If it comes to that, I'll probably do it, but try to look like I don't want to.'

'Well – have fun with your new friend,' said Helen, laughing.

I passed through security at the House of Commons and walked past the oil paintings of dead white men to the State Rooms. That day, the big news story was that the illegal immigrant with the pet cat had been made up, and May looked shattered as she entered. *Fair play for still coming,* I thought as she took the podium. *I almost feel sorry for you.*

'Good evening, and welcome to the launch of Diversity Role Models, which is working hard to stamp out homophobic –'

– and transphobic –

'– and transphobic bullying in schools, and I fully support its work.'

Don't include me, it makes it harder for me to hate you, I thought as May finished talking. Up stepped the next speaker, Roger Crouch. He explained how a game of Spin the Bottle on a Year 10 school trip generated rumours that his son, Dominic, was gay. Feeling unable to stop the bullying, Dominic went to the top of a tower block and texted 999 to say he was going to kill himself, only to be told that as he was not registered as a deaf user, no emergency service had been notified. Twenty minutes later, he jumped to his death. Since then, Roger had started a charity, Friends of Dominic Crouch, to fight discrimination in schools, and he had been touched at how positively the LGBT community had received his work – Stonewall had recently voted him their Hero of the Year. Once he was done, Suran, the founder of Diversity Role Models, introduced me to him.

'I can't imagine how you feel, but you're doing a great thing. Your speech was inspirational.'

'Thanks,' he replied. 'What do you do?'

I told him about the *Guardian* series, and my experiences at school. In Year 10, I had gone on a trip to the First World War battlefields. On the coach to Belgium, I sat with my friend Chris. We were behind two of the most unpopular boys in the school, and Chris starting joking that they were gay, doing camp impressions of them with suggestive noises. Another boy, Stephen, kept repeating 'Ace Bendover – Pet Defective!' until it got a response. It never did, but I joined in, convinced that if I didn't, Chris and the others would turn on me.

'I felt awful about how scared and lonely we must have made them feel,' I said. 'I resolved never to behave like that again, but I still found it easier to keep quiet and wait until I left school than to speak out. I guess that's why I do all this writing now, and come to these events – I'm just trying to make peace with my youth.'

Roger thanked me again, and we swapped contact cards. Seeing that Theresa May had fixed my handshake dilemma by leaving, I decided to 'network', suppressing my anxieties about how careerist it felt by telling myself it just meant talking to interesting people about things I cared about. I told Evan Davis, the host of BBC Radio 4's *Today* programme about my work, and how tired I was of repeatedly explaining what 'transsexual' and 'transgender' meant.

'Don't go into the media if you don't want to be typecast,' he said, smiling.

'Yeah, I know that *now*,' I replied.

'What do you write about?' asked a Labour MP. I told her what I'd written for the *Guardian*.

'Wow, that's great. You must get loads of work.'

'I spent this afternoon in Tower Hamlets Benefits Office.'

'*No!*' she replied.

'The bottom's fallen out of journalism. The Internet means it's easier to get into, but impossible to make any money. It's not like the 1990s when people were living it up in the Groucho Club. Now, it's like being a poet or something. Luckily, I'm not in it for that – I just *need* to write about certain subjects.'

That night, I woke at 3 a.m., a blog post about the need for Diversity Role Models almost fully formed. I wrote about the 'insidious effects of queer-bashing' at school – how I'd internalised the hatred and spat it back out at the boys on the bus, and how guilty I'd felt since, even though I'd told an old classmate years after leaving and he'd just said, 'Don't worry, they weren't gay.' *That wasn't the point*, I argued: unbroken, this cycle of abuse damages everyone, not just LGBT people. Because my school wasn't allowed to 'promote homosexuality', it wasn't until Dana International won the Eurovision Song Contest that the kids at Oakwood had a positive platform to discuss transsexual people. By then, I'd been scarred for life by years of social policing, self-repression and self-hatred.

I finished the post in three hours and sent it to the *New Statesman*. Two days later, I saw Roger sharing it on Facebook, quoting the line where I called him 'impassioned, articulate and dignified'. I thanked him for plugging my piece, and went back to looking for work.

——

I rushed around trying to get my life in order. I registered with a GP and landed a monthly contract at NHS London – the Strategic Health Authority, which managed the former PCTs across the city. My gender hadn't been an issue at the interview, and I let myself wonder if, even before the surgery, the transition might cease to be the dominant aspect of my life. The post was full-time, and I worried about when I might write, but it had its advantages. Seeing that Norwich was less than two hours by train, I treated myself to the thing I'd wanted most as a teenager, and could finally afford – a season ticket at City's home ground, Carrow Road.

Nobody in London hurled transphobic abuse at me, an effect, I thought, of it being late autumn, of my hormone therapy and of the welcome anonymity that came with the city. Living with Helen was fun: I felt comfortable enough in my body to be able to share a space with someone I trusted. Shrag were touring and the after-parties were often at ours, letting me catch up with Alice and Russell and other old friends and make some new ones. I liked the cultural life, too: Brighton's avant-garde Cinematheque had closed soon after I moved there, as had the Free Butt just before I left, but now I could see experimental movies, alternative bands and contemporary art all the time.

I saw that Terre Thaemlitz was playing at Café Oto in Dalston. 'Pansexual and transgender, Terre often refers to himself as "her" and is outspoken about gender issues and sexuality on the club scene,' ran the description, 'winning accolades for his challenging, experimental ambient music'. It sounded intelligent and ambitious, so I went, alone, for a show that was part lecture and part audiovisual performance about spirituality and the soul. The music was ethereal, soothing, absorbing; the film was touching yet hard-hitting. Thaemlitz talked about dealing with gender issues as a youth and trying to 'fix' them by finding religion – something I'd briefly considered when I was fourteen, only to find I wasn't capable of such belief.

On my way home, I suddenly felt shaky. I got back and knocked on Helen's door.

'Are you okay?' she asked.

'No.'

'What's wrong?'

'You know those cartoons where the Coyote chases the Road Runner off the edge of a cliff, and it's only when he stops to look down that he falls? I feel like that. I've got everything sorted and now all the stresses of the last few years are all catching up with me at once.'

She hugged me, and told me to forgive myself for struggling – *anyone* would find it difficult to stay strong all the time under the pressures I'd handled, especially alone, as I had.

'And you've done it all alone,' she said. 'When do you start your new job – Wednesday?' I nodded. 'Do something nice tomorrow and Tuesday.'

I followed her advice, going to an exhibition at the Tate Modern the next day. Later that week, I started at work. That Friday, I ate lunch at my desk, idly browsing the *Guardian* site. A headline caught my eye.

Father who set up anti-gay-bullying campaign after son's suicide found dead

Not Roger, please, not Roger, I thought. Sure enough, there was a picture of him with Dominic, and an article that described how the Gloucestershire police had found him at home following 'concerns for the welfare of a man at the address'.

I put down my sandwich, stunned, and looked around. People were dressed down, talking about their weekend plans. I knew nobody and was trying to keep my writing career quiet, worried that they wouldn't extend my monthly contract if they knew about my outside interests. So I told nobody about this double tragedy, and went home at 5:30 p.m., utterly traumatised. That night, I channelled my energy into a three-thousand-word blog post, airing my frustrations with being a trans woman in the mainstream media and about how much work I'd had to do for free. The next day I went to Brighton for the premiere of Ian McDonald's documentary *Justin*, about the life of Justin Fashanu and the campaign that I'd started with Jason and Paul of the Bandits.

I watched the opening scenes, nervously. There were shots of Jason going to the lockup garage in Shoreditch where Justin had died, and interviews with Justin's sister-in-law Marisol and niece Amal. I wondered where I would come in: back in May 2009, Ian had filmed me talking about why I'd left the campaign, and I worried about how he'd handle my transition. I hated the idea of Before and After footage, and of seeing the 'old' me on screen. This was quite recent, yet the person captured during our interview on BBC Radio and at the campaign launch just before I came out as transsexual seemed so distant: I spoke more stridently, not hiding my stubble, my hair shorter, thinning, an anxious, colourless stare on my face in every shot.

I watched to the end, tense. To my relief, Ian hadn't made my gender part of his film – it was not relevant to the story about Fashanu and football, and he kept the focus on the details of Justin's life and the events we'd organised to raise awareness. It felt weird seeing my old name credited, amplifying my sense of detachment, but I was relieved not to have been featured much.

I think Ian handled my transition as well as possible, not making it an issue, I told myself as I went back to London, feeling submerged by the huge crowds around Shoreditch as I walked home. The next morning, I went for breakfast at a friend's house nearby. I thought it would be intimate, but there were twenty people there. I'd been struggling with how many strangers had come into my life through Twitter and Facebook since *A Transgender Journey* began, trying to figure out what hopes, expectations and preconceptions they might have about me: I'd spent my first six weeks in London constantly meeting new people, and I couldn't handle any more.

I made an excuse, left and ran home. I was weeping as I opened the front door. Moments later, I was rolling on my bed, weeping, shrieking, hyperventilating, pressing my face into the pillow, smashing the mattress with my fists.

Helen rushed in.

'What's happened?'

I did all I could to sit up, and then fell on to her, crying. She put one hand round my shoulder and the other on my knee, waiting for me to collect myself. Once I could complete a sentence, I explained about Roger.

'It's not my tragedy, I know,' I said, still weeping as she made me a cup of tea. 'But it's such a brutal reminder – no matter what you do, you can't escape that kind of trauma.'

'Give yourself a break,' she replied. 'You're *always* doing stuff. Don't do any work today – just watch a movie or something. I'll be here if you need me.'

Weeping throughout, I watched Charlie Chaplin's *Limelight*, in which he played a washed-up former entertainer who saves a young dancer from suicide. I decided not to write for the foreseeable future – the first time I'd stopped since my second year in Manchester – and emailed my friend Tania, asking if she knew where I might find a therapist. She sent a link, and I spent my lunch break the next day browsing the London Psychotherapy Network.

I found an existential therapist 'concerned with exploring and clarifying your choices, values and meanings, and addressing how you deal with the inevitable challenges of life, how you might repeat patterns of behaviour, and how you might make different choices in the future'. *That sounds good*, I thought. I sent an email detailing my circumstances:

> *I'm looking for someone who won't ascribe my mental health problems to being transsexual, but instead help me understand and unpick this intertwining of my public and private lives.*

She wrote back, inviting me to discuss things further. I provided a brief summary from coming out as transsexual to Roger's death, and we agreed that I should attend an assessment to decide whether she would be able to help me disentangle the personal from the professional.

'Come on Monday at 4 p.m.,' she said. 'My practice is on Fleet Street.'

I found her office and rang the buzzer, climbing the five flights of stairs and arriving at her office breathless. I told her more about my life than I had told the Charing Cross psychiatric team, not afraid of jeopardising any treatment by saying too much, and she listened while I talked her through my transition and my writing about it.

'I've been built up as some sort of role model,' I said, 'and now I'm terrified of putting a foot wrong. I decided I wanted to be a writer when I was twenty and spent a decade getting a platform. Now I'm there, I can't say anything – one sentence in one article, even one tweet that people don't like and I might lose it again.'

'The core is that you're afraid of feeling vulnerable,' she replied. 'Of exposing yourself.'

'But that's all I do – in my journalism and in my life. Just by being myself, the world thinks I'm putting myself up to be shot at.'

Over the next few sessions, she told me how much I talked about work, using it to avoid my feelings. 'But I had to repress them so much!' I said, and instantly we were back to my youth, and how those years in the closet had set emotional patterns that had remained ever since. However much I tried to reshape my body, I couldn't change the way the media had shaped my world.

Date: 23/01/2012

Re: Admission for Surgery

I am pleased to confirm the arrangements for your admission to Charing Cross Hospital on Tuesday 17 JULY 2012 at 16:00. On the day of your admission, please go straight to the MARJORIE WARREN DAY & STAY ward on the Ground Floor, South Wing Annexe.

On receipt of this letter, PLEASE CONFIRM ACCEPTANCE OR CANCELLATION OF THE DATE ABOVE with the Admissions department.

There was a sticker near the bottom reading, 'Please stop your hormones 6 weeks before the admission date.' I didn't think twice about accepting: I'd stopped making any long-term plans, and just wanted the surgery done as soon as possible.

By this point, I had been on oestrogen for fifteen months. The Gender Trust handout had told me to expect major changes after the first year, but I'd been feeling disappointed at how little difference I'd noticed. Then, getting dressed for work one morning, I leant down to pull up my tights and felt my breasts weighing on my body for the first time.

Stunned, I stared at myself in the mirror. Suddenly, I could *see* that my cheeks were fuller, my skin softer and my hair thicker. *Maybe this is it: no more gender dysphoria after the surgery?* I exhaled, gently. *Is this how other people feel – in themselves? This* lightness, *unburdened by that disconnect between body and mind? One day, would I find that feeling hard to recall? What can it be like to have* never *felt that?*

I gladly stopped wearing the breast forms and went for a bra fitting, finding I'd been wearing ones several inches too small for three years. For a few weeks, I allowed myself to enjoy this hard-won comfort, struggling not to fret about the impending operation. But hard as I tried to relax, I couldn't help asking myself: *What* kind *of woman have I become?*

I'd taken a break from writing – there was little time anyway, in the office all week and going to watch Norwich every other Saturday. To maintain my profile, I had several talks lined up in February for LGBT History Month in London, Bradford, Sheffield and Manchester. The Manchester talk excited me most. I'd been back as Juliet once: to record a podcast about trans people and the media with Press for Change co-founder Christine Burns in December 2010. Now I was returning to Canal Street as a guest speaker at the Transgender Resource and Empowerment Centre, launched in 2009.

'It still looks exactly how I remember it,' I said to Joe as we walked by the water.

'It's dead in the evenings now, people don't come here any more,' he replied.

'Let me guess – the straight people who came after *Queer as Folk* got bored, and the old-style clubs didn't attract any younger people?'

'That's about it.'

'Maybe the younger gay guys here just don't feel the same need for labels, or for a scene,' I continued. 'Lucky them, I guess.'

We went to one of those bar/restaurants that had seemed so shiny and new back in 2000, and was now empty. I told Joe how I felt about the surgery.

'I just want it over so I can get on with my life,' I said. 'Helen asked about this when I moved in and I just said "Can I be crude for a moment?" She said yes, and I went, "I just want this fucking thing off my body right now." I was surprised by quite how strongly I felt.'

'Are you going to write about it?'

'My aim was to cover the social aspects of transsexual living and I've done that. I never liked those memoirs that built up to surgery as the be-all and end-all. I might put a statement on my own blog saying all that, and stand down.'

'Have you spoken to anyone else?'

'Yeah, Helen, and a few people from Trans Media Watch.'

'What did they say?'

'Helen reckoned I should finish it. One of the trans activists said I should think carefully about how the traditional narrative privileges those who want surgery and can access it. But she thought it might be worth doing if I could get away from that "everything's fine now" story and question *why* there's such interest.'

'I think you should carry on, too. There'll be people out there who *need* that information.'

'That's my instinct, too. It would be easy to avoid a compromise but it'd also be a cop-out, and even if doing that helped me, it wouldn't help anyone else.'

Joe accompanied me to TREC, where I explained to the audience – all trans apart from him – how we'd met, and supported each other's writing ever since. I spent an hour on how and why I'd written *A Transgender Journey* before taking questions. I referenced a *Guardian* article from 1992 about a feminist conference which mentioned 'three transsexuals' who did not speak, denying them a voice and focusing purely on what they wore.

Christine Burns put up her hand. 'I was one of those women,' she said, 'and I'm glad it's not like that any more.'

That seemed like an appropriate place to stop. Joe and I went back to his house.

'You were brilliant tonight,' he said. 'You should be proud of the column, too.'

'Thanks, that means a lot to me,' I replied. 'I blame *you* for all the stresses it caused me, you know. I never saw them coming.'

'I did. And I knew you'd cope with it.'

'It's been touch and go. But tonight's made up my mind – I'm going to finish it.'

———

I was happier in my body now, but hadn't I been a different person before I'd announced my transition and started living as Juliet – not just in name and body but also in spirit? Part of me missed the male persona I'd created, even if it had just been a survival tactic. Suddenly, I was feeling that division just as sharply as before I came out, and transition had done strange things to my sense of lived time. I felt both pubertal and prematurely aged, as if I'd existed twice.

Nostalgic for my time in Manchester, I went on Facebook. Dave was sharing a revamped Valentine Records site, and I followed a link to a Flickr page. There was Sarah's photo from 2004 of me with Joe and Joe from Performance, in my 1920s-style dress, headscarf and deep red lipstick. In it, I could see a path, not smooth but definitely continuous, between my early twenties and my early thirties. I looked at the person in the picture, and realised that however much the pressures of 'passing' had weighed on me, I still had the same opinions and politics, tastes and even style. As I'd promised my friends, I was still the same person – in fact, I felt more the same than ever.

———

I was starting to meet some of the broadsheet columnists I'd grown up reading. I saw Suzanne Moore at several events, immediately recognising her shock of red hair, telling her how impressed I was with her piece on Kate Bornstein from 1994 that I'd found in the *Guardian* archives –she'd been one of the few feminists to write positively about trans issues for them in the nineties. I met Deborah Orr, too. She took me out in Soho, and we ended up in a private members' club for writers.

I texted Phil and Steve.

'I'm in the Groucho!' I said. 'Looking out for the nineties lot with the champagne and the coke.'

Steve wrote back. 'Groucho, eh? Lah-de-dah!'

He's got a point, I realised as Deborah asked how things were with my journalism.

'I'm doing more for the *New Statesman*. They're the only ones who'll let me write what I used to. Art, film and literature stuff.'

'If you want to write about books, I've got a spare invite

for the *Times Literary Supplement* party. Come? It's at the Reform Club in Pall Mall.'

'Sure, why not?'

On the afternoon of the party, I got a message from Deborah.

'I can't make it now, but you should go. Just give my husband's name.'

I was unsure about attending. I felt conflicted about using the mainstream media to get my messages across, particularly as no publication had a perfect (or even good) record on trans issues. Now I'd put myself in a position where every time the *Guardian* ran something 'gender-critical', I felt personally responsible, or at least compromised. To try to retain *some* integrity, I'd made a rule for myself: no *Mail*, no Murdoch. Trans Media Watch had recently spoken at the Leveson Inquiry about how the *Sun* and the *Daily Mail* routinely outed trans people, publishing old names and photos, for no reason other than because they could. I wanted no part of either operation.

Going to the party doesn't mean working for them, I thought. *Turn it to your advantage: meet some interesting people, make some contacts and drink as much of their wine as you can.*

I put on a black dress with a ruffled neck that I'd bought in my favourite Brighton boutique and went to the venue, doing my makeup on the bus. It had been designed in the Classical style by architect Charles Barry as a clubhouse for those who'd supported the Great Reform Act of 1832, and later became the Liberal Party headquarters. It felt even more grandiose than the Commons, portraits of nineteenth-century politicians and huge mirrors on the stairs to the atrium, with its high glass roof, stone pillars and expansive balconies.

'What's your name, please?' asked the woman on reception.

'I'm down as Will Self,' I told her.

'Fine – just through there.'

I stood alone, sipping some white wine. I asked Christine, one of the organisers, who else might be there.

'Germaine Greer might be coming,' she said.

'God, really?' I replied. 'She's one of the most transphobic feminists around.'

In 1999, Greer had written that no transsexual woman – or 'sex-change', in her words – had 'ever begged for a uterus-and-ovaries transplant'. *Apart from Lili Elbe,* I thought, *but don't let that get in the way, will you?* Ten years later, Greer had written in the *Guardian* that 'other delusions may be challenged, but not a man's delusion that he is female'. *Yeah, nobody's ever challenged me, it's political correctness gone mad* … 'Don't worry, I won't glitter bomb her,' I told Christine, laughing, and as it turned out, I didn't see Greer. *Private Eye* editor and *Have I Got News for You* panellist Ian Hislop was there, though, alone with Culture Secretary Jeremy Hunt, but I had nothing to say to Hislop and nothing polite to say to Hunt. I did speak to a literary critic about Rayner Heppenstall, and briefly thought I might be able to hold my own with these people and fit into their world. But after a couple of hours, I'd had enough wine and got bored with introducing myself to people, only for them to realise I had nothing to offer them, smile weakly and then ignore me.

Walking down the stairs, I saw myself in the huge, clean mirrors. I stopped. I asked myself: *How did I get here?* I stared at the woman before me, and held out my hand towards her. *Is that me? Was this really what you dreamed of being when you decided to write, ten years ago? Maybe this is* exactly *who you wanted to be, but just couldn't admit it to yourself, because you were told identity politics weren't 'serious' and trans women weren't 'authentic'?* I looked at my opulent surroundings: weren't they everything I'd always hated? Unlike my trip to the Commons, when I'd been to support a charity, this was *just schmoozing. What would that person in the photograph, back in 2004, think of you?*

I'd thought going into arts journalism might be a better form of activism, showing trans people they didn't *have* to just talk about trans issues – but wasn't it cheating to use my transition as a springboard? *Even if you're more privileged than many other trans people, the playing field was hardly in your favour,* I told myself as I left. *Why shouldn't you use it to your advantage?* I'd felt like an outsider all evening, thinking about how comment journalism wasn't for me, with its strident, with-us-or-against-us arguments, and how tiresome I found it when prominent columnists claimed not to be part of 'the Establishment'. Even if my perspective was unusual within those circles, I was now definitely part of them.

I put on my iPod, and saw I'd had three songs on repeat: 'Soul Inside' by Soft Cell, 'Once in a Lifetime' by Talking Heads and 'Paint a Vulgar Picture' by the Smiths. I remembered how I used to criticise bands, comedians and writers for 'selling out' when I was a teenager, and saw that the reality was far more complicated: *If you articulate an outsider critique well enough, you stop being one.* I got the bus and took solace in Morrissey's sad, soothing refrain: *You could have said no, if you'd wanted to / You could have walked away, couldn't you ...*

———

I walked down Fulham Palace Road towards Charing Cross Hospital for my final pre-surgical appointment. Here, I was going to have my medical history examined to check my suitability for surgery, confirm my understanding of the techniques, and start to prepare for it.

The reception reminded me of East Surrey Hospital, where I'd had my first job in 1997 as a cleaner: stripped-down lilac walls, a child's drawing on a notice board the only concession to ornament. A nurse took my blood pressure, checked for MRSA by sticking cotton buds in my nostrils, and asked if I was diabetic or asthmatic before returning me to the front desk. A second nurse led me to another room.

'Are you on any medication at the moment?' she asked.

'Only my hormones, and I'm about to stop them,' I replied.

'Any allergies?'

'Hay-fever.'

'Any bad reactions to anaesthetics within your family?'

'Not that I know of.'

'Any family history of CJD?'

'CJD?' I said, thinking back to old *Daily Mail* covers about 'Mad Cow Disease'. 'I haven't heard of that since the late nineties.'

She checked my body mass index, measuring my weight against my height.

'Twenty-six kilos per metre,' she told me, 'so you're slightly overweight. Don't worry though, you'd only have a problem at thirty or over.' I sighed, relieved. 'Do you smoke?'

'No.'

'How many units of alcohol do you drink a week?'

'I don't tend to keep count,' I said.

She gave me a chart and we settled on fourteen. Then she handed me some notes to take to the clinic, saying: 'If you stop at the sweet shop, don't leave them behind as they've got all your personal details.'

Not stopping anywhere, I queued for my blood test. I got the all-clear and headed to the clinic for my appointment. An hour late, flustered, the nurse specialist called me in. I sat down, and she handed me a form:

Consent for operation of vaginoplasty
(this is the standard male to female gender reassignment operation)

In this operation

A neovagina is created by making a space between the rectum and the prostate and lining this with skin from the penis and scrotum.

The erectile tissue of the penis is largely removed as are the testicles and this is completely irreversible.

The urethra is shortened and its opening placed in a position to resemble female anatomy.

Neo labia minora and majora (inner and outer lips) are fashioned out of the penile and scrotal skin.

An innervated neoclitoris is fashioned out of the glans penis. This is placed under a small hood at the front of the new labia.

As I read the section on 'possible important complications', the nurse explained them, drawing diagrams to make sure I understood. She said there had been no cases of rectal damage in the last year, and introduced me to the Perspex dilators I'd need to use to keep the neovagina open, saying that besides the signed consent form, I should bring a mirror to hospital to help me learn how to use them. I sat with my teeth gritted, fists clenched and toes curled, hoping every time the nurse drew breath that she'd finished talking. By the end, I guessed she'd spoken for about two hours. I checked my watch: twenty-five minutes.

Then I left, thinking that however much I wanted or

needed it, and however dramatically it had been portrayed in memoirs or documentaries, for me, this just felt like a routine operation. It would take out two months of my life at most. I got home, lay on the sofa and tried to relax.

———

That March, my grandmother had died, aged ninety-seven. I was about to leave for East Surrey Hospital when Mum called to say it was too late. I wept, explaining how much I'd miss her to Helen, and how conflicted I'd felt about not feeling able to tell her who I really was. The most important thing was that we'd loved each other – she'd always made me feel I fitted into the family, with her love of travelling, music and German literature. Her final act of kindness was to leave me some money.

I knew I'd need it to get me through the summer, as I lost my job the following week. NHS London could only afford to keep one of two temps: I suspected my impending surgery was why they didn't choose me – they wouldn't want to retain someone who would have to leave in a few months. I signed on, walking in driving rain to Tower Hamlets Jobcentre, a weathered concrete and glass building so depressing it could have served no other function.

I sat upstairs, tweeting about how the Union Jacks they'd plastered across it to celebrate the Jubilee and the Olympics made it feel like a low-rent *Fatherland*, and then showed my 'job-seeking activity' to my caseworker.

'None of this counts,' she insisted, eyeing the list of websites I'd been on, people I'd called or emailed. 'If you don't apply for five jobs a week then we'll sanction you.'

'Nobody's going to give me a job now,' I replied. 'I'm having surgery soon, and then I'll be out of work for at least eight weeks.'

'Can't you delay it?'

'I don't know how long I'd have to be in a permanent job before they'd be prepared to pay for me to have two months off. And if I find something temporary and then quit, it'll just make it harder for me to get anything once I've recovered.'

'Perhaps you could go on Employment and Support Allowance?'

'I can't until I've actually *had* the operation. I'll do what I can but my hopes aren't high.'

I tried to get more freelance work, worrying about how any paid commissions would affect my benefits, and applied for journalistic jobs that I found funny. I sent my CV to the *Sun* for a features editor post, explaining how I'd bring my knowledge of transgender history, radical politics and avant-garde culture to their readership. This seemed *hilarious*, I told Chris Borg, until I remembered I'd put my name and all my contact details on it.

'Don't worry,' he said. 'They'd have got them anyway.'

———

I continued signing on. Walking to the Jobcentre one afternoon, a man on a motorbike pulled up alongside me, smiling.

'She-male?'

'Leave me alone.'

'No, you don't understand. I like she-males.'

'I don't care.'

'I just want to take you for dinner.'

'*Leave me alone.*'

I put my earphones back in and walked away. To my amazement, he drove past me on my return, waving at me on Dunbridge Street. *Fuck*, I thought. *He's stalking me and he's round the corner from my house.*

Over the next few months, he struck up several

conversations with me, putting me on edge even when I didn't see him, and I wondered if the vulnerability I felt transmitted itself to other men in the area. One Friday night in early June, I came home from seeing Julia Holter at Café Oto. Tired, I took a shortcut from Whitechapel rather than sticking to the main road. I glanced up Buckhurst Street to check nobody was there, and was nearly home when I heard a voice.

'Don't you remember me?' I stopped, and he walked towards me. 'I'm Gino.'

I'd met so many people recently that I wasn't sure. I froze momentarily. He grabbed my face and kissed me. I held him off.

'What are you doing tonight?'

'I'm going home.'

He paused. 'Are you a man or a girl?'

I waved my arm and walked away.

'Can I stick my dick inside you?'

Before I reached my front door, I tweeted the exchange. A flurry of people asked if I was okay: I was drained and distressed, but alright. Then I realised that I'd not foreseen sympathy because I'd come to *expect* this sort of treatment; above all, I felt relief that it hadn't been worse. I mentioned it on Facebook, too, and several trans women spoke about how, in these people's eyes, we were something less than male or female – that those points where men are attracted to us when we 'pass' and then repulsed when we don't are the most terrifying: *I'm a broken man so they don't fear a violent response, but I'm not a 'real' woman so they won't treat me with even the tiny modicum of respect that they might have for cisgender women. In that moment, all bets are off.*

I was reluctant to report it, but friends urged me to. One woman said it was more about 'telling yourself that you deserve better' than initiating legal proceedings; another suggested sending anonymous details to Galop, who monitor LGBT hate crime. But, as someone else pointed out, this was at its origin an example of the misogynistic abuse that all women face. I agreed, but reported it anyway. *What else could I do?*

————

Tania took me to my favourite greasy spoon café on Bethnal Green Road.

'How are you feeling?' she asked.

'I don't even know any more, I've been asked this so much. Weirdly, my therapist said I'd barely touched on it. I said I was excited to finally be doing it, but worried about how long I'll take to recover. But I trust the medics, and my parents will look after me.'

'What have your friends said?'

'I saw Phil and Steve in Brighton over the weekend. Steve just went, 'Can I have your balls?' I tried to explain that if I asked, not only did I think they'd say no to that, but also that they'd cancel the whole gig. I couldn't tell if his look of disappointment was genuine or not.' She laughed. 'Otherwise, they've just asked if I'm sure I'm doing the right thing, and tried to reassure me that I'll be alright.'

'You're comfortable with what they'll do?'

'I've re-read everything they gave me. I'm glad I'll be asleep through it, obviously. I came off the dole and tried to get on Employment Support Allowance but they said I'd need the surgeon to sign something. I told them I'd be out of London for a month – they said I could backdate it but I don't trust them not to fuck it up.'

'Or try to catch you out somehow.'

'Exactly. To be honest, everything's been so chaotic since I moved here that I'm almost glad to have a break, even if it's forced. Hopefully that guy will think I've left and stop following me home.'

We finished our lunch and walked back to my house. I'd left a suitcase by the door, with some clothes and books, my laptop with some films and TV programmes on it, a mirror and toiletries.

'Are you sure you've got everything?' asked Tania.

'The consent form's in my bag,' I replied. 'Anything else, one of my friends can bring. We'd better go, I don't want to be late again.'

I ran upstairs and went on Facebook.

This is the time. Lovely Tania Glyde is taking me to hospital. See you all soon x

I knocked on Helen's door to tell her I was leaving. She hugged me goodbye, and then Tania and I walked quietly to Whitechapel Tube. We got the District Line towards Richmond, counting off the stops. Aldgate East, Tower Hill, Monument … 'I always forget how slow this is,' I said as we crawled through Cannon Street, Mansion House, Blackfriars, Temple, each stop within a minute of the last.

Tania held my hand until we got off at Barons Court, and we walked up to Charing Cross Hospital.

I entered the Marjorie Warren ward, checked in at reception and found my bed on F Bay.

'I got you a soft toy,' said Tania, handing me a little tiger. 'You're going to need one, trust me. There's nothing more you can do now – just surrender yourself to the nurses …'

Before and After

Steven Ansell had been the last of my friends to turn up for my leaving party in Brighton, the Saturday night before I moved to London. He marched into the Lion & Lobster at 2 a.m. with a huge grin on his face, gave me a massive hug and then handed me an envelope.

'I wasn't sure whether to do this because, you know ... things have changed,' he said as I opened it. 'But then I thought – fuck it.'

Steve had made a card with a photograph of us at his home in Horsham, during a practice for our punk band, the Cheated. From the Norwich shirt I was wearing, I dated it to autumn 1996 when we had both just turned fifteen. We had the same floppy fringe, with short back and sides: Steve was holding an acoustic guitar, looking earnestly at the camera; I had a microphone and a pensive stare, wearing denim jeans and Doc Martens boots. Inside, he had written, 'I call this "portrait of two young anarchists" – Happy 30th!'

'I wrote a song on that guitar this week for the new Blood Red Shoes album,' he told me as I stared at the picture. 'I hope this is okay, anyway.'

'I know I look different now but I'm still the same person, and I've never wanted to deny my past. I'd rather people didn't edge around it,' I replied. 'Thank you so much!'

———

Steve's gift made me think about the fascination with the 'Before & After' image in mainstream media coverage of transsexual and transgender people. I first became aware of it long before my surgery – in fact, before I'd even left school. I remember one article in a women's magazine about someone 'Born a Man'. At the time I didn't consider how stupid this phrase was: I was too dazzled by the photographs of a person reclining, her palm resting where her forehead met her long, blonde hair. 'Now I'm a Beautiful Woman!' screamed the headline. In her pre-transitional past, the woman looked like a boy, neither exceptionally attractive nor unattractive. Now, she could have been a model. There was barely any detail on the treatments that helped her change her appearance, though: clearly, the photographs *were* the story.

In the *Sunday People*, I saw an ad for a company called Transformation. 'From He To She ... Instantly!' it promised, above photos of a stubbly, balding man and a glamorous woman in heavy makeup, a brown wig and a pretty dress. The advert was selling feminising products to male-to-female cross-dressers and transsexual women. I was sceptical about what they were offering to stop facial hair growth or develop a bust, knowing these would require more than putting cream on my face or stuffing something inside a bra. But while the women's magazine feature seemed from another world – I knew I could never look like that person, nor was it my dream – this advert made me feel like transition might be possible, even if I didn't know how.

Later, I saw that Before & After photographs have the effect of masking processes of change even as they ostensibly reveal them. When used in stories about unfamiliar people, these images are sensationalist, trying to make readers marvel at how it might be possible to move between male and female, usually using the most typically masculine and feminine pictures for maximum effect. Their shortcomings were exposed when US transsexual people such as Alexis Arquette, Chaz Bono and Lana Wachowski, already in the public eye, came out. In particular with Arquette, who had played cross-dresser Georgette in *Last Exit to Brooklyn*, there was no point in pretending she had changed overnight;

instead, media outlets studied old images to see which 'signs' they had missed.

Before & After pictures have been part of print coverage of transsexuality from the start. In January 1937, less than a decade after the earliest surgeries in Berlin, American bodybuilding magazine *Physical Culture* ran one of the first articles on the subject, 'Can Sex in Humans Be Changed?' Its opening paragraph was relaxed about the possibility of radical social change, suggesting that 'the old landmarks are going, nothing is static, everything flows ... Life is created in the laboratory [and] Sex is no longer immutable.' The writer, Donald Furthman Wickets, went on to look at historical ideas of 'male' and 'female', and the role of hormones in determining them.

There were two shots of Britain's first surgically transsexual man, Mark Weston: one in a white shirt, tie and tank top with Alberta Bray, 'a former girl chum to whom he is now married', and the other as 'Great Britain's girl [javelin] champion' during the 1920s, the only clear difference being that he had grown some stubble. There was a single image of Zdenek Koubkov of Czechoslovakia, who had won the Women's 100m at the 1932 Olympic Games as Zdeneka Koubkova, but had since transitioned, and was shown wearing a suit and lifting his hat to show off his close-cropped hair. The pronouns 'he' and 'him' were used throughout. Despite its scientific tone, the piece offered little sense of what happened physically to the athletes: readers were told no more than that, in both cases, 'the miracle was accomplished by surgery and duly acknowledged by law'.

Weston and Koubkov did not become international news. It was only after the Second World War, as photographs on newspaper covers became commonplace, that transsexuality developed into a mass media phenomenon. On 1 December

1952, the *New York Daily Times* ran the sensational story of Christine Jorgensen under the headline 'Ex-GI Becomes Blonde Beauty', with contrasting images of her as a soldier and then as a glamorous woman dominating the spread. Instantly, Jorgensen became internationally famous, working as an actress, singer and transgender rights advocate.

In *Transgender History* (2008), Susan Stryker wrote about how the fascination with Jorgensen 'had to do with the mid-twentieth-century awe for scientific technology, which now could not only split atoms but also, apparently, turn a man into a woman'. Stryker also noted that Jorgensen was the first American transsexual woman to become prominent after the war gave the United States a new geopolitical importance, and changed women's relationships with paid labour and domestic work. Now, it wasn't just gender roles that were in flux, but gender itself. What would happen if men could become women, and vice versa?

The transsexual phenomenon, as Dr Harry Benjamin called it in his influential 1967 book of the same name about the gender reassignment process, did not destroy American society. Looking at the *New York Daily Times'* pictures of Jorgensen now, they come nowhere near justifying the attention-grabbing 'Operations Transform Bronx Youth' subheading. Jorgensen's facial structure barely altered between 1943 and 1952; her hairline, eyes, nose, lips and chin looked the same, with the main differences being in her clothes and makeup.

Despite their contrasting styles, both *Physical Culture* and the *New York Daily Times* tried to show radical discontinuity between 'male' and 'female' to make their stories more powerful, emphasising the otherworldliness, if not the anarchic intentions, of those crossing them. But I found more truth in *Becoming*, a flipbook by Berlin-based artist Yishay Garbasz.

Garbasz regularly photographed herself as a standing nude after starting gender reassignment, installing 28 images as a zoetrope in the 2010 Busan Biennale, and choosing 87 of 911 pictures for her book. Each was taken before a white backdrop without makeup, emphasising the incremental changes to her frame; in this context, even her sex reassignment surgery in 2008 did not appear abrupt or incongruous, but rather assimilated into the physical landscape that she presented.

As I had aimed to do in my writing, Yishay had taken control of the conceit and exposed the potentially limitless terrain contained within it. By the time I had my sex reassignment surgery in 2012, I'd seen this demystification so often that I found it strange to see such pictures in print – and never stranger than when someone I'd known by a male name at sixth-form college in Horsham became famous as a female model, with tabloid newspaper spreads yet again carrying Before & After photos. I recognised her from the opening catwalk shot long before I got to the image of her as a boy, or the text about her struggle to realise herself as a transsexual woman rather than a gay man, and then navigate the pathway.

At that point, I thought back to the photo Steve had given me and how I looked now, and about the media that I had struggled so hard to change since I saw that first set of pictures in that women's magazine. I marvelled at how much and how little had changed.

10

'I'll take that, Jules. Don't do any lifting,' said Dad, throwing my suitcase into his car. I'd spent twenty-four hours at the house after returning from my seven-day hospital stay, mostly still and serene, doing as much packing as I could manage before my parents arrived to drive me back to Horley.

We weren't out of London when I felt a searing pain between my legs. Not wanting to worry them, I tried to be stoic: I would take my painkillers and see how I felt in the morning. A few hours later, I woke in agony. I looked down. My vagina was bright yellow, and it stank.

Dad drove me to the nearest Urgent Treatment Centre. I stretched out my legs, trying to do *anything* that might make it hurt less, and struggled through reception to see a nurse.

'I've never dealt with this before,' she said. 'I'm not sure A&E at East Surrey will be able to treat you. You might need to go back to Charing Cross.'

Thinking about a long drive back to London in hateful heat – the summer rains had ceded to blistering temperatures a few days before the Olympic Games were to start – I held back tears. Eventually, we managed to contact the GIC's nurse specialist, who said this could be handled with antibiotics – as I'd have known if I'd re-read the 'Going Home After Your Vaginoplasty Operation' leaflet from my pre-surgical consultation.

A senior doctor inspected me.

'The bruising above the wound is infected. Haemotopia. Don't worry, it's easily treated.'

He wrote a prescription and sent me home. By the following Monday, the cocktail of drugs had completely floored me. I spent the afternoon in bed, struggling to reassure myself that however bad I felt, and however little I'd been sleeping, things *would* get better – eventually. With the infection clearing up, Mum advised me to stop the new medication early. I trusted her, and there were no more complications.

With limited movement, I spent my time reading, or finding films, TV shows and old football to watch on YouTube as I dilated. Ten days after surgery, Mum said I was 'spending too much time in my room' and encouraged me to go outside.

She took my hand and led me to the top of our road. 'It hurts too much,' I said, and I staggered back. I returned to bed, and looked at Twitter on my BlackBerry. *Everyone's on about the Olympics, even people who don't like sport,* I thought. *A month ago, you all thought this would be awful, you were talking about how they were putting missiles on people's houses, driving poor people out of London, making unemployed people work there for free* ... Deep down, I resented the Games taking place just two Tube stops from my house, and not being able to go. I refused to watch anything except the football, and thought about the other things I was going to miss, particularly the gig to celebrate Shrag's final album, and the launch of Joe's third novel, *The Adult.*

I tried to imagine when taking several months out like this wouldn't have been a problem. I couldn't, but I still felt bitter. I began to loathe social media, too. I'd relied on it in hospital, reaching out at my loneliest, most painful moments, but now, Facebook served as a constant reminder of just what a great time everyone else was having. Twitter made me even more unhappy. I'd enjoyed it when I first joined, finding new books, films, art and writers, doing years' worth of 'networking' in six months, making friends in London and feeling part of so many conversations, even sensing that old power structures were being challenged by those traditionally excluded.

Now, I began to disengage. I'd grown annoyed with myself for becoming so addicted – I often woke at 3 a.m. and reached straight for my smartphone to make sure I didn't miss anything, or irritated friends at the pub by constantly turning to it. I'd found myself thinking in aphorisms, getting frustrated when they barely got any retweets. I became even more alienated when some stupid offhand remark proved far more popular than my blog posts. I tired of the endless arguments between journalists and activists – often, I liked people on both 'sides', and couldn't be bothered to keep track of who I was meant to hate now, and why. Yet I couldn't break with the relentless barrage of bad news, bad tempers and assumptions of bad faith that Twitter relentlessly threw at me.

Even though I now had the anatomy I'd always wanted, it was impossible to feel comfortable while I felt like this: sharp pains as nerve endings reconnected; a dull, throbbing ache; an unbearable pushing sensation at the base of the affected area which stayed constant for weeks; and plenty of discharge for the first month.

As the surgical team had advised, I took two baths a day, passing the time by listening to the radio. One afternoon, BBC6 Music played Joy Division's 'Love Will Tear Us Apart'. As I heard its opening bars – Ian Curtis's guitar strums, Peter Hook's insistent bass line, then Stephen Morris's *motorik* drums and that dreamlike keyboard melody, played by Bernard Sumner – my entire transition flashed through my mind: a huge, traumatic circle that had somehow led me back here, where I'd spend so many lonely hours obsessing over this band. I sank into the water and wept.

———

Once again, crying felt cathartic. I started to resume my usual activities – the first of which was writing. One afternoon, Mum knocked on my door.

'Come in,' I said, and she sat on my bed.

'What are you doing?'

'My account of the surgery. While it's fresh in my mind.'

'Can I see it?' she asked.

'You want to read it?'

'Of course, I read all your *Guardian* pieces. I look at your Twitter, too.'

'*What?*' I replied, trying to decide if I was mortified at the thought of her looking at everything I posted, or if my stance was that if she went on there, she would have to take responsibility for anything she didn't like.

'I just wanted to keep up with you in hospital,' she told me. 'I'm not interested when you start going on about weird art.'

I finished the piece in two days and showed it to her. Then I sent it to my editor at the *Guardian* and started on something else.

Slowly, my world expanded beyond my bedroom. Several friends came to visit, drinking tea with me in our lounge. Corinne arrived from Horsham with her baby son, Henry. We talked fondly about that night at the Harlequin, a decade ago, and about how different our paths had been since. A few nights later, Dad drove me to the Black Horse, our local, to meet Phil, Paul and Mark, who had travelled from Brighton. After the intensity of the last year, it was quietly beautiful to drink in a country pub with three of my oldest friends, and for a couple of hours, I felt like I was back in my sixth-form days, when little else mattered besides the fact that, as outsiders in small suburban towns, we'd found each other.

Later that week, Mum took me into town. She parked near the High Street, and we walked towards Frillies, the little lingerie store that was one of Horley's few remaining independent shops. I'd always seen it advertised in the *Horley Life* when I'd delivered the paper as a teen, but I'd never been in. Under these circumstances, there seemed to be something marvellous about going somewhere so modest, especially as Mum opened the door and spoke to the assistant.

'My daughter needs to buy some new bras. Could you arrange a fitting for her?' she said. Now I could see that she understood my transition as a process in which far more had been gained than lost. The assistant measured me and then offered plenty of choices. I picked a few, we paid and I threw my arms around Mum. We went to buy some makeup together at Boots, had a cup of tea and went home, closer than we'd ever been.

——

I met Tania as she got off the train.

'You excited about the tour?' I said. 'Here you'll see Horley Station Bookshop. It's unique in not stocking any books.' We laughed. 'From the train, you'll have seen the big Waitrose. Apparently Wikipedia is wrong, it's not the biggest in Europe. It's not even that big, really.'

We walked down the hill towards the town. Seeing how slowly I was moving, Tania put her arm around me.

'It's weird being back – I've not really returned for about ten years, and even then, I was either at my parents' house or the station. Mentally I left when I was about fourteen. Once I stopped playing football with the hard lads, the only way to get through school was to hide during break times and think about how I'd get out. As soon as I went to college I cut myself off from everyone I knew, and left as soon as I could.'

'Was there anything you liked about it?'

'There was a great record shop. It used to sell CD singles to kids walking home from school and that subsidised them selling me Mark Stewart records for a fiver. That's long gone. I used to go to the little library when I was back from university. One time, I looked at the Gay and Lesbian section of *The Rough Guide to San Francisco* and someone had torn out the pages.'

'Wow,' said Tania. 'That's terrible.'

'I was furious! *It's so homophobic here, Tory bastards*, I thought. Then I told my friend Alice in Brighton about it and she just said, "Did it ever occur to you that someone might have torn out the pages because they wanted to go there?" Obviously, it hadn't.'

We walked past a parade of charity shops to the High Street and sat at a café, looking at the handful of estate agents and betting shops, reading the *Gatwick and Horley Mirror*. Most of the news concerned other towns nearby, and as we went to the little bookshop, I told Tania how I'd gone to Horsham – hardly a metropolis – as a sixth-former in search of more culture.

'I don't see what your problem is,' she replied. 'The book-shop's got *Fifty Shades of Grey* in stock now. As if it were difficult to get hold of. That's enough, isn't it?'

'I remember buying the *Guardian* in the newsagent near my house. I took the only copy to the desk and the bloke just turned to his side and went "Intellectual?" I only wanted the TV guide and the football bit. It's like the whole town was designed by the *Daily Mail*.'

We walked back up to the Collingwood and Batchelor department store, marvelling at the little chinaware sets before getting another cup of tea.

'These last two weeks have made me feel better about the place,' I said. 'Nobody's given me any hassle – perhaps people are so unaware about the whole thing they don't even notice me. Or perhaps they deserve more credit than I give them.' I stirred my tea with a spoon. 'I don't think I'll hang out here too often, but I'm glad to have at least one nice memory of it.'

'You look tired,' she replied. 'Are you alright?'

'I should go and lie down. We've seen most of the town twice anyway.'

I walked Tania back to the station and called my parents, asking them to drive me home.

A week later, they took me back to London with several bags of food, lots of new clothes and a newfound sense of peace with my past. I rested for the afternoon before going to Shoreditch, where Joe Stretch was a judge at Literary Death Match.

'You look a lot better than when I last saw you,' he said. 'How's the recovery?'

'Getting here was hard work, even though it's only a half-hour walk. I'm dehydrated, and still not that mobile, but most of the stitches are out, the scars are going down and I'm getting used to how it looks. I think it all works.'

'It's incredible, isn't it?' said Joe.

'I'm a miracle of science,' I replied.

'*You're a miracle of science*. How does that feel?'

'It's absolute agony.'

He laughed, and we hugged. Then we spent the rest of the night talking about literature, politics and music, just like we used to. The next morning, we had breakfast in Bethnal Green.

'The season starts tomorrow,' he said. 'Who have you got?'

'We're away at Fulham, would you believe?' I replied. 'Down the road from Charing Cross.'

'You going?'

'My mates usually come down from Norwich for this one, so I told them to get me a ticket and sell it if I wasn't up to it. I think it'll be alright, as long as I rest today.'

'It'll mean a lot to you,' Joe told me. 'I reckon you should go.'

The next morning, I took the Tube to Hammersmith, walking gingerly but victoriously past the hospital on my way to the pub. My friends cheered as I entered.

'I think it's fucking brilliant that you've made it,' said Rich.

'Well, I'm knackered from the journey but you lot will look after me, right?'

'Of course,' said Tim, raising his glass. 'You excited about the first game of the season?'

'It's not my first game,' I said, laughing. 'I went to watch Horley Town play Holmesdale in the preliminary qualifying round of the FA Cup last weekend.'

'How did that go?' asked Ben.

'We won 5–1.'

'*We?*'

'Yeah, *we*,' I replied. 'I played for them, so why not?' I smiled. 'Anyway – it was mostly alright, apart from Horley's winger put the ball out. Chris and I were the only people behind the goal, so I ran to get it. Soon wished I hadn't.'

They smiled, and we talked about City's prospects under new manager Chris Hughton as we walked to the ground. It was the warmest day of the year, and I kept asking my friends to slow down, faltering in the thirty-degree heat. Lee and Martin helped me up the stairs to our seats, and I stood with my fellow fans, clapping, cheering and singing as the teams ran on to the pitch.

Instantly, I realised this wouldn't be the glorious comeback that I'd planned. Fulham dominated from the start, making several chances. The stewards kept telling us to sit down, but whenever Fulham broke into City's penalty area, everyone stood again – this happened at every match, but I hadn't thought about how painful it would be, a month to the day after surgery. After twenty-five minutes, Fulham took the lead. Fifteen minutes later, their striker, Petrić, burst through on goal. Norwich's defender Ryan Bennett slid in from behind to put the ball out of play.

'Jesus, did you see that?' I asked Martin. 'Best tackle I've ever seen!'

We watched as Fulham's winger put the ball down for the corner. The cross came in and Petrić headed it into the net.

'Fuck this, I'm getting a drink,' said Martin. 'Want anything?'

'I've *got* to have some water, I'm dying,' I replied.

'You sure you don't want anything stronger? There's another forty-five minutes of this bollocks.'

'I'm not drinking until I stop taking painkillers – water will be fine.'

I sat down at half-time, exhausted. As the second half kicked off, I wondered where Martin was. Just as Petrić made it 3–0, he returned with several drinks.

'Sorry, Juliet,' he said. 'They only had beer.'

The second half just got worse. A few minutes before the end, Fulham got a penalty. We left as Sidwell scored it, putting his team 5–0 up, and as we walked back to the pub, I tried to tell myself that the fact I'd made it to the match, and made it *through*, was more important than the result. For the next two days I could hardly do anything, but the following weekend, I mustered the energy to travel to Norwich for a 0–0 draw with QPR, and I barely missed a home game all season.

———

Eight weeks after surgery, I made my last visit to the GIC's surgical team. They asked a few questions about my health – which, I said, had been no worse than expected after the infection cleared up. Then I lay on a table as they examined me.

'There are no serious complications, but there's some granulation tissue from over-healing,' said the surgeon. 'We can fix that with silver nitrate.' The surgeon held up a silver rod, and I started breathing heavily, worried I'd start hyperventilating. 'Just relax, this won't hurt any more than your dilation.' They did the injection and discharged me, and I arranged my final appointment with the psychiatric team. There was another long wait – seven months – but this time, I wasn't bothered. After all, they've given me everything I'd needed.

In the meantime, I returned to psychotherapy, and my therapist asked how I felt about the end of the physical process.

'When I was young, I played computer games a lot. I spent three years on *Bounder*, where you had to get this tennis ball across rooftops in levels that got harder. All that time, I wondered what would happen at the end. I was hoping for a nice little sequence. When I finally completed the same, it just went back to the start. And this feels like that.'

'What do you mean?' she asked.

'Well … I'm pleased, or at least satisfied that doing all this will make my life better but it doesn't fix everything, does it? I've still got to get a job, work out what to write once the *Guardian* thing finishes, find somewhere to live that I can actually afford, and deal with my depression. And that's just fixing *my* stuff. I mean, I can have as many operations as I like, David Cameron is still prime minister.'

I was still struggling to sleep, keeping a pillow between my legs because lying on my side hurt too much. I came off the painkillers, deciding that constant low-level soreness might be better than the intense discomfort of the constipation they caused, and immediately found myself enduring the kind of nightmares I'd not had since I ditched my anti-depressants. One night, I had the horrific realisation: *it's still there! What the fuck? All that waiting and anxiety, all that pain, how is this even* – then I woke, caught my breath and remembered the transsexual women who'd had sex reassignment surgery before me, and asked, *Have you had the Dream yet?*

My mental health got worse, though. Transsexual friends had warned me to look out for post-surgical depression, and I'd been quite blasé about it.

'I've dealt with it all my life,' I said. 'How bad can it be?'

'Seriously, this is different,' they replied, and I learned the hard way.

I'd long functioned with depression and anxiety, but it rarely stopped me doing what I cared about. This didn't feel like the kind of psychological problem that I could discuss with a therapist: it was far more visceral, jumping into the void left by my gender dysphoria, equally difficult to put into words, complete with the throbbing headaches and crushing sense of worthlessness that I hadn't felt since my teens. I just wanted to sleep; when I couldn't, I lay on my bed with my arm over my face, listening to the bleakest music I could find.

I cancelled as many social obligations as I could, not wanting to see anyone. I spoke on a Trans Media Watch panel and left as soon as I'd done my bit, struggling even to answer a text message that asked, 'Are you alright?'

'You're not yourself,' I was told, and it was true. I felt like I was living in black and white again, the fragile confidence that I'd found through taking on such huge battles shattered. In the past, I'd tried to suppress my depression by forcing myself to do things I didn't enjoy, and to have 'fun'. Later, and particularly since I'd built up a following online, I'd reacted against that, being open about my mental health issues to let anyone who felt similar know they weren't alone. After weeks of isolation, I wanted to find some middle ground, and resolved to do whatever I could to lift myself.

I forced myself to resume some of my usual activities, going to see friends at gigs, galleries and cinemas, but the outside world seemed determined to make it difficult to find any sort of normality. My operation had been provided on the NHS, but still cost thousands in lost earnings, and I'd had no income since entering the hospital. I'd submitted my ESA application on returning to London, but heard nothing for weeks.

I called the Hackney Benefit Centre.

'We've got your name and address,' they said, 'but no other details.'

I was confused.

'Ah – I know what this is. I think I've got a protected characteristic under the Equality Act of 2010.' This was met with silence. 'I've just had gender reassignment. The protection is supposed to mean I don't have to tell you that, but obviously I do so you can sort this out.'

It wasn't until late September that I got a letter:

YOUR CLAIM FOR EMPLOYMENT AND SUPPORT
ALLOWANCE

I am pleased to tell you we can pay Employment and
Support Allowance from 17 July 2012.
You will get £49.00 a week.
We have used the tax years ending 5 April 2010 and 5 April
2011 to assess your claim.
To continue to receive Employment and Support Allow-
ance you may need to attend a Work Capability Assessment.
You must provide Medical certificates until a Work Capa-
bility Assessment is carried out.

I'd spent six months since leaving NHS London feeling
besieged by the brown envelopes that arrived with baffling
regularity, saying my benefits would start or stop or go up or
down. Now, I got one from Tower Hamlets Benefits Office,
telling me that as I'd not claimed JSA or ESA since July, they
would interview me under caution on suspicion of Housing
Benefit fraud. I found a lawyer who told me how to explain
everything to the benefits officer, and left with £76 to pay the
council and a £600 legal bill.

My ESA ended, and I signed on again. The Jobcentre had
moved, their shiny new premises somehow making the lived
reality of the government and the tabloids' demonisation of
people on benefits even more dispiriting. One afternoon,
I couldn't find a pen and asked to borrow one. 'Sorry, but
claimants aren't allowed to use our pens,' said the clerk.
'Don't worry, I've got one,' I sighed. Not seeing any plausible jobs in journalism, I decided to ask my agency to find me
part-time admin work and think about writing from there.

———

By November, life finally seemed to be calming down. After spending twenty minutes outside my house, my stalker apologised and promised to leave me alone, keeping his word. I felt over the worst of the depression after some cathartic chats with women who'd had similar experiences after giving birth, and the physical pain was fading. The 'phantom limb' feeling had vanished before I left the hospital, and I was no longer so dehydrated, sleeping properly. I still couldn't play sport so I exercised by taking long walks, but otherwise I'd resumed all my usual activities.

Gradually, I stepped down the number of dilations. One afternoon, I was lying on my bed holding the Perspex inside me, and realised I'd been thinking about sex the whole time. I'd not been watching anything particularly erotic – another Adam Curtis documentary about how clever people had thought something about global politics but were wrong – and I realised: *You've found your clitoris. And it* works!

I went to a sex shop during a trip to Brighton and bought a vibrator, the same length as my dilators but slightly wider. It had two speeds – the fastest was definitely more fun – and my entire body tingled as I turned it off and on, lying on my bed and laughing. Finally, I stopped missing my old orgasms, feeling thrilled instead about these new ones, and more amazed than ever by medical technology eighty years after Dr Hirschfeld's first breakthroughs.

Later that month, I got a call from my temp agency.

'We think we've found something for you,' they said. 'Personal assistant at an NHS Trust, covering maternity for a year. Three days a week for now, full-time in January. Sound good?'

'Yes, perfect.'

'And you're available to start immediately?'

'Absolutely. Where's it based?'

'Do you know Charing Cross Hospital?'

I laughed, grimly, and accepted the job – however weird it would feel to work there, I wanted to get out of the house and needed the money. So I travelled to Hammersmith several times a week, heading past the Marjorie Warren ward to my little office on the second floor of the prefabricated Education Centre at the back of the complex. Sometimes, I watched people walk nervously to the adjacent clinic, worrying about what they'd heard about it, perhaps from *A Transgender Journey* or maybe even *A Change of Sex*, wondering if they'd said the right things or worn the right clothes to reach the next stage, as had I and so many others.

I was relieved to be through that, but still not over the aftershocks from the Real Life Experience, and my depression hit its cruellest point, making me feel like I'd never had a pleasurable moment in my life. During some downtime at work – and there was plenty – I drafted an email to myself, listing every time that I had ever felt happy. I came up with plenty, and stopped, recognising this as a little step towards getting better.

I published a *Transgender Journey* post on my recovery, and as I'd promised myself, started to think about what I might do next. I gave up on the idea of earning a living from journalism, and decided to concentrate not on what might make money or what was politically useful, but what I enjoyed. My friend Ventiko, an artist/photographer based in New York, was bringing her Animamus Art Salon to London and asked me to present something at Brixton East. Trying to introduce more self-criticism into the form I'd used, I wrote a *Manifesto for Confessional Journalism*.

Never humiliate or sensationalise yourself or others known to you, and do not write anything unkind about your own body, although you may test its limits: think of confessional journalism, and everything else in your life, as a form of performance art.

That was how I'd come to think of *A Transgender Journey* – as a performance project in which I'd publicly constituted an identity, with my tweets from the hospital forming part of the work. I felt much more comfortable appearing in such a small space than on the *Guardian* website: I told the tiny crowd that 'the confessional journalist should not be a careerist', aiming 'to appear at small literary or journalistic events, or art galleries, before an audience of no more than twenty-five people'. They weren't sure if I was joking or not, and in truth, neither was I.

I tried to interview *Daily Mail* columnist Liz Jones, who wrote weekly about every aspect of her life, complicating it so much that in one article, she highlighted how no High Street bank would offer her an account for fear that she would denigrate them. Recently, she had generated controversy by writing about how she wanted a baby but her partner didn't, so she tried to steal some of his sperm from a discarded condom. Convinced by her level of detail, I considered the zero sum game of trying to shock: if Jones wanted to continue driving traffic to *Mail Online* by outraging Internet liberals, leftists and feminists, she would have to keep topping this anecdote without stretching her boundaries of credulity, or mental health, past the breaking point. *Wouldn't it be fascinating to talk about those tensions?* Jones declined my request but I wrote about her anyway, concluding that sustaining nourishing individual relationships was far harder than doing so with people online, not least because I could step back from those whenever I wished.

The final *Transgender Journey* article went online on 29 November. In closing, I wrote, 'I believe there are as many gender identities as there are people, all unique, all constantly being explored in conscious and unconscious ways.' I had said all I wanted in that format, and craved a break from the world of blogging, comment journalism and social media.

I'd thought my exhaustion and exasperation with Twitter would fade, and that I'd regain enthusiasm for the connections it offered. I didn't: having confessed so much in my series, I had nothing more to give. Walking home from the Close-Up DVD library on Brick Lane, looking at my phone and disdainfully going through the cavalcade of people's actions and opinions, it suddenly felt like a radical gesture to just watch the films I'd rented and *not* broadcast about them.

Then I had a beautiful realisation: I didn't *need* to be a 'public figure' for the whole of 2013. *Write about the culture you love, turn the* Guardian *thing into a book, and keep out of the trans culture wars,* I told myself, insisting I deserved a break.

Yet eight days into the New Year, I realised 'keeping out of the trans culture wars' was no longer possible. I'd been off social media, partly because it was blocked at work and my phone got little reception there, but I saw that people were angry about Suzanne Moore's article on the *New Statesman* site entitled 'Seeing Red: The Power of Female Anger'. I often became frustrated with people on Twitter picking out single words or phrases in attacking otherwise strong pieces; I always thought it might be better to build on positive aspects. However, I agreed that Suzanne's line about women 'being angry with ourselves for not being happier, not being loved properly and not having the ideal body shape – that of a Brazilian transsexual' ended on the wrong note. Besides adding little to her point, the statement ignored the fact that the 'Brazilian transsexual' she was most likely referencing, Givenchy model Lea T, had been publicly disowned by her father, ex-international footballer Toninho Cerezo. It also ignored the reality that the murder rates for trans people in Brazil were horrific: thirty-six were recorded on the Transgender Day of Remembrance website for 2012, many killed in brutally sexualised ways, some unnamed as their bodies were left unidentifiable.

People pointed out to Suzanne that she hadn't accounted for the realities of their lives – some calmly, others with angry threats. I watched it get nastier, surviving the usual twenty-four-hour life of these Twitterstorms. Suzanne's remark that 'people can lop their dicks off and be more feminist than me' didn't help; nor did various comment pieces written about it, illustrating a new landscape in which journalism and blogging, comments sections and social media had coalesced, filling the infinite space of the Internet with self-sustaining controversies.

In an industry where personal connections were so important, I'd never felt so compromised: I liked Suzanne, and had defended her against online abuse. The offending piece had appeared where I now published most of my work, and she regularly wrote for the *Guardian*, whose record on trans issues I'd struggled so hard to improve. I was gearing up to move – Helen had left already, I hadn't clicked with my new short-term flatmate and I'd decided to live alone again – and I was trying to remove as many sources of drama from my life as possible. By the end of the week, however, it had become impossible to remain detached.

I intervened just once, to say that I'd been on Twitter for two and a half years and this had been the most dispiriting week yet. I spent Saturday in Norwich, failing to stop my mind from wandering back to the fracas during an interminable, freezing 0–0 draw against Newcastle. I hoped to use

Sunday to start planning my move to Leytonstone but when I went on Twitter that morning, I saw this wouldn't happen. My timeline was in meltdown, with everyone furious about Julie Burchill's interjection, published in the *Observer* and cross-posted on to the *Guardian*'s *Comment Is Free* site, entitled 'Transsexuals Should Cut It Out'.

It opened with the assertion that she was still Julie from the block despite eating lobster and drinking champagne, and closed with the threat that 'shims, she-males, whatever you're calling yourselves these days – *don't* threaten or bully we lowly natural-born women, I warn you.' In between was a tirade of transphobic insults, centring around the baffling generalisation that all trans people had PhDs, with such remarks as 'after having one's nuts taken off ... by endless decades in academia', adding '(See what I did there?)' for anyone who'd not encountered these clichés in TV comedies, *Daily Mail* editorials or school playgrounds.

I wrote to the *Observer*'s readers' editor, turning my email into an open letter on my blog. I said I felt like I'd wasted my time in writing for the *Guardian* and that I'd never felt so let down by so many people, although the one thing I could say for Burchill was that I wasn't disappointed in her. The *Guardian* asked me to respond, but I'd already spent all morning online, where several friends had remarked, 'They probably think they can get Juliet to do something and that'll make it alright'. I also had a *New Statesman* piece to finish about trans people, pronouns and respectful language. I suggested Roz Kaveney, whose long fight against transphobia in LGBT and feminist circles made her better placed. Her line 'Once you decide that some people's lives are not real, it becomes okay to abuse them; for people without the outlet of writing for a national newspaper, it becomes okay to shout things in the street, or worse' said everything I would have.

Meanwhile, I quietly put feminists who wanted to counter Burchill's slurs in touch with like-minded editors, and helped the *Guardian*'s Patrick Barkham with an article on the history of transgender rights, perfectly happy not to be quoted.

Before Sunday was out, the *Observer* announced that Burchill's article was subject to an internal inquiry. I wasn't surprised: *Guardian* editor Alan Rusbridger had spent all day on Twitter dissociating his newspaper from it, telling anyone he could that it was 'actually an *Observer* piece'. The next day, the *Guardian* deleted it from their website, with the editors explaining that they could not defend it in its published form, if not how it had reached print in the first place, given Burchill's history on this subject. Rather than asking if her tract was politically useful or had any artistic merit, established columnists made endless accusations of censorship, failing to differentiate between the right to free speech and the privilege of an influential platform. Then Toby Young republished it in the *Daily Telegraph*: Burchill had been silenced by getting the same piece published in two national newspapers within twenty-four hours.

After the Press Complaints Commission declared that it could take no action against Burchill or the *Observer* as her article attacked a group rather than individuals, I could assess the incident properly. It had been useful in showing outsiders just what we had faced from the 'liberal' press for years, taking transphobic feminism to its logical conclusion, far more visibly than the passages on 'total rape' in *The Transsexual Empire*. It also showed how many people now took transphobia seriously, and were prepared to fight such abuses of power.

Worse was to come, though. The Burchill fiasco had been unkind and unfair, but ultimately ridiculous, and I'd hoped that now, people at the *Guardian/Observer* would understand that the need for people to feel safe and respected might need to be considered at times, and that columnists might show a little more responsibility in their work. That hope soon proved misplaced. The *Daily Mail* seemed to have stepped up their hostile coverage of trans people since the Leveson Inquiry, and, unlike Burchill, one of their leading columnists singled an individual out. A primary school teacher in Accrington who had recently decided to transition went back after the Christmas break as a woman, and her employer told the children and their parents that she would be known as Lucy Meadows. A local newspaper reported a father saying that his three sons were 'too young to be dealing with that'; Richard Littlejohn picked up on this in the *Mail*, writing an editorial headed 'He's Not Just in the Wrong Body, He's in the Wrong Job', asking whether anyone had thought of the 'devastating effect' that Meadows's gender reassignment would have on her pupils.

Shortly thereafter, Meadows killed herself, having been hounded by journalists near her home. Now someone had to tell her pupils why their teacher had died. The inquest heard that her note had made no reference to the coverage, citing her debts, the deaths of her parents and someone she had loved and the stresses of her job. Commentators were quick to insist that Littlejohn should not be blamed, but the coroner insisted that media attention had contributed, saying, 'Her only crime was to be different ... And yet the press saw fit to treat her in the way that they did.' Strangely enough, Littlejohn's article seemed to have vanished from the website, but unlike the *Observer*, the *Mail* didn't provide an explanation.

I pieced this together in the office, reading blogs and newspaper sites, having seen flashes of a story about press harassment that week but not registered the details until its awful conclusion. I recognised it immediately as a tragedy that had been coming for decades. Walking furiously down Fulham Palace Road that Thursday evening, I realised that other people would write rapid response pieces about Meadows's specific circumstances the next day. I decided to spend the weekend writing a manifesto about the standoff between trans people and the press, reaching the sad conclusion that the situation was self-perpetuating because most of us felt too hurt by the mainstream media to engage with it, let alone participate in it. I wrote the piece in one sitting and then submitted it to the *New Statesman*, shaking and feeling sick as I pressed 'send'.

The following morning, as I stood at Earl's Court changing trains to get to Charing Cross Hospital, I got an email telling me the piece was online. I shared it on Twitter, telling myself that even if I couldn't untangle my personal and professional lives, or feel confident that I could opt out of this circular struggle, I'd done my best in the face of such terrible provocations. I sat down, shaking, hoping that both broadsheet and tabloid transphobia had come to a head and that editors, writers and readers might at least pause for reflection.

─────

Back in the office, bored, I called Joe. I told him I was settling into my flat and had started to play football again – the final stage of my recovery – and explained what had happened.

'The question of how Richard Littlejohn sleeps at night is one of the great mysteries of the Western world,' he said. 'For you, at least, have things calmed down now?'

'I think it's more that everything that could have happened *has* happened,' I replied. 'It's weird being on an even keel – I sort of miss the chaos. I've got my final Gender Clinic appointment today, perhaps I'll feel different after that. I'd better go actually, it's in five minutes.'

'How is everything?' asked my secondary clinician.

'Fine,' I replied. 'Things with my family have never been better, and I'm back in work.'

'Okay, good. What about your mental health?'

'That's as good as it's going to get, I think.'

'And physically? No issues?'

'No, that's all alright.'

'Well, if you're happy with everything, then we can discharge you. You can get re-referred if you ever need to.'

She wrote my name and NHS number on a slip, and for a fleeting second, I felt in love with her. I handed the paper to reception, wondering if this was what Simone de Beauvoir meant when she said a woman was not born but made. Then I pressed the button to open the door and walked down the stairs for the last time.

I stepped out into the April sun. *I should celebrate*, I thought. I looked around at the launderette and the Conservative Club on Greyhound Road, Pizza Express across the street and the Southern Belle in front of me. *Treat yourself to lunch at least.*

I went alone into the pub. It was empty, but they still played rock music far too loud. I settled on breaded halloumi with chilli and sour cream and sat in the corner. I glanced at Twitter on my BlackBerry, putting it away when my food arrived. Resting my head on my palm and my elbow on the table, I picked up a stick and dipped it in the cream, watching the goals from the weekend's Premier League games on the big screen. I bit off the end, sighed and ate the rest of the stick. I ate two more, pushed away the bowl, got up and left. I walked back to the Education Centre, climbed the stairs and opened the door to my office.

I pressed CTRL, ALT and DELETE and entered my password to unlock my PC. I had no new emails, so I went on the *Guardian* website, but there was nothing new that I wanted to read. I let go of the mouse, drummed my fingers on my desk and then gently reclined into my chair, letting the day go by.

Epilogue

SHEILA HETI: *Why did you want to end the book with a conversation?*

JULIET JACQUES: I wanted to cover what happened after my final Gender Identity Clinic appointment in April 2013. And as so much of what has happened since then has had to do with my relationship to the media, I thought the format of this epilogue should be a magazine-style interview. Also, I wanted to explicitly mention a problem I had with the media – transition being portrayed like a mythical hero's journey. To me it didn't feel like that, rather a bunch of hoops to jump through while working in boring jobs.

After I finished the *Guardian* series, I felt so burnt out. I scaled back my social life and Internet presence, and my feelings about the transition changed. I became so angry about how long the Real Life Experience took, and how difficult it was. Writing this book, I arrived at a more nostalgic attitude about certain aspects of my life, particularly my pre-transitional explorations of gender.

The narrative concludes on a deliberately flat note. People might have expected me to leave the clinic and jump in the air, and a film might have finished by freezing on that moment, but life just went on. What else could have happened, apart from me going back to the office and thinking: *what now?* It really was that anticlimactic. But while the transition had to close there, the book didn't. I thought this might be a way of showing that life didn't end at that point.

You close with that line from 'Once in a Lifetime' by Talking Heads ...

I was obsessed with that song when I was thirteen – the idea of an experience that's both transcendent and mundane, and then fades into the past. Back then, I couldn't have imagined just how apt it would seem in my early thirties, but here we are.

It was the perfect line to end on. Can you talk about writing the book?

I started in September 2012. I hadn't finished the *Guardian* series then, so I've been constantly intertwining my personal and professional lives for six years. The proposal got commissioned in July 2013, but the finished book is nothing like those sample chapters.

Initially, I wanted to directly address the readers about their expectations for trans narratives and how they'd been conditioned to read them. But the format of a memoir is so personal, relying on an intimate bond with readers – the trust that the writer is honest, letting them into experiences they wouldn't otherwise have. I needed to find a middle ground. The first draft didn't work because whenever I came up against an experience that was traumatic to recall, I recoiled and would fall back on some sort of distancing device. I finished that draft in May 2014 and, apart from sharing some bits to friends, only showed it to my editor.

Can you say a bit more about those distancing techniques?

In the *Guardian*, I described a trip to a sperm bank. Thinking of that audience who were perhaps reading because they wanted lurid 'body shock' material, I talked instead about an old Commodore Amiga game called *Balance of Power* where you played as the United States or the USSR, trying to increase your global sphere of influence without starting a nuclear war. I always picked the Soviet Union without knowing why, and I'd soon get bored and invade Tanzania for no reason. The screen would go black and some text would appear: 'You have ignited a nuclear war. And no, there is no animated display of a mushroom cloud with parts of bodies flying through the air. We do not reward failure.' In the column I said that just as the game wouldn't reward failure, I would not indulge voyeurism. While some readers might have been affronted, some might have found it funny. I wanted to challenge people like that in this book, but it didn't feel like it worked as well in print as it did online.

Initially, I tried to write two chapters on my childhood. They didn't work: I couldn't get the register right. That whole time I was in Horley I was not telling anyone about my gender, so I had ten thousand words in which there couldn't be any interactions with people about it. It made more sense to start at university, threading the childhood stuff back through. That was when we hit on the structure of personal chapters alternating with theoretical interludes, ending with this process of reflection.

Several interesting things happened between those two drafts. One was that I wrote a long essay for the *New Statesman* about the conflict between trans people and radical feminism, including my relationship with the media. It was well received, even trending on Twitter, which gave me the confidence to include more culture and theory in the book.

Because of that, I got invited to Bishkek, the capital of Kyrgyzstan, to speak at the PEN International Congress, on a panel to oppose laws that bar discussion of LGBTQI [lesbian, gay, bisexual, transgender, queer and intersex] people in Russia, Nigeria and Iran. The laws were being debated in the Kyrgyz parliament, which made me feel more of a political *need* for the book.

Finally, in November, Dalkey Archive Press asked me to interview Jean-Philippe Toussaint for an event. Toussaint is my favourite contemporary author: his novels are detached yet heartfelt, shifting from the mundane realities of life to grand philosophical reflections without you even noticing – his prose is so subtle. We discussed his volume of essays titled *Urgency and Patience* about how and why he writes: that evening reminded me of my passion for writing, and helped me rediscover my voice. Then I began the final draft, finishing in February this year. I did eighty thousand words in four months, but I really enjoyed it, immersing myself as Toussaint advised.

One of the most painful moments in the book is the suicide note you wrote, where you say you had tried to give life some meaning through writing, and that you hoped to leave the world a little better than when you found it. How much of that desire – to leave the world a better place – is in your mind when you're writing? Is there a way in which having that thought is helpful, but another way in which it's kind of oppressive?

If you thought like that about everything you did, you'd go insane – which, I suppose, I did. Sometimes I'll take on a commission thinking, 'If I do this, it'll buy me a few days to do what I love.' Usually, this means short fiction. I worked for the NHS until last summer, and the fundamental principle there was: *do no harm*. I try to apply that to writing. Not every piece I write is going to contribute to a grand aim, but hopefully, enough of them do.

I wrote in the book about the anxieties of being a trans advocate, but a lot of it has been great. The thing I enjoyed the most came in 2013, where I was asked to speak to a sixth-form Feminist and LGBT Society. The invitation came from my old college in Horsham. I had such a happy time there: I told a few people I was 'a cross-dresser' and felt comfortable experimenting a little (although later I met Ryan, whose experience of transitioning there was not positive). So it was wonderful to see how much things were improving, with these teenagers creating spaces for themselves.

If you'd told me in 1998 that one day I'd come back and speak to a society like that, which included trans people, I doubt I'd have even understood what you were describing. I had a beautiful afternoon, talking with them about their cultural references, gender politics and ambitions. I got back in touch with several teachers. Perhaps they wondered what had happened to me. Because of my name change, they wouldn't have known.

It also felt so good because with the *Guardian* series, I was aiming at people like the sixteen-to-eighteen-year-old me – people interested in language, gender and politics – and trying to make those things accessible without talking down to them.

Elsewhere, speaking to the Bishkek Feminist Collective – all under thirty, I think – about the situation for trans people in Britain, they told me about how hard it is to get gender recognition or surgery in Kyrgyzstan. One of my favourite moments came when Selbi, translating between English and Russian, asked, 'Did you respond to the Julie Burchill scandal?' I laughed – that Burchill piece was so noxious that it stank all the way to central Asia. I didn't think when I started that people in Kyrgyzstan would be invested in these arguments, but they are.

Did you ever feel any resentment about having to write this book? There are many places where you discuss the onus on trans people to convey their experiences and write autobiographically. Were there any points where you thought, 'Why do I have to do this?'

Definitely. Having written my life story once already, I found it incredibly frustrating that if I wanted to be a literary writer and journalist, I had to cannibalise myself a second time before I could do anything else. Initially, I wanted to write a wider history of trans people in Britain, as well as short stories, but all I could get publishers to consider was a personal story. This became more annoying with my awareness that once the book came out, I'd be accused of overshadowing collective politics with a self-centred publication, and reinforcing stereotypes of trans people as individualistic.

Plenty of times I've wanted to write about other things, but trans writing has taken precedence – partly because I felt the need to do it, partly because other people seemed to feel I should use my platform to address our political problems, and partly because editors reach for the first name they associate with certain topics, and with trans topics, that's sometimes me. The way I've tried to handle it is to cover other subjects as much as possible, only returning to trans issues when I feel it's absolutely imperative.

I hope this book fulfils the same aims as my journalism on the subject – providing a better understanding of trans living, some sort of reference point. Every time I think there's no further need for this sort of writing, the situation changes.

I thought after Burchill and Littlejohn, things were calming down, so why do I need to do this? Then the situation changed again – the transphobic radical feminist perspective pushed back into the mainstream and there was a need to create a weightier counter to that.

Can you talk about your relationship to radical feminism, and to feminism in general? Do you consider yourself a feminist? You wrote about Germaine Greer and a certain line of feminism that you say 'hates' trans people.

I discovered transphobic feminism through the *Guardian*, after seeing one or two post-punk bands allude to Janice Raymond. To me, that *was* feminism. I hadn't read any theory besides Valerie Solanas or studied feminist politics. I could have done in Manchester and I wish I had now. Instead, I had this modernist/socialist background that was scornful of what it called 'identity politics', a position I later saw as prejudiced in itself.

When I read Bornstein, Stone and others, I thought of them as transgender theorists. I didn't connect them with feminism, even though they were responding to that discourse. I read them alone rather than through any sort of community, so that was how I framed things when I started writing around these issues – seeing trans and queer people on one side and feminism on the other. I knew nothing of third- or fourth-wave feminist efforts to integrate these sides, besides knowing a bit about Judith Butler, who I'd not yet read.

It was only when I joined Twitter that I got a following of people who identified as feminists and learned about transfeminism, cyber-feminism and intersectionality. I had to give myself a crash course. If I hadn't, the articles probably wouldn't have worked.

Maybe because I spent my twenties feeling so excluded, I find the word 'feminist' difficult to apply to myself. And perhaps after working through so much trans terminology, I'm fatigued with labels in general. But feminism has done a lot to shape my writing: *A Transgender Journey* was an attempt to counter socialist, conservative and feminist transphobia at the same time.

You read something like *The Transsexual Empire* now and you really are floored by its depth of hatred. But in 1980, the US National Center for Health Care Technology commissioned Janice Raymond to write a paper about medical care for trans people to help them make evidence-based decisions on the efficacy of treatment. Her paper was very hostile to gender reassignment, and Medicare didn't fund hormones or surgery until May 2014. It resulted in thirty years of people not being able to access those services unless they were wealthy.

In the book, I talk about Julie Bindel's piece about rape crisis centres, and about the time I was nearly sexually assaulted in 2012. The Equality Act of 2010 tries to secure certain trans rights, but also talks about conflicting needs – the example it uses are centres for survivors of rape or domestic violence being allowed to exclude trans women. That means we don't have anywhere to go that feels safe, especially given the coalition government's assault on services for LGBT people and women. I don't know what the right answer is, but I do wonder how that discussion might look if trans people hadn't been characterised as walking rapes, and if the people doing that hadn't had the ear of policy makers.

My tactic has been to acknowledge that there's no way around the fundamental problem with a certain brand of feminism refusing to accept our identities, so I try to appeal to an audience not immersed in those arguments, saying, 'What's the fairest perspective on this?' It's an effort to make sure that trans perspectives on trans lives reach people in influential positions.

There's an interesting line in the book where you say, 'If you articulate an outsider critique well enough, you stop being one.' What's your relationship to being an insider or outsider after being embraced as a voice by people in the trans community, and politicians who invite you to their events and want you as a spokesperson?

I've felt like an outsider from an early age – first in my family, then at school and in my home town, then at university, then in every job I've ever had. So a big problem came when I felt that considering myself an outsider wasn't tenable any more. There was this strange mixture of fascination and repulsion in going to places like the House of Commons. I've noticed that there are many ways I feel like an insider in terms of where I'm published, who I've met, and the opportunities I've had. But I sometimes still feel like an outsider *within* those circles, because my perspective and frame of reference make me feel like I don't fit in.

I think I'm through with those swanky liberal LGBT events now – I'm now far more selective about what I'll go to. But there's a great line in a Lydie Salvayre novel about the narrator's voluntary reclusion meaning that people don't invite her to things. Remaining an outsider while keeping your hand in physical and online communities enough to ensure you're not forgotten, and that you keep up with the discussion enough to remain relevant, is incredibly difficult.

First-person opinion journalism has exploded in the last five years, and there are so many people doing these sorts of pieces now that I can sustain regular slots in mainstream media outlets but I still feel relatively marginal just because I don't write that often, and when I do, it's not on the expected topics. Perhaps it's more important to keep questioning the power dynamics of the industry, and to make sure that what I write is sincere, not a performance, and done for the right reasons.

What would the wrong reasons be?

Fame and money!

I remember being seventeen years old and sitting with a friend outside a used bookshop and saying I'd never take any money from my writing because I thought it would corrupt me. It's nice to have that memory as an anchor. Obviously I do take money from writing, but it puts the brakes on going ahead with decisions I might make if I didn't have that memory.

I talk in the book about an arbitrary position I took – 'No *Mail*, no Murdoch' – but it was easy as they weren't asking. Aged seventeen, I was obsessed with the Manic Street Preachers. Their latest album had just come out [*This Is My Truth, Tell Me Yours*] and it seemed to have stepped away from the post-punk sound and radical politics of their earlier albums, especially *The Holy Bible*. I thought, 'Oh, they've sold out, that's awful.'

It's easy to make those judgements when you're a teenager, but this tightrope between art and commerce is so complicated when you're in it, and you have to take a relativist view. If you refuse to write for anyone who you have *any* political problem with, then you can't work at all. My politics aren't just about trans issues, but when I came to the mainstream media, every place was transphobic. Then it gets even harder, because if I want to use that media to change things, I'm forced to ask, 'What level of transphobia is acceptable?' Which is absurd. Deciding how to handle this is far harder than sitting in a sixth-form common room banging on about Bill Hicks.

About six months ago, you sent me some photographs of you and your friends – including Joe – in your teens and early twenties, and I replied by sending you some pictures of my friends around the same time. We could have been in the same circle. There was such an aesthetic similarity. That was a wonderful moment – we were across the ocean but shared so many cultural touchstones – the Smiths, certain avant-garde films and writers. It really struck me, reading your book, how hugely your coming to under-standing and acceptance of yourself revolved around looking at representations of people in art – not only trans people, but people with non-mainstream identities. There were the positive, inspiring models like Morrissey, Priscilla, I Shot Andy Warhol *and Almodóvar films, then there were things like* Ace Ventura. *I wondered if you could talk about that, and if part of your motivation in writing the book was to present another model to help other people make sense of themselves?*

Partly due to social prejudice, enshrined in Section 28, I saw little choice but to apprehend my identity through culture. I was at the mercy of those who edited newspaper articles, and wrote and directed films and TV programmes, and their representations of trans people and gender identity. The more mainstream places probably wouldn't have involved trans people on the creative side, and certainly wouldn't have cast them as trans characters, but would have put them on chat shows like Jerry Springer or Ricki Lake. So I had to find pop culture's queer underground, and Morrissey and

Warhol were my routes in. I wonder how much of it was that I felt I had no other option, and how much was that I'm more interested in a certain type of culture than most people. I'm sure there are plenty of trans people who are left cold by these things – you can probably be trans and never see an Almodóvar film and you'll be alright.

While writing this book, I realised how angry I was about liberal and conservative politics here, but last year, two trans politicians who came out were involved with the far-right UK Independence Party, so I don't think being trans has to be pinned to a certain politics or mindset. I wanted to give a sincere expression of how I realised *my* identity, which I couldn't have done without writing extensively about art, film, music and literature. I wanted to present a model different to the one Jan Morris offered in *Conundrum*. My favourite trans-sexual memoir is Jayne County's, where she lives immersed in US counterculture, summing up her decision not to have surgery in a single sentence. She reminded me that everyone's experience is different – having something to react against can be as useful as having something to identify with.

One of the motivations of your book seems to be to cut down this phrase – 'trapped in the wrong body' – as a dominant way that people who don't know much about trans people think about them. You really demonstrate why it's not apt.

The conclusion that I and people like CN Lester reached at the same time was: *what if we're not trapped in the wrong body but trapped in the wrong society?*

If I'd been allowed to transition in my early teens, then my adolescent and adult life would have been much easier. Kate Bornstein was questioning this phrase twenty years ago, but I still see it in mainstream media as a way to convey gender dysphoria. I understand why it exists as a shorthand, but never felt 'trapped' by my body. I said in the *Guardian* that transitioning was about 're-launching the symbiotic relationship between my body and mind from a starting point that felt right'. I stand by that.

There's so much in the book about struggling for money and taking low-paying jobs. There are two factors: one is being a writer, particularly one who writes online a lot, which isn't lucrative; the other is being trans and experiencing discrimination and this affecting your income. I wonder where you are in your relationship to making a living as a writer, especially with your growing audience.

Things haven't changed that much. Writing online is nowhere near as lucrative as some people think. When I was writing for the *Guardian,* a lot of the criticism seemed to spring from the assumption that every time I published something, it would add another storey to my house, and that I was spending any spare money on getting wasted in the Groucho Club, which wasn't the case (with one exception).

One of the things I think the Internet has done is make it less difficult for diverse voices to break in: I think the *Guardian* took a chance on me because I was cheap. Securing this representation is important, but I wouldn't recommend trying to make a career from blogging. Most people I know who do so for prominent publications have day jobs.

There's another factor between my writing and my gender – my mental health. Some of my problems were attendant on my dysphoria, some not, but depression and anxiety were big barriers. You throw that in with my politics – opposed to everything from a radical left position – and it's not a recipe for a happy relationship with capitalism.

I'm really interested in artists' and writers' relationship with capitalism. It seems that now, the more money you make, the more people esteem you. That feels new. It used to feel that an artist's inability or refusal to be assimilated into that world, or be branded, was a mark of specialness. Thinking about your future, where do you hope to situate yourself?

This has been a constant tension, because there's a demand for me to write about trans issues that comes from both outside and within myself, and there's a need for it. We need as many trans writers, artists and 'possibility models' (as Laverne Cox puts it) as possible, and given how typecasting works, it would be the most economically sensible option to pursue that. But there's an exhaustion that comes with that burden of representation.

It's a balance. I *do* still want to write about gender identity, but primarily about underground literature, film and art. I'm still trying to find a way of organising my life that lets me pursue all of these, as well as the more creative forms of writing that I always wanted to do.

You quote Agrado in All about My Mother saying, 'The more you resemble what you've dreamed of being, the more authentic you are.' I love that quote. The question of authenticity is so troublesome, but that's the best definition I've seen. I wonder to what extent you're close now, not just in your body but in your life and your place in the world, to what you dreamed you would be?

What I loved about Agrado's definition is that it places the emphasis on being true to oneself, rather than worrying about other people's judgements about whether I'm 'authentic' or not. In the Internet age, I think it's less relevant anyway.

Online, you can be whoever you want, for however long it suits.

When I think about who I dreamed of being when I saw that film, aged twenty, it wasn't that I had a certain conception of my body, because I was still figuring that out, but I had an idea of what sort of person I wanted to be – a writer. I wanted to have friends in the arts, I wanted to live in a city, and in a weird way I have become exactly that person. My favourite bit in the book is when I leave that *Times* party and think, 'Who am I? How did I get here?'

Much as I loved these underground artists and writers, I never wanted to be wilfully obscure, but I didn't like the idea of being mainstream either. My imagined path involved making films, writing plays and stories. I ended up taking such a circuitous route that I barely recognised my destination once I arrived.

In another section you write, 'I focused on the minutiae of existence, rather than my big ambitions, understanding that realising the latter would be impossible without taking care of the former. I made a point of cleaning my teeth twice a day, and playing football with friends.' Maybe that winds up being circuitous, but on the other hand, if you focus on day-to-day desires and needs, you get to where you want to be, naturally.

It's easy to forget how important the body is, especially for trans people. Before I get to the city, street, house or bedroom I live in, I spend more time in my body than anywhere else, and if that's not right then I can't do much else.

I had huge ideals when I was twenty-one. I tried to write a play about Anglo-American foreign policy as seen by a schizophrenic man, but I couldn't. The gulf between that ambition and my life experience made it impossible. Back then, Joe told me I put too much pressure on my writing, and on myself, which wasn't healthy, and the mental state I got into made it impossible to do anything. I remember writing all this down in 2014, thinking, 'Look at you, selling out your big ambitions', but actually I was putting myself in a better position to realise them.

Where does fiction fit into this?

I think fiction is a field in which trans people have not been well represented. In literary fiction, trans characters tend to be written by outsiders – to illustrate their wider points about gender, or to make things more exotic. They're often not realistic. They rarely have a rich inner life, and none of them spoke to me. I think it's a matter of doing what trans people did first with autobiography and then with theory: creating something by ourselves, largely for ourselves, but not exclusively, which describes the realities of our lives.

I think fiction is an exciting way of doing that. The problem I've had with journalism is that while it can be widely read, particularly by people in government – which can lead more directly to political change than fiction – you're tied to real people and events. What I love about fiction is that you can invent one big lie, but after that, you can be far more truthful because you're not worrying about treading on toes in the same way.

I would have loved this book to have blended fiction and autobiography, like your novel *How Should a Person Be*, but because I was commissioned to write a memoir, I had to stick to facts. I recalled as much dialogue as possible, and drafted lots with friends and interviewed several people to make it feel as 'truthful' as possible, even if it wasn't exactly what was said.

Near the end, you say 'It's weird being on an even keel, I sort of miss the chaos.' Do you feel the chaos has passed?

The lack of stability that came with transition itself feels like it's resolved, although it has some effects on my employment prospects, since I couldn't focus on a career in my twenties like many people. If I go somewhere now, I don't feel being trans has to be a big issue, and I like it not to be. Getting misgendered or heckled in the street happens rarely; and in situations where I don't have to speak, hardly at all. Some days I feel good about where I am physically, others less so, but that's still not the same as gender dysphoria, with its all-consuming sense that my body and the way I was expected to behave because of it were fundamentally wrong. I feel less weighed down than I used to, but I'll always have a transsexual history. I've learned to be proud of that, though.

The media stuff remains a constant process of victory and defeat, so that still feels chaotic. I've been on the front line for five years and I want to move away from it. Psychologically it's been draining.

Withdrawing from social media, especially Twitter with its bitter arguments, has helped. I think it's terrible for writing. I can't think of anything less healthy for an author than being able to measure their audience down to the last digit, not just in general but for each piece. As someone who's devoted to shining a light on marginal culture, Twitter is a disaster. It was one thing to suspect no one was reading when I wrote for *Filmwaves*. It's quite another for Twitter to tell me that two people 'favourited' my blog on Croatian artist Sanja Iveković.

There's such a compelling quality in the book where we have a sense of being with you through your days, so I thought I'd ask in closing: what was your day like yesterday?

What *was* my day like yesterday? I went back to my therapist for the first time in eighteen months, partly to discuss the effect that writing the book had had on me, and what it was like to return to all the memories in it. Then I did a podcast where I talked about my relationship with the media, then went for a drink with friends in Leytonstone.

It seems like it was a nice day.

It was pleasant enough.